CRIMINAL LAW

IN

IRELAND

by

Sean E. Quinn, B.A. (Hons), H. Dip. in Ed.
of King's Inns,
Barrister-at-Law.
Lecturer in Law,
Regional Technical College, Letterkenny, Co. Donegal.

MAGH ITHA TEORANTA
1988

Published in 1988 by
Magh Itha Teoranta
31 Elgin Heights, Bray, Co. Wicklow, Ireland

British Library Cataloguing in Publication Data

Quinn, Sean E.
    Criminal Law in Ireland

ISBN 1 871509 00 9

TO THE MEMORY

of

MY PARENTS

Ena
(Nee McLaughlin)

and

Daniel Joseph

PREFACE

The writing of this book has grown out of my need to have available a textbook on criminal law for my students.

The book is aimed at those who are studying criminal law. I hope that it will be useful to others working in the area of criminal law, and also that it will prove a good reference for a layperson.

The criminal law that applies in Ireland(twenty-six counties) today is the criminal law that developed in England over many centuries. As stated in the text this has in large measure been superseded in England itself. Nearly seventy years after the establishment of the Irish Free State this is inexcusable. Serious consideration should be given to the codification of the criminal law.

The law is stated as known to me in June 1988, any errors are my own.

I would like to thank Anne for her patience.

S. O'C.   July 1988

SUMMARY OF CONTENTS

CONTENTS

PART I CRIME

Chapter 1 INTRODUCTION

Chapter 2 CLASSIFICATION OF CRIMES

Chapter 3 CRIMINAL PARTICIPATION AND ASSOCIATION

Chapter 4 DEFENCES TO CRIMINAL RESPONSIBILITY

PART III OFFENCES AGAINST PROPERTY

TABLE OF CASES

The abbreviations "R. V", "A. G. V", "D.P.P. V", "The People V" and "The State V" are omitted in the following table

TABLE OF STATUTES

Chapter 1

INTRODUCTION
Criminal Law is a branch of "public law", i.e. that law which is concerned with the relationship of members of the community with the State. It is concerned essentially with those acts or omissions which are known as crimes.

The definition of crime
A crime may be defined as: an act or omission, forbidden by the State, which is punishable after due process of law. There are therefore three essentials of a crime; firstly that it is a harm, brought about by human act or omission, which the State desires to prevent; secondly that punishment is a method of prevention, punishment could be death, imprisonment, fine, or community service; thirdly that legal proceedings are employed to decide whether the accused did cause the harm, and is according to law to be punished for doing so.

Crime and tort
The difference between a crime and a tort is that while they are both wrongs, a crime is a public wrong and a tort is a private wrong. In the case of a private wrong, it is for the injured party to initiate legal proceedings on his own behalf for the purpose of compensating him or restoring him to the position in which, but for, the injury, he would have been. He may at any time after the institution of legal proceedings abandon or compromise his claim. Whenever a criminal wrong has been committed, then whether or not it involves a civil wrong, the offender becomes liable to punishment by the State, not for the purpose of compensation to anyone who may have been injured but as a penalty for the crime and in order to deter the offender and others.

Sources
The sources of criminal law in Ireland are:
    (1) The common law as it developed in England,
    (2) Statutes of the Westminster parliament, and
    (3) Statutes of the Oireachtas.
The common law as it came to be applied in Ireland, was largely

1

unaffected by the establishment of the Irish Free State. Indeed as the pace of legislative change is slower in Ireland than in England, the common law is today more intact in Ireland than in England.

During the nineteenth century, the Westminster parliament sought to reform and codify much of the criminal law. The result is that today in Ireland the majority of the offence against the person and property date from that period of change.

The Oireachtas where it has introduced legislative changes, has tended to copy what has taken place in the Westminster parliament. As for example the changes in the area of burglary, robbery and rape. Even the newer area of law such as Road Traffic and Drugs contain strong similarities. While the supremacy of the Constitution does make for differences, a decision of the House of Lords is still very persuasive in the area of case law.

Hence the Criminal Law that applies in Ireland is not Irish Criminal Law, but it consists in the main of the common law of England as applied to Ireland and the many statutes passed prior to the establishment of the Irish Free State.

It is to be noted that the following statutes which contain a very large amount of criminal law still apply in Ireland :

Accessories and Abettors Act 1861
Larceny Act 1861
Malicious Damage Act 1861
Offences Against the Person Act 1861
False Personation Act 1874
Falsification of Accounts Act 1875
Customs Consolidation Act 1876
Criminal Law Amendment Act 1885
Punishment of Incest Act 1908
Post Office Act 1908
Forgery Act 1913
Prevention of Corruption Act 1916
Larceny Act 1916

They have been largely replaced and updated in England. The modern English statutes effecting the above and the common law itself are the following:

Children and Young Persons Act 1933
Customs and Excise Act 1952
Post Office Act 1953
Sexual Offences Act 1961

Homicide Act 1957
Suicide Act 1961
Criminal Law Act 1967
Theft Act 1968
Criminal Damage Act 1971
Forgery and Counterfeiting Act 1981
Criminal Attempts Act 1981
This comparison speaks for itself.

Codification of criminal law

The introduction of the Code napoleon in 1804 and its later spread throughout continental Europe, encouraged the codification of criminal law. The codification of criminal law, was seriously considered in England later in the century. In 1878 a Criminal Code Bill, which had been drafted by Sir James Fitzjames Stephens was introduced in parliament; it was reintroduced in 1879 after it had been recast by a committee of judges, and again in 1880, with a few further alterations. Had the Bill been passed it would have recast the law in a briefer and more precise shape. Many reforms have been effected piecemeal in England since and are contained in the statues listed above. In 1985 in England the Law Commission has issued a report "Codification of the Criminal Law".It contains a draft of the projected criminal code, Part I of which deals with "General Principles of Liability"; Part II is concerned with specific offence and deals with offences against the person and offences of damage to property. There are no moves towards codification in Ireland.

CRIMINAL RESPONSIBILITY

Actus non facit reum nisi mens sit rea

This maxim properly translated means "an act does not make a man guilty of a crime, unless his mind be also guilty." It draws attention to, the two essential elements of a criminal offence and means that a criminal act must be accompanied by a criminal state of mind.

Actus reus

The actus reus is the necessary act which must have been committed for the crime to be proved. The act includes

3

conduct, its result and the surrounding circumstances. It is this conduct which together with the mens rea makes the crime.

Examples of such conduct would be:

(a) A physical act, as in assault,

(b) Words, as in incitement, conspiracy, or blackmail,

(c) An omission, as can result in manslaughter, or misprision of felony see R V Instan below.

(d) Possession, as in the case of controlled drugs or seditious documents,

(e) A state of affairs, as being found by night with housebreaking implements,

(f) Conduct of others as in vicarious liability.

Where a criminal offence requires specific consequences of certain conduct it must be established that such consequences have been caused by the accused person.

Consider the following cases:

R. V. Michael (1840)

The accused intending to murder a child, gave laudanum to the child's nurse so that it would be administered as a medicine. The nurse decided not to administer it, later however her five year old daughter did administer it and the child died. The accused was convicted of murder.

R. V. White (1910)

The accused put cyanide into his mother's drink intending to kill her. She was found dead later having sipped from the glass, but medical evidence showed that she died from a heart attack and not the poison. The accused was found guilty of attempted murder.

Mens rea

Mens rea is the essential element of a criminal offence. At common law mens rea is always required for an offence (though see below), in the case of an offence created by statute, unless the statute specifically rules out mens rea, the courts will hold that mens rea is required, because of the principle that, the interpretation of the statute which is most favourable to the accused must be adopted. It is necessary to distinguish between a number of different mental attitudes which an accused may have in respect of the offence charged:

Motive: Any motive that a person may have for the commission of a crime is not relevant, be it good or bad. It may however be relevant, as circumstantial evidence, or in deciding punishment on conviction.

R V Hicklin (1868)

The defendant was convicted of having in his possession copies of an obscene book. On appeal his conviction was quashed on the ground that the books were not kept by the defendant for gain nor to prejudice good morals. By way of case stated it was held, that although the motive of the defendant was an honest one nevertheless he had the intention which constituted the criminality of the act.

Intention: Intention as it has been interpreted by the courts can be considered of two types.

(a) Direct Intention where a person desires to bring about a certain objective and subsequently tries to bring about that objective.

(b) Oblique Intention where a person desires to bring about a certain objective and in order to bring about that objective, he must do something else which he does not desire to do.

Recklessness: Reckless as to whether or not a result is to be caused is sufficient. A person who does not intend to cause a particular result may take an unjustifiable risk of causing it and if he does so, he may be held to be reckless, however not all risk-taking constitutes recklessness.

Negligence: Negligence has a narrow application in the area of criminal law. In this case the test is objective; would a reasonable man have realized that there was some risk involved.

Blameless inadvertence : A person may reasonably fail to foresee the harm that would follow from his actions.

In general, in order to establish the criminal responsibility of an accused for an offence at common law. It must be shown; that the conduct contributed to the actus reus; and that the accused foresaw at the time of that conduct that it would result in consequences, including those which did occur.

STRICT AND VICARIOUS LIABILITY

There are two categories of cases from which the requirement of mens rea is excluded; statutory offences involving what is called strict liability, and statutory offences committed by a servant in the course of carrying out his master's duties, which were not authorized and where vicarious liability attaches to the master.

5

Strict liability

The presumption of mens rea is liable to be displaced by the words of the statute creating the offence , or by the subject matter with which it deals. The courts have attempted to classify on general lines the cases which are exceptions from the general rule;

(a) Acts which might not be considered criminal in any real sense, but are acts which in the public interest are prohibited under a penalty,

(b) Public nuisances,

(c) Case in which although the proceedings are criminal in form, it is really only a summary mode of enforcing a civil right.

The following cases illustrate the position;

Woodrow (1846)

The accused was found guilty of having in his possession adulterated tobacco, although he did not know that it was adulterated. The statute was for the protection of the revenue and there was absent from it "knowingly" or any similar words.

R V Prince (1875)

A reasonable belief that a girl was over sixteen years was no defence to a charge under section 55 of the Offences Against the Persons Act 1861, by which it was a misdemeanour to take an unmarried girl under sixteen years out of the possession and against the will of her father and mother.

R V Bishop (1880)

The accused advertised in the newspapers for patients suffering from "hysteria, nervousness and perverseness" and received into her house several young women so described, who were in fact lunatics. She was convicted of receiving lunatics into her house, it not being an asylum or hospital registered under the act. An honest belief on the part of the accused that the women were no lunatics was not material.

Cundy V LeCocq (1884)

A licensed victualler, had sold liquor to a drunken person, in contravention of the Licensing Act 1872, section 13. He was convicted despite a bona fide mistake as to the condition of the person served.

The courts in their construction of a statute will have regard to what can be seen as a danger to society in the offence charged, the greater the degree of danger to society in the offence charged. The greater the degree of danger the more likely is the offence to be interpreted as one of strict liability. Examples of these type of offences is to be found in; the Misuse of Drugs Acts, the Road Traffic Acts and the Offences Against the State Acts.

Offences of strict liability are strict but they are not absolute and the general defences that there are available to a person charged with any other criminal offence are available equally on a charge on a charge of an offence of strict liability. Because of the drastic effects of a statute imposing strict liability, the same statutes provide statutory offences, i.e. section 29 of the Misuse of Drugs Acts, see later.

Vicarious Liability

Vicarious liability arises where a person is held legally responsible for the wrongful acts of another. A person may be held liable for the acts of another, where he has delegated to him the performance of certain duties imposed on himself by statute; or a master may be held liable because acts which are done by a servant, may in law be the master's acts.

Where there has been a general delegation authority by a master to his servant, the master will generally be liable for the servant's infringements of a statute which concerns the running of a business.

Allen V Whitehead (1930)

The respondent was the occupier and licence of a refreshment house which was open day and night. He employed a manager, on eight consecutive nights, women known by the manager to be prostitutes, had been to the refreshment house and had remained there contrary to the respondent's instructions, given after a previous warning by the police. The respondent though he rarely visited the the refreshment house and was unaware of what had taken place was convicted under the Metropolitan Police Act 1839, with knowingly permitting or suffering prostitutes in a place where refreshments are sold and consumed.

Where there has been a delegation of authority it must be complete;

O'Reilly V Keatinge (1971)

A motor vehicle belonging to the accused was stationary in Meath Street, Dublin and his brother who was in charge of the vehicle, sold ice-cream to passers by. The accused was charged with engaging in a form of stall trading, with holding a street traders licence, contrary to the Street Trading Act 1926. It was held that the defendant as the seller in law contravened the statute.

At common law there is no general principle that a master is vicariously liable for a crime committed by his servant:

Devlin V Nugent (1942)

The accused was charged with permitting intoxicating liquor to be consumed at his hotel premises at a time prohibited by the Intoxicating Liquor Act 1927. The drink had been supplied and served by the hall porter, without knowledge or permission of the accused. The drink that was supplied was from a receptacle used by the night porter and the hall porter had no authority or permission, except when acting as the night porter, to take drink from the receptacle. The accused was not convicted.

R V Huggins (1730)

A prison warden had been charged with the murder of a prisoner. The death had been caused by his servant without his knowledge. He was acquitted

An exception to this general rule is the offence of public nuisance, the objection of the law being to prevent the nuisance from being continued;

R V Stephens (1866)

An accused was held liable for the obstruction by his servants of the navigation of a public river by depositing rubbish therein.

Evening Standard Case (1954)

An inaccurate report of the evidence of a criminal trial was telephoned in by a reporter and the defendant newspaper published it. It was held that the newspaper was liable for contempt

It may also be that vicarious liability extends at common law to charge of criminal libel against the proprietor of newspaper in respect of libels published by his servants, section 7 of the Libel Act 1843 provides a defence where such a publication was made without authority.

There can be no vicarious liability for attempting to commit an offence, or for the aiding or abetting of an offence.

PROOF

In a criminal trial the burden of proof is on the prosecution to prove their case beyond a reasonable doubt.

Woolmington V Director of Public Prosecutions (1935)
Viscount Sankey L.J. ".. Throughout the web of the English criminal law one golden thread is always to be seen, that it is the duty of the prosecution to prove the prisoner's guilt, subject to matters as to the defence of insanity and subject also to any statutory exceptions. If, at the end of, and on the whole of, the case there is a reasonable doubt, created by the evidence given by either prosecution or the prisoner, whether the prisoner killed the deceased with malicious intention, the prosecution has not made out the case, and the prisoner is entitled to an acquittal. ..."

The People V McMahon (1946)
In the Court of Criminal Appeal, Maguire P. in reference to the Woolmington case stated: " The court is of opinion that this principle is a true one, and as applicable as to the facts of this case, imposes on the prosecution the necessity of negativing every supposition consistent with the innocence of the accused." The principle is subject to modification during the course of a criminal trial, whenever the defence is one of insanity, or because the definition of the crime so enacts, or one of the matters to be proved lies peculiarly within the knowledge of the defendant.

The principle is subject to modification; during the course of a criminal trial, whenever the defence is one of insanity, or because the definition of the crime so enacts, or one of the matters to be proved lies peculiarly within the knowledge of the defendant.

The People V Hayes (1967)
Where the defence of insanity is raised by an accused, the onus is on him to establish that defence, which he may do so on the balance of probabilities.

The onus of proof has been shifted by statute in a number of instances; The Larceny Act 1916, section 28 which creates the offence of being found by night in possession of housebreaking implements, if a person charged with such an offence proves that his trade is such that one would expect him to be in possession of the implements, he is entitled to be acquitted. The Road Traffic Act 1961, section 38 which prohibits driving without a driving licence, presumes until the contrary is proved by the defendant, that he did not hold a driving licence.

Facts peculiarly within the knowledge of a party;

The People (A.G.) V Shribman and Samuels (1946)
The accused were charged with conspiring to export certain articles without a licence such as was required by the Emergency Powers (Control of Export) Order 1940. The Court of Criminal Appeal held that the existence of a licence was a matter peculiarly within the knowledge of the accused.

Where a plea of self-defence is raised the onus is still the prosecution to prove guilt beyond reasonable doubt, there is no question of an accused having to establish his defence in such a way to raise a doubt as to his guilt.

The People (A. G.) V Quinn (1965)
Walsh J. stated in the Supreme Court ".....the only question the jury has to consider is whether they are satisfied beyond reasonable doubt that the accused killed the deceased (if it be a case of homicide) and whether the jury is satisfied beyond reasonable doubt that the prosecution has negatived the issue of self-defence. If the jury is not satisfied beyond reasonable doubt on both of these matters the accused may be acquitted."

The People (A. G.) V Byrne (1974)
It was held by the Court of Criminal Appeal that, it is essential that the jury should be told that the accused is entitled to the benefit of any doubt and that where two views on a matter are justified, they should adopt the view which is favourable to the accused, unless the prosecution has established the conflicting view beyond reasonable doubt.

Chapter 2

CLASSIFICATION OF CRIMES

Criminal offences may be classified as those that are minor and those that are non-minor.

Non minor offences

At common law offences are either felonies or misdemeanours; treason the most serious felonies is in a separate category, and is considered later.

Felonies

In the early days of the common law all crimes were felonies, for which the punishment was death and forfeiture of all property.

Examples of felonies are; murder, manslaughter, burglary, larceny, bigamy and rape. As time passed the punishment in respect of felonies became less severe.

A felony differs from a misdemeanour in that :

(1) Originally, all felonies produced a forfeiture; whilst no misdemeanours did. But all forfeiture for felony and treason were abolished by the Forfeiture Act 1870.

(2) Originally all felonies (except petty larceny) were punished with death; whilst no misdemeanour was.

(3) Where a felony has been committed any person, who reasonably suspects any other of being the felon may arrest him.

(4) A person seeing a felony being committed, is required to arrest the felon

(5) Where a person is convicted of a felony, he loses his public office, or pension, cannot vote in an election, or sit in the Oireachtas, until he is pardoned or worked out his sentence.

(6) No civil proceedings can be instituted for loss or damage arising out of the commission of a felony, until the criminal proceedings are completed.

(7) Where a felon is killed as a felon the excuse or justification is available.

(8) It is only in the case of felonies that the distinction is drawn between the four classes of participation in a crime.

Formerly all felonies were triable only on indictment, now by the Criminal Justice Act 1951 many lesser felonies may be dealt with summarily in the District Court.

Misdemeanours

The common law judges, in order to avoid the harshness of the penalty in the case of felonies, created a lesser class of offence known as a misdemeanour. The penalty for a misdemeanour has been either fine of imprisonment. In addition to offences having evolved as misdemeanours at common law, offences have been declared to be so by statute. "Assault" is a misdemeanour at common law, while "Malicious Wounding" is declared to be a misdemeanour in section 20 of the Offences Against the Person Act 1861. There is no maximum punishment for a misdemeanour, and there are felonies which are subject to a lessor penalty than some misdemeanours as is contained in the Larceny Act 1916.

Today the distinction between those crimes that are are classed as either felonies of misdemeanours has become blurred, the modern practise in the creation of offences, is to refer simply to an "offence" and a distinction is made as between punishment on convictions on indictment, and a summary conviction

Minor Offence

The Constitution of Ireland at Article 38.2 provides that; Minor offences may be tried by courts of summary jurisdiction. The Constitution does not go on to define a minor offence, nor has the Oireachtas legislated as to the meaning of a minor offence, however it is clearly an offence to be dealt with otherwise than by a court sitting with a jury. It follows then that minor offences must be sought amongst those many offences which are triable summarily before the District Court.

The courts have considered the question what is a minor offence and how it is to be distinguished from the non-minor offences.

Melling V. O' Mathghamhna (1962)

The Supreme Court was of the view that the punishment an offence might attract was a criterion for deciding whether or not an offence is minor.

Conroy V. Attorney-General (1965)
It was held that the making of a disqualification order under the Road Traffic Act 1961, section 26 was not a punishment..
Kostan V. Ireland (1978)
It was held that the forfeiture of fish and gear, which might be worth up to £100,000 was not minor.
L'Henryenat V The Attorney General (1983)
It was held by the High Court that the existence of a penalty involving a forfeiture of property does not, per se, remove the corresponding offence from the category of minor offences.
The State (Rollinson) V James (1984)
It was held by the Supreme Court that, a penalty of £500 as laid down by the Finance Act 1926 did not make an offence non-minor.

In both the Melling and the Conroy case the Supreme Court have been prepared to accept imprisonment of up to six months as being a minor punishment. The other Melling criteria for considering whether or not an offence is minor are; the moral guilt involved, the state of the law when the Constitution was enacted, and public opinion at the time of that enactment.

The present classification of crimes is unsatisfactory, and other than treason does not enlighten us as to any particular crimes, for that we have to examine the offences themselves.

Chapter 3

CRIMINAL PARTICIPATION AND ASSOCIATION

PARTICIPATION IN A CRIME

Four categories of participation in a felony exist :
        (a) as a principal in the first degree;
        (b) as a principal in the second degree;
        (c) as an accessory before the fact;
        (d) as an accessory after the fact.

Principal in the first degree
A principal in the first degree is the actual perpetrator of the offence.

It is not necessary that he be present when the offence takes place, nor is it necessary that the act be carried out by his own hand, the felony may be committed by the hand of an innocent agent. If a man sends a six year old child into a shop to steal something for him, the man and not the child is the principal in the first degree in this theft. An animal may be employed as an innocent agent, anyone who sets a dog on people is himself guilty of assaulting them.
R V Butt (1884)
The accused made a false statement to his employer's book-keeper, knowing that such statement would be recorded in the accounts. He was convicted as principal for falsifying his employer's accounts.
See also *R V Michael* above.

There may be more than one principal in the first degree, a person may have been simultaneously assaulted by two or more people. Or both parents may have sent their child into a shop to steal for them.

Principal in the second degree
A principle in the second degree is one by whom the perpetrator of the offence is aided and abetted at the time of its commission. "Aiding and Abetting" involves giving help or encouragement during the commission of the offence. Some

14

actual encouragement must be given, mere presence is not sufficient. Presence may be actual presence at the scene of the crime such as to be an eye-witness or it may be an constructive presence,as where the aider and abettor is some distance away, but near enough to give whatever help is required. A person cannot be guilty of aiding and abetting in the commission of an offence, if the facts which constitute such offence is unknown to him.

The aided and abettor is liable with the principle for such crimes as were done in execution of their common purpose, which need not necessarily be arranged beforehand, between the principals which must exist at the time of the commission of the offence.

A principal in the second degree is liable to the same punishment as the principle in the first degree.

Accessory before the fact

An accessory before the fact is a person, who though absent at the time that the offence was committed, procures, counsels, commands another to commit a felony. Where one felony is counseled but another is committed, the accessory before the fact is only liable where the felony counseled was likely to lead to the offence that was committed.

Example; if A hires B to kill C by stabbing him and B then kills C by administering poison, A is an accessory to the murder. On the other hand if A instigates B to steal C`s car and in order to do so B kills C, A is not an accessory to that murder.

Accessory after the fact

An accessory after the fact is one who has no prior connection with the felony, but who known the felony has been committed, subsequently shelters one of the felons (including an accessory) in any way to secure their escape from justice. There must be an intention to help the felon to escape justice, active assistance to the felon is required, mere failure to report the felons presence will not suffice. However a wife who aides, assists, or hides her husband knowing him to have committed a felon is not an accessory.

Thus abstaining from arresting a known felon, and so allowing him to escape, is not enough to make a person guilty as an accessory of the felony itself (but it does make him guilty of misprision of felony).

The Accessories and Abettors Act 1861

Section 2 of the Act provides that an accessory before the fact shall be punished in all respects as if he were the principal felon.

Section 4 of the Act provides that other than where it is especially enacted, as in the case of murder, an accessory after the fact is liable to two years imprisonment.

In the case of a misdemeanour an accessory after the fact involves no criminal responsibility,

Section 8 of the Act provides, that whosoever shall aid, abet, counsel, or procure the commission of any misdemeanour shall be liable to be tried, indicted and punished as a principal offender.

Today therefore the only important surviving difference between the various modes of participation in a crime as laid down by the common law is in the case of an accessory after the fact. We shall see later that particular statutes make particular provision in this area.

CRIMINAL ASSOCIATION

Misprision of felony

Misprision of felony occurs where a person, knowing that a felony has taken place does not give information to the authorities that might lead to the felon's arrest, or does himself make an attempt to arrest the felon, or where a person during the commission of a felony fails to act or stands passively.

There is no duty of disclosure in the case of a legal adviser, doctor, clergyman or servant, where the commission of a felony has been disclosed to them in a professional capacity. Also an employer is entitled to give an employee a second chance.

Misprision of felony is a misdemeanour at common law punishable by fine and imprisonment. Active concealment or personal gain is not essential for this offence. Misprision of felony is a passive offence, if a person were to render active assistance he would be an accessory after the fact. In the case of a misdemeanour there is no offence of misprision.

Compounding a felony

Compounding a felony occurs where a person for valuable consideration, enters into agreement with a felon not to prosecute him. It occurs where a person who has been stolen from, enters into an agreement with the thief that in return for not prosecuting him, the stolen goods shall be returned. It is committed by the bare act of agreement.

Compounding a felony is a misdemeanour at common law and in the following statutes :

It is an offence under the Larceny Act 1861 at section 102 to advertise a reward for the return of any property lost or stolen, on the basis that no questions will be asked.

It is an offence under the Larceny Act 1916 at section 5(3) for any person; to corruptly take any money or reward, directly or indirectly, under pretence or upon account of aiding any person to recover any stolen dog. This is punishable by eighteen months imprisonment.

This is a more serious offence than misprision of felony, for it includes that offence and goes further. All other members of the community are permitted by law to prosecute for this crime, even though a person may have suffered no injury and indeed has no concern with the crime.

Chapter 4

DEFENCES TO CRIMINAL RESPONSIBILITY

It has been seen that mens rea, is a necessary element in every criminal offence. If it is absent the commission of an actus reus produces no criminal responsibility. However there are situations when the presence of mens rea may be negated, as well as special defences which apply in the case of particular crimes, there are certain defences which apply in the case of crimes generally, which will now be considered.

INFANCY

Seven years and under
There is an irrebuttable presumption that an infant under eight years is doli incapax (incapable of knowing right from wrong and incapable of forming a wrongful or felonious intent). He cannot therefore be guilty of any crime.
Walters V Lunt (1951)
A seven year old child helped himself to certain goods and took them home. His parents, were charged with receiving stolen goods from him, knowing them to be stolen. It was held that they could not be convicted since the child, being under age, could not have been guilty of stealing and therefore the goods were not stolen.

Over seven and under fourteen years
There is a presumption that an infant in this age group is doli incapax however this presumption may be rebutted by proof of "mischievous discretion", that is the infant was able to distinguish between right and wrong and that he knew that what he was doing was morally wrong.

Before there can be a conviction of such an infant, it must be shown by evidence, independent of the evidence of the offence that at the time he had formed a malicious intent. On its own the knowledge by the infant that the act was against the law is not sufficient.

Proof of the "mischievous discretion" required to rebut the

18

presumption has been considered in the following cases :

Leahy V Limerick County Council (1952)
Damage was caused to a house by children and there was no evidence as to what their ages were. It was held that the onus was on the respondents to show that the persons who did the damage were *doli incapax* by reason of age, either by conclusive presumption of law or one which is rebuttable. This was overruled by the Monagle case below.

Green V Cavan County Council C.C. (1959)
The applicant sought damages for malicious injury to sluice gates, around which oil had collected, and which had been set on fire and destroyed by two children, one of twelve years and the other of seven years. It was held that the applicant was entitled to compensation for malicious injuries.

Monagle V Donegal County Council (1961)
The applicant brought proceeding for the loss of property destroyed as a result of fire caused it was alleged, by the malicious act of a boy of about eight years and six months. The respondent appealed against a judgement in favour of the applicant. It was held by the High Court that the onus is on the applicant to satisfy the court by evidence that if a fire was caused by children, such children were not doli incapax either because they were over fourteen years or, if between seven and fourteen years, that they appreciated the consequences of what they were doing.

Accordingly for a crime to be proved, it is necessary to prove that the infant committed the act and that the infant knew that what he was doing was wrong.

There is an irrebuttable presumption that a boy under the age of fourteen years is incapable of committing rape, see chapter on sexual offences.

Over fourteen years
An infant in this age group has full criminal responsibility. The only limitation on this is in the area of punishment; an infant under seventeen years cannot suffer the death penalty. Infants between fifteen and seventeen years are known as young persons and those over seventeen years are known as juvenile adults.

19

INTOXICATION

In the early years of the nineteenth century, self-induced drunkenness was regarded not as an excuse for the commission of a crime, but rather as aggravating guilt. The trend today is that drunkenness may be pleaded where it is claimed to have negated the mens rea for the offence charged.

D. P. P. V Beard (1920)

The accused placed his hand over the mouth of a girl in furtherance of rape. He unintentionally killed her by pressing his thumb on her throat when trying to prevent her from screaming. Beard was drunk at the time of the offence. The law relating to drunkenness was reviewed in this case and the following are the principle points made in the course of the judgement:

1. If the accused was actually insane within the meaning of the McNaghten rules when he committed the alleged crime, then although his insanity was the result of alcoholic excess, he has as complete a defence as he would have had if it had been induced by any other means; but, where insanity is not pleaded, the jury should not be told to consider whether the accused knew that what he was doing was wrong.

2. Evidence of drunkenness rendering the accused incapable of forming the specific intent essential to constitute the crime charged should be taken into consideration with the other facts proved in order to determine whether or not he had this intent.

3. Evidence of drunkenness falling short of a proved incapacity in the accused to form the intent necessary to constitute the crime in question, and merely establishing that his mind was affected by drink so that readily gave way to some violent passion, affords no defence.

Attorney General (N.I.) V. Gallagher (1963)

Gallagher was charged with the murder of his wife. Having decided to kill her, he bought a knife and a bottle of whiskey. After drinking the whiskey he killed her. His defence was that he was either insane or so drunk as to be incapable of forming the intent necessary for murder. In the House of Lords it was stated that :

"If a man while sane and sober forms an intention to kill and makes preparation for it, knowing it is the wrong thing to do, and them gets himself drunk as to give himself dutch courage to

do the killing, and whilst drunk carries out his intention, he cannot rely on this self-induced drunkenness as a defence to a charge of murder, nor even as reducing it to manslaughter."
Director of Public Prosecutions V Majeskie (1976)
A number of charges were brought against the accused. of assaults occasioning actual bodily harm (section 47). The accused claimed that he had been acting under the influence of a combination of drugs and alcohol. The jury were directed that self-induced intoxication was no defence to assault.. The House of Lords reaffirmed the rules laid down in Beard and Gallagher and held that in crimes of basic intent, as distinct from specific intent, self-induced intoxication provided no defence; it was irrelevant to offences of basic intent such as assault.

A crime of basic intent, is, a crime whose definition expresses, or more often implies, a mens rea which does not go beyond the actus reus. It is a reckless course of conduct and recklessness is enough to constitute the necessary mens rea in crimes of basic intent. Crimes of "basic intent" or "general intent" include rape, manslaughter, assault occasioning actual bodily harm and malicious wounding.

Self induced intoxication could be a defence to a charge of a crime of "special" or "specific" intent, that is a crime where the prosecution has to prove that the purpose for the commission of the act extends to the intent expressed or implied in the definition of that crime. Crimes of "specific intent" include larceny, receiving, murder and wounding with intent.

The principals governing intoxication by alcohol and by drugs are the same. Involuntary drunkenness by mistake or by negligence or malice of others or through a weakened physical condition following lack of sleep or food or deprivation of blood, in which circumstances a person would be more affected by a small quantity of drink, would afford a defence.

MISTAKE

The law regarding mistake is summarized in the following maxim: *ignorantia facti excusat; ignorantia jurit non excusat* (ignorance of the fact excuses; ignorance of the law does not excuse); It has long been established that ignorance of the law is no excuse:

R. V Bailey (1800)
The accused was charged and convicted under a statute passed when he was at sea, at a time when he could not have known that the law in question existed.

Mistake is a defence because it prevents an accused from having the necessary mens rea, which the law requires for the offence with which he is charged. However when strict liability is imposed by the law in relation to an offence, as in the case of many of the road traffic offences then a mistake no matter how reasonable will not excuse. The mistake that is relevant is a mistake as to ignorance of fact. The mistake must be such that, had the facts been as the accused supposed them to be, he would not have been convicted of the offence charged.

Even where threats of physical violence are used to obtain possession of what is bona fide believed to be one's own property or property to which one is entitled, no offence is committed. An old case where a mistake of fact negatived criminal liability was;

R. V. Levett (1638)
Levett under the impression that thieves were in his house, thrust his rapier into the deceased, believing that she was one of them. He was charged with unlawful homicide, however it was resolved that it was not manslaughter; for he did it ignorantly, without the intention to hurt the deceased.

In general mistake must be a reasonable one, however doubt has been cast on this by the English case of *D. P. P. V Morgan (1975)*, see chapter 8 on sexual offences.

INSANITY

It is important to note that "insanity" in law is not the same as "insanity" in the medical sense. Since 1843, the McNaughten rules have been recognized as the main authoritative statement of the law on insanity. In 1843 Daniel McNaughten shot Edward Drummond who was secretary to the Prime Minister of England, Sir Robert Peel, believing his victim to be the Prime Minister. McNaughten was acquitted on the ground of insanity and, following his acquittal a debate took place in the House of Lords the consequence of which was a series of questions was put to the Law Lords. The answers given by the judges are known as the <u>McNaughten Rules</u>.

The Rules may be summarized as follows :

1. Every person is presumed to be sane, and to possess a sufficient degree of reason to be responsible for his crimes until the contrary is proved to the satisfaction of a jury.

2. To establish a defence on the ground of insanity, it must be clearly proved that at the time of the committing of the act, the party accused was labouring under such a defect of reason, from disease of mind, as not to know the nature and quality of the act he was doing; or if he did know it, that he did not know what he was doing was wrong

3. If the accused was conscious that the act was one which he ought not to do and if that act was at the same time contrary to the law of the land, he is punishable.

4. Where a person under an insane delusion as to existing facts commits an offence in consequence thereof, and making the assumption that he labours under such partial delusion only, and is not in other respects insane, he must be considered in the same situation as to responsibility as if the facts with respect to which the delusion exists were real.

The presumption of sanity may be rebutted by evidence which satisfies a jury on the balance of probabilities that the accused was insane at the time of his commission of the offence.

Attorney General V Boylan (1937)

It was contended on behalf of the accused that the judge should have told the jury that if the result of the evidence was to leave them in doubt as to the sanity of the accused they should give him the benefit of the doubt and find him to be insane. It was held by the Court of Criminal Appeal, that the contention was unsustainable.

The People (A.G.) V Fennell 1 (1940)

It was held by the Court of Criminal Appeal that an accused must establish clearly his insanity to the satisfaction of the jury.

The Attorney General V Leo O'Brien (1936)

It was pointed out that the McNaughten Rules were framed in answer to questions asked specifically with regard to "persons afflicted with insane delusions".

The attempt to give wide and general application to the rules has accordingly run into difficulties.

Doyle V Wicklow County Council (1974)

A youth had set fire to abattoir. It was established that he had caused the damage deliberately, there was also evidence that he was suffering from a mental disorder which prompted him to set fire as a means of protest against the slaughter of animals in the belief that he was justified in doing so, although he knew his act to be contrary to law. Griffin J. stated on behalf of the Supreme Court "In my opinion, the McNaughten rules do not provide the sole and exclusive test for determining the sanity or insanity of an accused." He made reference to the following case in his judgement :

The People (A. G.) V Hayes (1967)

Henchy J. said "In the normal case, tried in accordance with the McNaughten rules, the test is solely one of knowledge: did he know the nature and quality of his act or did he know that the act was wrong? The rules do not take into account the capacity of a man on the basis of his knowledge to act or refrain from acting, and I believe it to be correct psychiatric science to accept that certain mental diseases, such as paranoia or schizophrenia, in certain cases enable a man to understand the morality or immorality of his act or the legality or illegality of it, or the nature and quality of it, but nevertheless prevent him from exercising a free volition as to whether he should or should not do that act. ...., but if it is open to the jury to say, as say they must, on the evidence that this man understands the nature and quality of his act, and understands its wrongfulness, morally and legally, but that nevertheless he was debarred from refraining from assaulting his wife fatally because of a defect of reason, due to mental illness, it seem to me that it would be unjust, in the circumstances of this case, not to allow the jury to consider the case on those grounds." This was adopted by Griffin J. in the Supreme Court in the

Doyle case as a correct statement of the law on insanity.

Accordingly Irresistible impulse is part of the law in Ireland. A person is said to act under an irresistible impulse to do an act when from disease of the mind he is incapable of restraining himself from doing it, although he may know at the time of committing it that the act was wrong.

An accused found guilty but insane will be kept in custody during the pleasure of the Government.

SELF DEFENCE

The use of force is lawful for the necessary defence of self or others or property; but the justification is limited by the necessity of the occasion and the use of unnecessary force is an assault. "If one man strikes another a blow, or does that which amounts to an assault on him, that other has a right to defend himself, and to strike a blow in his defence without waiting until he is struck, but he has no right to revenge himself; and if when all danger is past he strikes a blow not necessary for his defence, he commits an assault and battery." (Russell on Crime).

R V Rose (1884)

The accused, heard his mother scream "murder" and saw his father, a powerful and aggressive man pressing his mother against the bannisters at the top of the stairs in such a way that it seemed that the father was about to cut her throat with a knife, although no knife was ever found. He shot his father and was charged with murder. He was acquitted, the jury having been directed that the law of self-defence extended to the defence of parents and children and if the accused had acted in the honest belief, held on reasonable grounds, that shooting his father was the only way of saving his mother's life, he should be acquitted.

Devlin V Armstrong (1971)

The accused incited a crowd who had been stoning the police to build a barricade to keep the police out of the Bogside, to defend the barricade and throw petrol bombs. She claimed to have done this in the honest and reasonable belief that the police were going to enter the Bogside and assault people and damage property. It was held that she had no defence on the basis of self-defence because there was no sufficiently close relationship between herself and the people of the Bogside, whom she claimed to be defending.

Attorney General V Thomas Keatley (1954)

A man has a right to defend any man by reasonable force against unlawful force ."There is of course, implicit in this statement the requirements to be deduced from the passage already quoted (above) that the use of force is necessary and that no more force than is necessary is used. These two matters are eminently questions of fact to be decided, in a criminal trial, by the jury .

Attorney General V Christopher Dwyer (1972)

This was a point of law stated for the opinion of the Supreme Court; "Where a person, subject to a violent and felonious attack, endeavours by of self defence, to prevent the consummation of that attack by force, but, in doing so, exercises more force than is necessary but no more than he honestly believes to be necessary in the circumstances whether such person is guilty of manslaughter and not murder." This question was answered by the court in the affirmative. In their consideration of the question the Supreme Court distinguished between the above type of self defence and what it called a full self defence. "A homicide is not unlawful if it is committed in the execution or advancement of justice or in reasonable self defence of person or property, or in order to prevent the commission of an atrocious crime, or by misadventure. In the case of such self defence, the homicide is justifiable and is therefore not unlawful."

"In such a case where the evidence in the trial discloses a possible defence of self-defence, the onus remains throughout on the prosecution to establish that the accused is guilty of the offence charged:......the homicide is not unlawful if the accused believed on reasonable grounds that his life was in danger and that the force used by him was reasonably necessary for his protection. In such a case he is entitled to a complete acquittal."

See also the consideration of self defence in chapter 7, and see *The D. P. P. V Kelso* in the same chapter.

DURESS

This may be considered under three headings :

> Duress per minas
> Duress per neccessitatem
> Marital coercion

Duress per minas

Duress per minas (by threats) was considered in the case of:

Attorney General V Whelan (1934)
"Threats of immediate death or serious personal violence so great as to overbear the ordinary powers of human resistance should be accepted as a justification for acts which would otherwise be criminal"

It must be shown that the overpowering of the will was operative at the time of the crime and that the accused had no opportunity to escape from the threat.

Duress has not been a general defence in cases of murder. However in the case of :

Director of Public Prosecution V Lynch (1975)
It was held that on a charge of murder it is open to a accused as a principal in the second degree to plead duress. Any threat must be to a person; threats to property no matter how grave will not suffice.

Where duress is raised as a defence, it is for the prosecution to negative it. A jury should be directed to consider whether the will of the accused, subjectively considered was overborne and whether his action under duress were reasonable.

Duress may be more often raised, as a mitigation not of the offence, but of the punishment.

A.G. V Farnan & Others (1933)
The Central Criminal Court held, that, when by special verdict a jury finds that an offence has been committed under duress the verdict is not a verdict of "not guilty", but is merely to be taken into account in mitigation of punishment.

Duress per neccessitatem

Duress per neccessitatem (coercion of necessity) is an uncertain defence :

R. V Dudley and Stephens (1884)
Two men who had been shipwrecked after eighteen days
without food killed a boy who was with them and ate him.
The defence of necessity failed, however their sentence of
death was commuted to six months imprisonment.

Necessity may be relevant in mitigation of sentence, but
otherwise it is a questionable defence in law.
R V Bourne (1939)
The defendant was a gynaecologist who had performed an
abortion on a young girl who had been raped. He was charged
under section 58 of the Offences Against the Person Act 1861.
He claimed that he had formed the opinion that without the
operation the girl would have become a physical wreck. The
jury was directed that the word "unlawfully" in the section
meant that no person could be guilty of the offence unless it
was proved that the act was not done in good faith for the
purpose of preserving the life of the mother. The defendant was
found not guilty.

Marital coercion
At common law it was presumed that a married woman acted
under the coercion of her husband, in the commission by her of
a crime, when the offence was committed in the presence of
her husband. In the People V Murray and Murray (1977), see
below; it was held that there is no presumption of marital
coercion, where a wife is charged with murder.

DIPLOMATIC IMMUNITY

The Diplomatic Relations and Immunities Act 1967 gives
force of law to the provisions of the Vienna Conventions on
Diplomatic Relations signed on 18th April 1961 and 24th April
1963. Total inviolability is extended to the person of a
Diplomatic Agent his private residence, papers and property.
He is not liable to any form of arrest, detention or prosecution,
and his persons at all times must be treated with respect.

Diplomatic Agent means the head of a diplomatic mission and
members of the diplomatic staff of the mission. The members of
the family of a diplomatic agent, forming part of his household,
if they are not Irish citizens enjoy the same privileges and

immunities.

Diplomats are specially privileged against prosecution for any breach of the criminal law. Such diplomatic immunity may be expressly waived by the diplomat's own Government. The immunity extended to any kind of offence.

OBEDIENCE TO ORDERS

In certain circumstances obedience to orders of a superior may negative mens rea; the following cases illustrate.

R.   V.   James   (1837)

The accused was charged with having unlawfully and maliciously obstructed an airway in a mine. He had done so in accordance with his masters instructions and believed that he was acting lawfully. He was deemed to be an innocent agent and found not guilty.

Keighley   V.   Bell (1866)

In relation to the military, Willes J.   stated   " an officer or soldiers acting under the orders of his superior not being necessarily or manifestly illegal would be justified by his orders "

Accordingly this "defence" can only really apply where the accused is an innocent agent.

CORPORATIONS

In general corporations are placed in the same position as individuals. A corporation cannot be found guilty of an offence where death or imprisonment is the only punishment. There are in addition a number of personal offences for   which a corporation could not be indicted, The Offences Against the State Act 1939 and The Road Traffic Act 1961 provide for corporate liability.

Chapter 5

THE INCHOATE OFFENCES

ATTEMPT

It is a misdemeanour at common law to attempt to commit an offence, whether such offence was a crime at common law or by statute. An attempt is a proximate act towards the carrying out of an indictable offence.

Mens rea

The *mens rea* of attempt is the intent to carry out the complete offence, so that the mens rea of attempt is essentially that of the complete crime.

(a) It must be shown that the person accused of an attempt to commit a crime intended or foresaw those consequences of conduct contained expressly or implicitly in the definition of the crime.

(b) It must be proved that the person accused of attempt intended those consequences referred to in (a), even though a lesser degree of mens rea might be sufficient if he were charged with the completed crime.

R V Whybrow (1951)

The accused, by a device which he had constructed, administered an electric shock to his wife while she was in a bath. The trial judge directed the jury that, if he did so with intent to kill his wife or to do her grievous bodily harm, he would be guilty of attempted murder. The Court of Criminal Appeal held that this was a wrong direction. An intent to kill had to be proved. "But if the charge is one of attempted murder, the intent becomes the principal ingredient of the crime."

Actus reus

The *actus reus* of attempt is when some act is carried out; which may be regarded as a movement towards the commission of the offence and such act cannot be regarded as having any other purpose.

Eagleton (1855)

Parke, B. "The mere intention to commit a misdemeanour is not criminal. Some act is required, and we do not think that all acts towards committing a misdemeanour are indictable. Acts remotely leading towards the commission of the offence are not to be considered as attempts to commit it, but acts immediately connected with it are ..."

How are these acts to be distinguished?

R V Taylor (1859)

The accused approached a haystack and lit a match. On noticing that he was being watched, he extinguished the match.The jury were told that the facts warranted their finding the accused guilty of an attempt to burn the haystack if they thought that he intended to set fire to it.

R V Button (1900)

The accused, a very good runner, entered for two races in the name of Sims, stating, untruthfully, that he had never run a race. He was given a start in each of the races and won, but did not claim the prize money when questions were raised as to who he really was. He was convicted of attempting to obtain money by false pretences. On appeal; Mathew, J. stated "The pretences which the prisoner made were not too remote, and the conviction was good."

R V Robinson (1915)

The accused was a jeweller who, after insuring his stock against theft, tied himself up and called for assistance, telling the police that he had been attacked and his safe robbed. Subsequently he admitted that he had hoped to make a claim on the insurers. He was convicted on a charge of attempting to obtain money by false pretences. On appeal Lord Reading C.J. stated "... we think that the appellant's act was only remotely connected with the commission of the full offence, and not immediately connected with it...We think the conviction must be quashed.."

The People (A. G.) V Thornton (1952)

On a charge of an attempt to procure the miscarriage of a girl. It was held by the Court of Criminal Appeal that on a charge based on an alleged attempt to commit a crime, the jury should be informed by the trial judge that a mere desire to commit the crime, or a desire followed by an intention to do so, is not sufficient to constitute an attempt.

It appear therefore that the *actus reus* of an attempt to

commit an offence exists when an accused performs an act which may be regarded as a movement towards the commission of the offence, and the performance of that act cannot reasonably be interpreted as having any other objective than the commission of the offence.

Attempts at treason, murder and arson are declared to be felonies by statute.

CONSPIRACY

Conspiracy is a misdemeanour at common law. All conspiracies are misdemeanours, even conspiracy to murder.

Conspiracy is an agreement between two or more persons to carry out an unlawful purpose.

The following points arise :
<ul>
<li>(a) the act of agreement,</li>
<li>(b) the persons agreeing,</li>
<li>(c) the purpose agreed upon.</li>
</ul>

The agreement

A mere intention is not sufficient, it is necessary that there be an actual agreement between parties. Once agreement has been reached, the offence is complete even though no further act is done in pursuance of the agreement or where the parties had not settled the means to be employed.

Such an agreement can be inferred from the subsequent conduct of the persons involved. Anything said, done or written by any one of the accused in execution of their common purpose is admissible in evidence against all of them. Proof of the conspiracy in most cases depends on inferences to be drawn from the conduct of the parties. Only rarely will direct evidence of the agreement be available.

Two persons

The name of the crime indicates that it is one of combination, a man cannot by himself con-spire. Husband and wife cannot be guilty of conspiring together. However, a husband and wife and a third party can be convicted of conspiring together.

R V McDonnell (1966)

McDonnell was charged with his own limited company, for the conduct of whose affairs he was solely responsible. On a motion to quash the indictment it was held that as a matter of law the one man responsible for the affairs of a limited company cannot be convicted of conspiring with that company.

One person may be convicted alone of conspiracy with persons who are unknown or not in custody, or dead, or whose trial has been postponed. But if two persons are jointly indicted for conspiring together both must be convicted or both acquitted; so also if three persons are jointly indicted for conspiring together and two are acquitted.

There does not have to be direct communication between the alleged conspirators. The existence of the conspiracy may be shown by the detached acts of the several conspirators.

An unlawful purpose

"Unlawful" as used in conspiracy has never been clearly defined. It has not been interpreted as meaning solely criminal. However an agreement to commit any indictable or summary offence is a conspiracy.

Some examples of conspiracies are :
(1) Agreement to commit any criminal offence
(2) Agreement to commit any fraudulent or malicious tort,
(3) Agreement to prevent the course of justice,
(4) Agreement to effect a lawful purpose with a corrupt intent, or by improper means.

Shaw V D. P. P. (1963)
Shaw and others published a "Ladies Directory" containing details of prostitutes and was charged with conspiring with the prostitutes to corrupt public morals. The House of Lords held that there was such an offence at common law and upheld the conviction.

Scott V Commissioner of Police (1974)
Scott agreed with others to copy certain films without permission and without paying fees, so as to enable him to make "pirate" copies and to distribute them commercially. He was convicted with conspiracy to defraud and appealed unsuccessfully to the Court of Appeal. He had submitted that since the count did not include an element of deceit, it was bad in law. In the House of Lords; Viscount Dilhorne stated: "... it is clearly the law that an agreement by two or more by dishonesty to deprive a person of something which is his or to which he is or would be or might be entitled and an agreement by two or more by dishonesty to injure some proprietary right of his, suffices to constitute the offence of conspiracy to defraud."

Penalty

It has been held that a higher sentence should not be passed for conspiracy than could be passed for the substantive offence except in very exceptional cases. The Offences Against the Person Act 1861 at section 4 provides that conspiracy to murder is punishable by ten years imprisonment.

INCITEMENT / SOLICITING

Incitement is a misdemeanour at common law. It is to incite or solicit any other person to commit a crime, even though it is not committed. A definite act of solicitation is essential.
R V Higgins (1801)
The defendant was convicted of soliciting and inciting another to steal from his master, although there was no evidence that anything had been stolen. On appeal it was held that the mere act of solicitation was a sufficient act to constitute the actus reus of a crime.

Communication
The incitement must be communicated.The offence may not only be committed by an individual personally, but also by an incitement in a newspaper.
Wilson V Danny Quastel Ltd. (1966)
Lord Parker C.J. stated "There can be no incitement of anyone unless the incitement, whether by words or written matter, reaches the man whom it is said is being incited"

Inciting the impossible
It is irrelevant that the crime incited is impossible of commission;
R V McDonough (1963)
The defendant mistakenly believed that there were some stolen lamb carcasses in cold storage at a meat market. He offered them for sale to butchers, acknowledging that they were stolen. The Court of Appeal upheld his conviction for soliciting (inciting) the butchers to handle stolen property.
R V Fitzmaurice (1983)
The defendant's father had asked him to recruit people to commit a robbery. He recruited one person who recruited two

others and put them in touch with his father. Unknown to the defendant, no crime was to be committed. His father planned to claim reward money for preventing a robbery. He was convicted of incitement to rob. The person he recruited had already been acquitted of conspiracy on the grounds of impossibility. The Court of Appeal declared that the fact that the conspiracy had been impossible did not necessarily mean that the incitement would be. The offence he had incited had not itself been impossible to commit at the time he incited it, and therefore he was liable. He would not have been liable had it been physically impossible at any time.

Attempt
An attempt at incitement is also an offence. If the crime is committed the person is liable as an accessory before the fact in the case of a felony or as a principal in the case of a misdemeanour. It is not an offence to incite someone to be an accessory before the fact to a crime.

Statutory offences of inciting
Incitement of particular crimes are contained in the relevant statutes; as for example Offences Against the Person Act 1861, section 4 incitement to murder and the Misuse of Drugs Act 1977, section 21(1); soliciting or inciting any other person to commit an offence under that Act, which is punishable in the same way as the substantive offence. Others are considered in the following chapters.

Chapter 6

HOMICIDE

Homicide is the killing of a human being by a human being. Not all homicides are a breach of the criminal law. A number of circumstances variously described as either excusable or justifiable are considered to be lawful.

They are :

Execution
Where death is caused in the execution of the lawful sentence of a competent court, as in the case of the hangman where a person has been sentenced to death for capital murder.

Advancement of justice
Death may be caused where force is used in carrying out a lawful arrest or in the suppression of a riot. However the force used must have been reasonable in the circumstances.

Misadventure
Death may be caused where a person is doing a lawful act without negligence. This excuse applies in the case of sports such as boxing or football, however the force used must not be excessive. Another instance of this would be a patient dying in surgery, where there had been no negligence.

Self-defence
The Offences Against the Person Act 1861 at section 7 provides that; No punishment shall be incurred by any person who shall kill another by misfortune or in his own defence, or in any other manner without felony, see self defence in chapter 4 above.

Chance-medley
Where in any chance-medley(i.e. sudden combat) one person stops fighting, but the other continues his assault, and the former one having having no other means of escape, kills his assailant, the necessity of self-defence prevents the homicide from being a felony.

A homicide that is not justifiable at law, or excusable by the law is an unlawful or felonious homicide. Such crimes are as follows : Murder, Capital Murder, Manslaughter, Suicide, Infanticide and Genocide. Infanticide is considered in chapter 10 and Genocide is considered in chapter 28.

MURDER

Murder has been described by Coke as "...when any man of sound memory, and of the age of discretion, unlawfully killeth within any county of the realm any reasonable creature in *rerum natura* under the king's peace, with malice aforethought, either expressed by the party or implied by law, so as the party wounded, or hurt, ... die of the wound or hurt, ... within a year and a day after the same."
These ingredients of murder must be examined as they apply not only to murder but to the other unlawful homicides as well.

any man
This means a person to whom criminal responsibility may be attached, see chapter 4 above.

unlawfully
This is to distinguish murder from the non-felonious homicides referred to above.

killeth
The killing must be unlawful and not excusable or justifiable.

within any county
The Offences Against the Person Act 1861 at section 9 provides that; in relation to murder or manslaughter a person may be tried in Ireland, where the offence has been committed abroad. See also jurisdiction which is considered later.

any reasonable creature
This means a human being, "reasonable" does not mean sane but human, it does not include an unborn child. A child is considered to be "in being" when it has an existence independent of its mother, it is not necessary for the umbilical cord to be cut for this to be so. Injuries inflicted before birth, or during birth

which cause death before birth are not murder, however an injury inflicted before birth, which causes death after birth may be murder.

the king's peace
All persons are free to live their lives peacefully. The only exclusion from this would be the killing of an enemy alien during the actual course of war.

malice aforethought
This was the mens rea of murder at common law, it is considered below.

within a year and a day
The prosecution must prove that the death of the victim occurred within a year and a day of the injuries inflicted by the accused.

Malice aforethought
This was the mens rea of murder at common law, it has now been altered by statute.

At common law malice had been categorized as follows :
Express malice; this consists of an intention to kill, the particular person who was killed, or a person other than the one who was killed.

Universal or general malice: this consists of an intention to kill some person but not caring who is killed, as where a gun would be fired into a crowd of people.

Implied malice; this consists of an intention to cause grievous bodily harm which resulted in a killing.

Constructive malice: this consists of the intention to either commit a felony, or oppose a police officer, which results in a killing.

The Criminal Justice Act 1964 at section 4 provides :

(1) Where a person kills another unlawfully the killing shall not be murder unless the accused person intended to kill, or cause serious injury to, some person, whether the person actually killed or not.

(2) The accused person shall be presumed to have intended the natural and probable consequences of his conduct; but this presumption may be rebutted.

The People (A. G) V Dwyer (1972)
The Supreme Court held that where an accused pleads

self-defence to a charge of murder, the jury must be informed that if such accused used more force than was reasonably necessary, but no more than he honestly believed to be necessary, they should return a verdict of manslaughter.

The question of causation

The killing may be by any cause whatsoever. If a person does any act, of which the probable consequences may be and eventually is death, such a killing may be murder, although the deceased was not struck by such person. Thus in murder(as in the case of manslaughter) a person will be held liable not only in cases of direct violence, but also where an act on their part led through a chain of events to a death.

The principals as to causation can be illustrated by reference to case law:

Where an actual killing is not caused solely by the accused this will not necessarily exempt him from liability, see R   V Lowe below.

R. V Wall (1802)

Governor Wall was tried and executed in 1802 for the murder of Sergeant Armstrong nearly twenty years earlier for sentencing him to an illegal flogging ; though death might not have resulted but for the deceased having drank alcohol whilst he was ill.

Where death is caused partly by an accused and partly by the conduct of others, a court may hold that the death is too remote.

R. V Jordan (1956)

The accused had stabbed the deceased who had died in hospital not having received normal treatment. His conviction was quashed because at the time of his death, the original wound caused by the stabbing had nearly healed.

R. V Blaue (1975)

The accused stabbed the victim who was taken to hospital. The victim who was taken to hospital. The victim, a Jehovah's Witness, was informed that without a blood transfusion she would probably die. She refused and died. The accused appealed against his conviction for manslaughter on the grounds that the victim's refusal to accept a blood transfusion broke the chain of causation. The court dismissed the appeal, the refusal to accept the blood transfusion did not break the chain of causation.

If a person under an apprehension of personal violence does an act which causes his death, as for example jumps out a window or into a river, the person who threatened is answerable for the consequences, see R V Halliday below.

A killing may be caused by mental suffering or shock.

R. V Tower (1874)

The accused violently assaulted a young girl who was holding a four and half months old child in her arms. The screams of the girl so frightened the child that it cried till it was black in the face. From that day it had convulsions and died a month later. It was held that there was evidence to go to the jury of manslaughter.

Absence of body

The absence of a body, will not stand in the way of a conviction for murder :

Attorney General V E. & R. Edwards (1935)

This was a trial for the murder of an illegitimate infant. The trial judge certified that it was a fit case for appeal on the grounds that the body had not been found and that no medical evidence had, or could have been tendered that the infant had died a violent death, and whether the jury, in the absence of direct evidence of a killing, and on the facts before them, were entitled to infer that the infant had been murdered. It was held by the Court of Criminal Appeal, that the verdict could not be set aside.

Attorney General V Ball

The accused was indicted for matricide. He made a statement to the effect that his mother had committed suicide and that he had put her body into the sea. A bloodstained hatchet was found in the house and a very large amount of blood was splashed about. It was held that there was evidence sufficient to go to the jury that the deceased met her death an the hands of the accused.

See also *The People (A.G.) V Thomas (1954)* in chapter 30.

The People (Attorney General) V Cadden

It was held by the Court of Criminal Appeal, that a jury may convict on purely circumstantial evidence but to do this they must be satisfied that not only the circumstances were consistent with the prisoner having committed the act but also that the facts were such as to be inconsistent with any other rational conclusion than that he was the guilty person.

Attempts to murder

The Offence Against the Person Act 1861 creates a number of ancillary offence :

Section 4
All person who shall conspire, confederate, and agree to murder any person, and whosoever shall solicit, encourage, persuade, or endeavour to persuade, or shall purpose to any person, to murder any other person, shall be liable to ten years imprisonment.

Section 11
Whosoever shall administer to or cause to be administered to or to be taken by any person any poison or other destructive thing or shall by any means whatsoever wound or cause grievous bodily harm to any person, with intent to commit murder, shall be liable to life imprisonment

Section 12
Whosoever, by explosion shall destroy or damage any building with intent to commit murder, shall be liable to life imprisonment.

Section 13
Whosoever shall set fire to any ship or vessel with intent to commit murder shall be liable to life imprisonment.

Section 14
Whosoever shall attempt to administer to, any person any poison or other destructive thing, or shall shoot at any person, or shall attempt to drown, suffocate, or strangle any person, with intent to commit murder, shall be liable to life imprisonment.

The People (D.P.P.) V. Douglas & Hayes. (1985)
It was held by the Court of Criminal Appeal that; While it was anomalous that where a person shoots at another intending to cause serious injury and that person dies, the offence of murder has been committed, while if he does not die the offence of shooting with intent to murder has not been committed, section 14 of the 1861 Act specifically required proof of an intent to kill and it was irrelevant that the court of trial was satisfied that those who fired the shots would have been guilty of murder had any person been killed. In order to determine whether an intent to kill existed, a court may take into account that a reasonable man would have foreseen that the natural and probable consequence of the acts was to cause death and that the accused acted in reckless disregard of that likely outcome of the acts, but such factors of themselves would not constitute proof of such intent.

Section 15
Whosoever shall, by any means other than those specified above, attempt to commit murder, shall be liable to life imprisonment.

Section 16
Whosoever shall maliciously send, any letter or writing threatening to kill or murder any person, shall be liable to ten years imprisonment.

All of the above except the offence under section 4 are felonies, see also the offence of attempting to choke under section 21 below in chapter 7.

CAPITAL MURDER

The Criminal Justice Act 1964 at section 1(a) provides that :
A person shall be liable to suffer death for capital murder, namely -
(i) murder of a member of the Garda Siochana acting in the course of his duty, or
(ii) murder of a prison officer acting in the course of his duty, or
(iii) murder done in relation to certain offences under the

Offences Against the State Act 1939, or
(iv)murder, committed within the state for a political motive,
of the head of a foreign state or of a member of the
government of, or a diplomatic officer of, a foreign state;
(v) an offence by a person subject to military law.

The People (DPP) V Marie and Noel Murray (1977)
The accused who were husband and wife, escaped in a car after
an armed robbery. The driver of a private car, who was
passing at the time, pursed the robbers in his car until
eventually the robbers' car stopped and the accused ran away
from it. The pursuer stopped his car and ran after and overtook
the husband. When he was about to seize the husband, the wife
shot and killed him. The pursuer was a member of the Garda
Siochana who was not in uniform and who was not on duty. The
accused were convicted in the Special Criminal Court of capital
murder and sentenced to death. On a final appeal from the Court
of Criminal Appeal it was held by the Supreme Court :
1   The offence of capital murder is a new statutory offence
which requires proof of *mens rea* in relation to each of its
constituent elements.
2   That the requisite *mens rea* to support a conviction for
capital murder may be established by proof of the specific
intention mentioned in section 4 of the 1964 Act as applied
to a victim known by the accused at the time of the killing
to be a policeman acting in the course of his duty.
The People V Murtagh (1966)
It was held that in the case of capital murder, where the
penalty is death and in the case of murder where the penalty is
penal servitude for life, no lesser penalty can be pronounced.
The State V McMullen (1925)
It was held that if a police officer is killed in the execution of
his duty by a person at whom that duty is aimed, it is murder,
even though there was no premeditation and no intention to
cause his death.
The People (Attorney General) V. White (1947)
The accused was convicted and sentenced to death by the
Special Criminal Court for the murder of a detective garda,
while he, with other gardai, was seeking to arrest the accused
and another man. Shots were fired between the garda and the
accused and another man and the garda was killed. The ground
of arrest of the other man without a warrant, was his
membership of an illegal organization, but the garda did not

know the identity of the accused and no cause for his arrest was alleged by any witness in the course of the trial. It was held that the Special Criminal Court was entitled to find on the evidence, that the accused fired the fatal shot, but that in the circumstances proved and on the evidence, the offence committed was manslaughter and not murder.

MANSLAUGHTER

Manslaughter is the unlawful killing of another person without the particular malice aforesaid that is required for murder. Manslaughter is a felony at common law, for which the punishment is penal servitude for life, by section 5 of the Offences Against the Person Act 1861.

It is generally accepted that there are two forms of manslaughter, voluntary and involuntary.

Voluntary manslaughter

Voluntary manslaughter is an unlawful killing which is reduced from murder to manslaughter because of provocation. Such a killing may occur where where as the result of a quarrel two persons fight and as excessive and unreasonable force is used there is a death. Where a person used force in defence of his own life and its use was such as was necessary in the circumstances, he having no means of escape and no other means of resistance, then it is excusable homicide. Provocation may consist of violent assault accompanied by gross insults. It would also arise where one spouse finds another in the act of adultery and kills immediately. An unlawful imprisonment or an unlawful arrest may be a sufficient provocation to reduce to manslaughter a killing inflicted by the actual person imprisoned or arrested.

The provocation must be so recent and so strong, that the accused person at the time of the killing was not the master of himself. If there is time between the provocation and the killing for the blood to cool, the offence will be murder.

The distinction between the objective and the subjective condition of the accused has been considered by the courts; Did the accused lose his self-control? Were the circumstances such that a reasonable person would have lost his self-control? *The People V Sean MacEoin (1978)*
The Court of Criminal Appeal ruled that the subjective test is to

be applied in relation to provocation, was the accused actually provoked? Before the plea of provocation fails, the prosecution must prove beyond reasonable doubt :

(a) That the accused was not provoked to such an extent that having regard to his temperament, character and circumstances he lost his self-control at the time of the wrongful act, and

(b) That the force used was unreasonable and excessive having regard to the provocation.

Whether there was sufficient provocation or not is a matter of fact for the jury, but as to whether there is enough evidence of this is to be submitted to the jury is for the judge.

Involuntary manslaughter

Involuntary manslaughter is committed where a person brings about the death of another by acting in some unlawful manner, without the intention of killing or doing an act likely to kill.

It may arise in the following ways :

(a) By an unlawful act done with the intention of causing physical harm, or alarm to another, but not with the intention of causing death or grievous bodily harm(sometimes called constructive manslaughter); or

(b) By the intentional or grossly negligent omission to perform a legal duty, in which neither death nor grievous bodily harm was intended or known to be a likely consequence; or

(c) By a lawful act performed with criminal negligence.

An unlawful act

The accused is not guilty of murder because he lacks the necessary malice aforethought, however the unlawful act must be in the nature of an assault which does require mens rea.

The following cases illustrate this mode of involuntary manslaughter:

R V Connor (1885)

A Mother threw a piece of iron at a child with the intention of frightening him. It struck and killed another child. She was convicted of manslaughter.

R V Wild (1837)

The accused gave a guest who would not go a kick which resulted in his death. There was no intention of his intending to cause any serious harm, but he was convicted of manslaughter because " a kick is not a justifiable mode of turning a man out of your house, though he be a trespasser".

R V Larkin (1943)
The accused flourished an open razor, intending only to frighten a man who had been associating with his mistress. The mistress who had been drinking, swayed against the accused and her throat was cut by the razor. He was convicted of manslaughter.

Omission to perform a duty
Unless it is provided for specifically by statute, the common law imposes no duty upon a person to act in a particular way towards another.

In certain cases a person owes a legal duty to others and where his failure to perform that legal duty is coupled with criminal negligence as distinct from negligence generally and results in death, he is guilty of manslaughter. The legal duty must be owed by the accused person because of his custody of, or control over, the deceased person, who must have been helpless. The death that resulted must have been unintentional.

Such a legal duty would exist in the following circumstances:
(a) where there is a special relationship;
(b) where there is a voluntary assumption of responsibility;
(c) where there is a contractual duty;
(d) where there is a statutory duty;
(e) where a duty arises because of previous conduct.

Accordingly a person would have no legal duty to protect a stranger.

The following cases may be noted :

R V Instan (1893)
The accused, lived with her aunt, who was seventy-three years of age and a helpless invalid. During the final ten days of the aunt's life, the accused failed to supply her with food or medical attendance, thus accelerating her death. She was convicted of manslaughter.

R V Lowe (1850)
The accused a colliery engineer left his post, leaving in charge of the engine a boy who to his knowledge was unable to control it. As a result of which another was killed. The accused was convicted of manslaughter.

R V Senior (1899)
A member of a sect which believed that the acceptance of medical aid was tantamount to a lack of faith in God, omitted to obtain aid for his eight month old child who had pneumonia and died. Evidence was given which showed that the child's life

would have been saved by medical treatment. The father was convicted of manslaughter.

Act performed with criminal negligence
A person may be doing some act lawful in its nature, but doing it recklessly and therefore unlawfully. The degree of negligence must be much higher than that which might ground liability in tort.

A. G. V Dunleavy (1948)
It was stated that the trial judge should instruct the jury that manslaughter is a serious crime and that before convicting of manslaughter they must be satisfied that the fatal negligence was of a very high degree and was such as to involve a high degree of risk of substantial personal injury to others.

Because of the very high degree of negligence required for manslaughter in relation to motor accidents, the offence of dangerous driving causing death was created, see chapter 18.

It was held by the Court of Criminal Appeal, that the trial judge should see that the jury is given clearly to understand as follows:

(a) That negligence in this connection means failure to observe such a course of conduct as experience shows to be necessary if, in the circumstances, the risk of injury to others is to be avoided, i.e., failure to behave as a reasonable driver would;

(b) That the jury must be satisfied that negligence upon the part of the accused was responsible for the death in question;

(c) That there are different degrees of negligence, fraught with different legal consequences;

(d) That manslaughter is a felony and a very serious crime, and that before convicting of same the jury must be satisfied that the fatal negligence was of a very high degree, and was such as to involve, in a high degree, the risk or likelihood of substantial personal injury to others.

The following case was approved of.

Andrew V D.P.P. (1937)
It was held by the House of Lords that to kill a person while driving recklessly or at a speed or in a manner which was dangerous to the public was not manslaughter in the absence of "criminal negligence".

R V Dant (1865)
The accused turned out a very vicious and dangerous horse to

47

graze. It kicked a child on the head and killed her, he was convicted of manslaughter.

Attorney General V Maher

Accused drove a motor car without a licence and in the course of doing so killed a man. There was no evidence of culpable negligence. It was held that the evidence was not sufficient to uphold a charge of manslaughter.

Killing recklessly

The consideration of "recklessness" in a number of English cases, now casts doubt on the above category of involuntary manslaughter and points towards a category of "killing recklessly".

Killing recklessly arises, where the accused either

(a) recognises an obvious and serious risk of causing physical injury and nevertheless takes it, or

(b) gives no thought to the possibility of there being a serious risk of causing physical injury which would be obvious to a reasonable man.

See *Kong Cheuk Kwan V The Queen (1985)*

SUICIDE

Suicide is the taking of ones own life with malice aforethought and it is a felony. At common law no suicide could be buried in consecrated ground, a person who took their own life was buried on the highway, with a stake through his body and his goods were forfeited. Later a suicide was buried between the hours of nine and twelve at night, without any service.

The confiscation of goods of suicides was put to an end with the general abolition of forfeiture for felony by the Forfeiture Act 1870 and the Internments Act 1882 removed all penalties except the purely ecclesiastical one.

Attempted suicide

An attempt at suicide is a misdemeanour and by the Summary Jurisdiction (Ireland) Amendment Act 1871, section 9 as amended by section 85 of the Court of Justice Act 1936, such a charge may be tried summarily by a Justice of the District Court if the person charged shall confess and consent to be so tried.

Any person who instigates another to commit suicide is

guilty of murder.

Suicide pacts
R V Abbot (1903)
It was held that if two parties mutually agree to commit suicide, and only one accomplishes that object, the survivor is guilty of murder. This is known as a suicide pact.

Chapter 7

ASSAULT AND BATTERY

At common law assault and battery are distinct offences. Usually both offences are committed together and the entire transaction is described in law as "an assault and battery". This has been shortened in lay terms as "an assault" and even lawyers use "an assault" as synonymous with "battery". Hence it is common for the term "assault" to cover both.

ASSAULT
An assault is an act by which any person, intentionally, or possibly, recklessly, causes another person to fear the immediate application to himself of unlawful physical force. The mens rea of assault is the intention to create in the person's mind a belief in the immediate application of unlawful physical force. The actus reus is the creation in the mind of a person the belief that unlawful physical force is to be used immediately against him.
Tuberville V Savage (1669)
The plaintiff was alleged to have put his hand upon his sword and said "if it were not assize time, I would not take such language from you." It was held by the court that this was not an assault.
   Alarm is essential to an assault. Hence if a person is so far away, that he cannot possibly touch him, it is no assault, furthermore to constitute an assault there must be the means of carrying the threat into effect.
Stephens V Meyers (1830)
It was held to be an assault, where the defendant had advanced upon another with threats and clenched fists and, at the last moment, was prevented from striking him.
R V St.George (1840)
It was held that it was an assault to point an unloaded gun at someone who believed it to be loaded and was put in fear.

BATTERY
A battery is the actual intended use of unlawful force on another person without his consent. The mens rea of battery is the intention to apply unlawful physical force. The actus reus is

the actual application of unlawful physical force. No actual harm need be done or threatened. The slightest force will suffice as long as it was exercised in a hostile manner. The force applied or threatened need not involve immediate contact, it is sufficient if harm is done or threatened to a person's clothes without touching his skin, similarly the hostile force may be exercised directly or even indirectly, as by striking a horse thus making it throw its rider.

DEFENCES TO ASSAULT

The exercise of force against the person of another is not always unlawful. It may be shown by an accused that he was justified or excused in law by what he did, see also the consideration of self defence in chapter 4.

Misadventure
It is a good defence that the alleged assault happened by misadventure. There are many cases of accidents which cannot be set up as a defence in an action for trespass to the person, but which would certainly be a good defence upon an indictment. In general the same circumstances that would excuse a homicide, would also be a good defence in relation to assault.

Consent
As a general rule it is a good defence that the person complaining of assault or battery consented to the acts complained of, if such consent is freely given by a rational and sober person, knowing the nature of the act, unless the consent is to bodily injury or to acts likely or intended to do bodily harm or to an injury constituting a breach of the public peace.

It is unlawful to strike another person with such a degree of violence that bodily harm is a probable consequence, and consent cannot be a defence in such circumstances.

In the case of a surgical operation, carried out by a competent surgeon, however great the risk, the consent of the patient will be a full justification for what would otherwise be an aggravated assault.

Further exceptions to this general rule would be:
Blows given in the course of athletic contests. As in the case of a lawful sport, it is good defence that the alleged assault occurred during a friendly contest; or that it happened by accident whilst the accused was engaged in some sport or

51

game, which was not dangerous.

Blows given during innocent horseplay amongst friends or acquaintances.

Lawful chastisement

It is a good defence that the alleged battery was the correcting of a child by its parents, but such punishment must be of a moderate and reasonable nature. A schoolteacher was similarly entitled, but with the abolition of corporal punishment in schools, this is now questionable.

Self-defence

It is a good defence, in justification even of a wounding, that the accused was attacked first and committed the alleged assault in his own defence. It is not necessary that a person should wait to be actually struck before striking in self-defence. There is in such circumstances a duty to retreat, if possible.

Spouses may justify an assault in defence of one another, as may a parent in defence of his child, and a master in defence of his servant any force used in such circumstances, must be reasonable, for if it were excessive, or greater than was necessary for mere defence, or if it were after all danger was past and was by way of revenge, then there can be no justification.

The right of self defence extends to the defence of property. It is a good defence that the assault was committed, by the accused in defence of his property or possessions, but again any force used must be reasonable in the circumstances. Only after he has been requested to leave and on refusing to do so, may a trespasser be removed by force. However in the case of a burglar force may be used to expel such a person immediately. Also force may be used to resist anyone who attempts to take possession of a persons goods.

Execution of process

It is good defence that the accused was an officer of justice implementing a process. However no greater of force can be used than was necessary to secure the prisoner. A person may justify laying his hands upon another to prevent him from fighting, or committing a breach of the peace.

OFFENCES

At common law both assault and battery are misdemeanours, assault at common law is more often referred to as "common assault" the remainder of the law with regard to "Assaults" is principally contained in the Offences Against The Person Act 1861. By this Act the more serious offences are made felonies, while the lesser offences are ranked as misdemeanours.

Common assault

By section 42 of the Act, provision is made for the summary trial of common assault and of battery. The Criminal Justice Act 1951, section 11 provides that a person convicted of either common assault or battery shall be liable to a fine of £50 and or six months imprisonment.

By section 47 of the Act, whoever is convicted on indictment for a common assault is liable to one years imprisonment.

The State (Clancy) V Wine (1980)

It was held by the High Court, that where a person is charged with common assault, he may be prosecuted either summarily or upon indictment and that the mode of prosecution to be employed, is the choice of the prosecuting authority, and the person charged has no right to be consulted on the matter.

Wounding with intent

By section 18 of the Act : "Whosoever shall unlawfully and maliciously by any means whatsoever wound or cause any grievous bodily harm to any person, or shoot at any person, or , by drawing a trigger or in any, other manner, attempt to discharge any kind of loaded arms at any person, with intent, in any of the cases aforesaid, to maim, disfigure, or disable any person, or with intent to resist or prevent the lawful apprehension or detainer of any person, shall be guilty of felony..." and liable to life imprisonment.

This section creates four types of assault offences:
1. To "wound" any person,
2. To "cause grievous bodily harm" to any person,
3. To "shoot at" any person,
4. To attempt, "by drawing a trigger, or in any other manner,"to discharge any kind of loaded arms at any

person.

Each of these offences may be done with any of the following intents:

- (a) To maim,
- (b) To disfigure,
- (c) To disable,
- (d) To do some other grievous bodily harm,
- (e) To resist or prevent the lawful apprehension or detainer of any person.

To "maim" is to injure any part of a person's body, such as to render him less able to defend himself.

Foley V. Corporation of Dublin (1939)

A violent attack was made on a Garda, while he was seeking to bring disturbers of the public peace to justice. He sustained a fracture of his right jaw and his left jaw was broken. He lost five teeth and others were loosened. It was held by the High Court that the injuries suffered amounted to maiming under section 106 of the Grand Jury (Ir.) Act, 1836.

To "disfigure" is to do some external injury, which takes from a person's appearance.

To "disable" is to do something which creates a permanent disability and not just a temporary injury.

"Grievous bodily harm" means serious harm, but it need not be either permanent or dangerous.

The People (Attorney General) V Goulding (1964)

The applicant was charged under the Offences against the Person Act 1861 sections 18 and 20 Per O'Daly, C.J.: "It should be noted that in defining wounding with intent to do grievous bodily harm the trial Judge inadvertently said it was something that interfered with the health or comfort of another. This sets too low an onus upon the prosecution. "Grievous bodily harm" requires that the interference be a "serious" one.

Harm may be caused without personal contact, for example: if A breaks his leg from jumping out of a window to avoid an attack by B, then B will be liable. Whether in any particular case, the harm done was grievous is for a jury to decide.

To constitute a "wound" there must be a breaking of the whole skin, hence a mere scratch is not a wound, nor will it be sufficient that bones have been broken, if the skin is not also broken.

The People (A.G.) V. Messit (1974)
It was held by the Supreme Court that a wound, for the purposes of section 18 and 20, must include a severance of the entire skin. To constitute a maiming, disfiguring or disabling or other grievous bodily harm within Section 18, the injury must be a serious one though not necessarily a permanent one.

The intent is important in these offence and it is the above "intents" that distinguish between a charge under this section and what is to follow. The unlawful infliction of grievous bodily harm without "malice" is not an offence under this section, but would perhaps be a "common assault".

In order for there to be a conviction it is necessary for the appropriate intent to be proved. It is not necessary that the person whom it was intended to harm should be the one who was actually harmed.

Unlawful wounding
By section 20 of the Act, "Whosoever shall unlawfully and maliciously wound or inflict any grievous bodily harm upon any other person, either with or without any weapon or instrument, shall be guilty of a misdemeanour..." and liable to five years imprisonment.

The term "wound" and "grievous bodily harm" as used in this section have the same meaning as above, in section 18. With regard to "inflict" any injury which is held to constitute an assault, need not necessarily be inflicted directly. The absence of the word "assault" has the effect of giving this offence a wider construction than the above.
R V Martin (1881)
Shortly before the end of a performance in a theatre, the accused who intended to cause terror in the minds of the audience, turned off the lights on a staircase and placed an iron bar across one of the doorways. In the panic that followed a number of persons suffered injury. The accused was charged under section 20; he was convicted.
R V Halliday (1889)
The accused terrified his wife with threats of personal violence and in order to escape began to climb out the window, with the result that she fell and broke her leg. The conviction of the accused was upheld on appeal.
R V Cunningham (1957)
The meaning of "maliciously" was considered in this case; it

involves an actual intention to do the particular kind of harm which, in fact, was done, or recklessness as to whether such harm might occur or not.

Attempting to choke

By section 21 of the Act, "Whosoever shall, by any means whatsoever, attempt to, choke, suffocate, or strangle any other person, or shall, by any means calculated to, choke , suffocate, or strangle, attempt to render any other person insensible, unconscious, or incapable of resistance, with intent in any of such cases thereby to enable himself or any other person to commit, or with intent in any of such cases thereby to assist any other person in committing any indictable offence, shall be guilty of felony..." and shall be liable to life imprisonment.

Administering drugs

By section 22 of the Act, "Whosoever shall unlawfully apply or administer to or cause to be taken by, or attempt to apply or administer to or attempt to cause to be administered to or taken by, any person, any chloroform, laudanum, or other stupefying or overpowering drug, matter or thing, with intent in any of such cases thereby to enable himself or any other person to commit, or with intent in any such cases thereby to assist any other person in committing, any indictable offence, shall be guilty of felony,..." and liable to life imprisonment.

Administering poison

By section 23 of the Act, "Whosoever shall unlawfully and maliciously administer to or cause to be administered to or taken by any other person poison or other destructive or noxious thing so as thereby to endanger the life of such person, or so as thereby to inflict upon such person any grievous bodily harm, shall be guilty of felony..." and liable to ten years imprisonment.

It must be shown that; whatever was administered did endanger life or cause grievous bodily harm. Whether the thing administered is a "noxious thing" or not may depend on the quantity administered, some drugs being harmless in small quantities, and dangerous only in large quantities. It has been held that heroin is a "noxious thing".

By section 24 of the Act, "whosoever shall unlawfully and

maliciously administer to or cause to be administered to or taken by any other person any poison or other destructive or noxious thing, with intent to injure, aggrieve, or annoy such person, shall be guilty of misdemeanour..." and shall be liable to five years imprisonment.

R V Dones (1887)
The defendant squirted a solution of household ammonia during a fight. It was held that this was not "administering".
It need not be shown that "harm" has been caused in relation to, this offence. In respect of both offences it is necessary that "intent" be shown. Upon an indictment for either of the above, the jury may convict of a lesser offence under section 25.

Assault with intent
By section 38 of the Act, " Whosoever shall assault any person with intent to commit felony, or shall assault, resist, or wilfully obstruct a peace officer in the due execution of his duty, or any person acting in aid of such officer, or shall assault any person with intent to resist or prevent the lawful apprehension or detainer of himself or of any other person for any offence, shall be guilty of a misdemeanour,.." and shall be liable to two years imprisonment.

This section creates a number of offences:
1   Assault with intent to commit a felony,
2   Assaulting, resisting, or wilfully obstructing :
      (a) a peace officer in due execution of his duty,
      (b) a person, acting in aid of a peace officer in due execution of his duty,
3   Assaulting any person with intent, to   resist, or prevent, the lawful apprehension or detainer of :
      (a) himself, or
      (b) any other person.

An offence under this section may with the consent of the Director of Public Prosecutions be dealt with in the District Court.

R V Forbes and Webb (1865)
An accused was convicted of assaulting plain clothes policemen in the execution of their duty. His claim that he did not know that they were policemen was held irrelevant. "The offence was, not assaulting them knowing them to be in execution of their duty, but assaulting them being in the execution of their duty".

Assault occasioning actual bodily harm

By section 47 of the Act, "Whosoever shall be convicted upon an indictment of any assault occasioning actual bodily harm shall be liable,..." to three years imprisonment. The Criminal Justice Act 1951, section 2 provides that this offence may be tried summarily.

Actual bodily harm need not be an injury of a permanent nature; nor need it amount to grievous bodily harm, as mentioned above. The absence of any reference to "wound" or "inflict" in this section, gives the offence a narrower construction than other offences above.

R. V Miller (1954)

In relation to a charge under this section the Judge directed the jury that actual bodily harm meant "any hurt or injury calculated to interfere with the health and comfort" of the victim.

For this offence it is not necessary to prove, that the risk of injury was foreseen, the intent is the same as in the case of a common assault.

Assault with intent to rob

The Larceny Act 1916, section 23 (as amended by the Criminal Law (Jurisdiction) Act 1976) provides that the penalty for an assault with intent to rob is life imprisonment.

OTHER OFFENCES UPON THE PERSON

KIDNAPPING

This is an offence at common law committed, where any person of any age or either sex is stolen or carried away by force or fraud against the persons will. It has been held that the offence is committed if there is a carrying away of the person even for a short distance.

The Criminal Law Act 1976, section 11 declares that kidnapping is a felony and is punishable by life imprisonment. See also the offence of child stealing in chapter 8.

FALSE IMPRISONMENT

False imprisonment is the unlawful and total restraint of the personal liberty of another, whether by constraining him or compelling him to go to a particular place or by confining him in a prison or police station or private place, or by detaining him against his will in a public place.

The People V Edge (1943)

The Supreme Court held that a boy under fourteen years or a girl under sixteen years has not got the legal capacity to consent and such apparent consent would not be a valid defence to a charge of false imprisonment or kidnapping.

The Criminal Law Act 1976, section 11 declares that false imprisonment is a felony and punishable by life imprisonment.

It is not essential that a person be aware of his imprisonment, he may be either asleep or drunk. The offence may or may not involve an assault.

"False" means unlawful, where it is clear that no charges are to be leveled against an arrested person, he should be released at once. Any restraint must be completed in every direction, there is no false imprisonment, where a person is free to move in a particular direction.

Walters V W.H. Smith & Son (1914)

A private detective arrested the plaintiff on suspicion that he had stolen from one of the defendant's shops. He had not done so. It was held that in the case of a private citizen, an arrest for an already committed offence was lawful only if it could be proved that the offence had been committed, and that the person carrying out the arrest had reasonable and probable cause for his suspicion. The plaintiff was awarded damages.

Chapter 8

SEXUAL OFFENCES

RAPE

At common law rape is the unlawful carnal knowledge of a female without her consent. Although the offence is usually accompanied by violence, it is accepted that rape can be committed without any use of violence, as the essential is the lack of consent.

The Offences Against the Person Act 1861, section 48 declares rape to be a felony and the punishment to be life imprisonment.

The Criminal Law (Rape) Act 1981 amended the law relating to rape and indecent assault on females. By section 2(1) of that act a man commits rape if,

(a) he has unlawful sexual intercourse with a woman who at the time of the intercourse does not consent to it, and

(b) at the time he knows that she does not consent to the intercourse or he is reckless as to whether she does or does not consent to it,

By the 1861 Act, section 63; where it may be necessary to prove carnal knowledge, it shall not be necessary to prove the actual emission of seed in order to constitute a carnal knowledge, but the carnal knowledge shall be deemed complete upon proof of penetration only, the slightest penetration shall suffice and it is not necessary to prove that the hymen was ruptured.

It is to be noted that while the 1861 Act refers to "unlawful carnal knowledge", the 1981 Act refers to "unlawful sexual intercourse", presumably unlawful sexual intercourse, relates not to sexual intercourse, but means unlawful carnal knowledge as outlined in section 63 of the 1861 Act. Accordingly "unlawful sexual intercourse" includes sexual intercourse as is commonly understood, yet also includes acts which would not ordinarily amount to sexual intercourse.

The People (A. G.) V. Dermody (1956)

The appellant was charged with unlawful carnal knowledge, of a girl under fourteen years of age. In evidence she said that the man had put his private part "a wee bit" into hers, but the evidence showed that the hymen had not been ruptured. It was

60

held by the Court of Criminal Appeal, that the offence of rape , or unlawful carnal knowledge contrary to the Criminal Law Amendment Act 1935, could be sufficiently proved by proof of penetration, even though emission could not be proved.

Carnal Knowledge or sexual intercourse means vaginal intercourse, there is no offence of rape *per anum* or oral rape, however the former would be buggery and the latter would be an indecent assault.

Consent

The absence of the consent of the woman is an essential feature of the *actus reus* of rape, and it is for the prosecution to prove the absence of such consent. The question to be asked is, not was the act against the will of the woman, but was it without her consent.

(a) The Criminal Law Amendment Act 1885, at section 4 provides :

Whereas doubts have been entertained whether a man who induces a married woman to permit him to have connection with her by personating her husband is or is not guilty of rape, it is hereby enacted and declared that every such offender shall be deemed to be guilty of rape.

(b) Where consent is obtained by personal violence or by threats of personal violence there is no real consent.

(c) Consent obtained by fraud is no real consent :

R. V Flattery (1877)
The defendant professed to give surgical and medical advice. On the pretence that he was performing a surgical operation he had intercourse with a young girl, she offered no resistance. It was held that he was guilty of rape.

R. V Williams (1923)
The defendant had sexual intercourse with one of his pupils to whom he was giving singing lessons, by the pretence that it was a method of training her voice. The girl offered no resistance. It was held that he was guilty of rape.

(d) It is rape to have sexual intercourse with a woman, who is asleep or otherwise unconscious, as she is therefore unable to give or withhold consent. See R. V Mayers (1872)

(e) It is rape to have sexual intercourse with a woman due to plying her with drink. See Camplin (1845). However if the drunkenness is due to her own excesses, the offence may be indecent assault and not rape.

(f) The addition to the law brought about by section 2 of the

1981 Act above, occurred after the following case :

D. P. P. V Morgan (1976)

Morgan spent the evening with three friends and then invited them to his home to have sexual intercourse with his wife which, against her will each did. At their trial the accused claimed that even if she did not consent, nevertheless they had believed that she was consenting. The trial judge directed the jury that such a mistaken belief was a good defence provided that there had been reasonable grounds for such a belief. Subsequently the House of Lords held that the mens rea of rape was an intention to commit non-consensus intercourse and that therefore a mistaken belief, even if unreasonably held that the victim was consenting meant that the accused did not commit the offence.

(g) The question of consent does not arise in relation to defilement of young girls under the Criminal Law Amendment Act 1935 considered below.

Recklessness

The meaning of "reckless" in section 2(1)(b) of the 1981 Act has been considered by the English courts. The test of recklessness is a subjective one.

R V Satnam S. and Kewal S. (1984)

Bristow J. for the Court of Appeal stated that the word "reckless" in relation to rape involves a different concept to its use in relation to other crimes. In relation to offences against the person the foreseeability, or possible foreseeability, is as to the consequences of the criminal act. In the case of rape the foreseeability is as to the state of mind of the victim. In summing-up a case to a jury and to give a proper direction as to the issue of consent ".. the judge should, in dealing with the state of mind of the defendant, first of all direct the jury that before they could convict of rape the Crown had to prove either that the defendant knew that the woman did not want to have sexual intercourse, or was reckless as to whether she wanted to or not. If they were sure he knew she did not want to they should find him guilty of rape knowing there to be no consent. If they were not sure about that, then they would find him not guilty of such rape and should go on and consider reckless rape. If they thought he might genuinely have believed that she did want to, even though he was mistaken in his belief, they would find him not guilty...if...they were sure he had no genuine belief that she wanted to, they would find him guilty. If they came to the conclusion that he could not care less whether she wanted to or not, but pressed on regardless, then he would have been reckless and could not have believed that she wanted to, and they would find him guilty of reckless rape"

Husbands
A husband cannot, as principal in the first degree commit rape on his wife, a wife is irrebutably presumed to consent to sexual intercourse with her husband by virtue of the marriage contract. There are circumstances however, in which the wife's consent to sexual intercourse may be considered as having been revoked.
(a) Where a decree of nullity has been granted.
(b) Where a divorce a mensa et thora has been granted.
(c Where there is a separation agreement and, in particular where such an agreement contains a non-molestation clause.
(d) Where the husband is subject to an injunction forbidding him to interfere with his wife. See *R. V Clarke (1949)*
(e) Where a husband has given an undertaking to the court in order to avoid the issue of such an injunction referred to in (d).
A husband is not entitled to use physical violence or fear in order to have sexual intercourse with his wife, if he does so this amounts to an assault. See *R. V Miller (1949)*. A husband may be convicted as a principal in the second degree or as an aider and abettor of the rape of his wife by another.

Boys under fourteen years
The other person who cannot be convicted of rape is a boy under the age of fourteen years, he is irrebutably presumed incapable of rape, attempted rape, or of sodomy, whether he is or is not fully developed and actually did commit the offence. However if the facts prove that what would otherwise be rape was committed, he can be convicted of indecent assault. He may also be convicted, as may a woman, as an accessory to rape when he assists another to commit the offence.

Evidence
The Criminal Law (Rape) Act 1981 lays down restrictions on evidence at trials for rape offences. By section 3(1) of the Act; no evidence shall be introduced, except with the leave of the

judge, about any sexual experience of a complainant with a person other than the accused.

Sentencing
English case law, including a "Guidelines Judgment" and a recent decision of the Supreme Court has clarified the position here.

R V Roberts and Roberts (1982)
Lord Lane C.J. delivering the judgment of the Court of Appeal, stressed the seriousness of this particular crime which, other than in wholly exceptional circumstances, called for an immediate custodial sentence to mark the gravity of the offence, emphasize public disapproval, serve as a warning to others, punish the offender and, last but by no means least, to protect women.

R V Billam and Others (1986)
The Court of Appeal laid down the following guide-lines on appropriate sentences for rape and attempted rape :
1. At the top of the scale comes the defendant who has carried out a campaign of rape, committing the crime upon a number of different women or girls. A sentence of fifteen years or more may be appropriate. Where a defendant has perverted tendencies, a life sentence will not be inappropriate.
2. For rape committed by an adult without any aggravating or mitigating features, five years should be taken as the starting point in a contested case.
3. Where rape is committed by two or more men acting together, or by a man who has broken into or otherwise gained access to a place where the victim is living, or by a person who abducts the victim and holds her captive, the starting point should be eight years.
4. In the case of young offenders, there should be some reduction to reflect their youth.
5. The starting point for attempted rape should normally be less than for the completed offence.
6. Aggravating or mitigating factors.
    (i) Aggravating factors -
        (a) violence is used, over and above the force necessary to commit the rape, or
        (b) a weapon is used to frighten or wound the victim, or
        (c) the rape is repeated, or

64

(d) the rape has been carefully planned, or

(e) the defendant has previous convictions, or

(f) the victim is subjected to further sexual indignities or perversions, or

(g) the victim is either very old or very young, or

(h) the effect upon the victim, whether physical or mental, is of special seriousness.

(ii) Mitigating factors -

(a) a plea of guilty, or

(b) the victim behaved in a manner calculated to lead the defendant to believe that she would consent to sexual intercourse.

The Director of Public Prosecutions V Edward Tiernan (1988) The Attorney General had asked the Supreme Court to decide the guide-lines which courts should apply for rape when hearing this appeal. Finlay C.J. stated " While in every criminal case a judge must impose a sentence which, in his opinion, meets the particular circumstances of the case and of the accused person before him, it is not easy to imagine the circumstances which would justify departure from a substantial immediate custodial sentence for rape and I can only express the view that they would probably be wholly exceptional .... I have no doubt that in the case of rape, an admission of guilt made at an early stage followed by a plea of guilty can be a significant mitigating factor" In his judgement the Chief Justice referred to *R V Billam* above.

ATTEMPTED RAPE

If there is not sufficient evidence for a conviction for rape, an accused may be convicted of attempted rape. The penalty for attempted rape is seven years imprisonment, however not the provisions of the Criminal Law Amendment Act 1935, section 1 below with regard to a second or subsequent conviction of attempted rape of a girl under fifteen years of age.

OTHER OFFENCES INVOLVING SEXUAL INTERCOURSE

It can be seen from the above that, in order to constitute the offence of rape, it is always necessary that sexual intercourse should take place without the consent of the woman, however by the Criminal Law Amendment Act 1935, such an act when committed with a young girl is criminal, even though done with her consent

Defilement of girl under fifteen years of age
By section 1 of the Act; any person who unlawfully and carnally knows any girl under the age of fifteen years shall be guilty of a felony, for which the penalty is life imprisonment. An attempt at this offence is a misdemeanour, for which the penalty on first conviction is five years imprisonment or on a second or subsequent conviction is ten years imprisonment.

Defilement of a girl under seventeen years
By section 2 of the Act; any person who unlawfully and carnally knows any girl who is over the age of fifteen years and under the age of seventeen years shall be guilty of a misdemeanour, for which the penalty on first conviction is five years imprisonment or on a second or subsequent conviction is ten years imprisonment. An attempt at this offence is also a misdemeanour, for which the penalty on first conviction is two years imprisonment or on a second or subsequent conviction is five years imprisonment.

The above offences are of the same character as rape and the same principals of proof apply, with the exception that consent is no defence. See *A. G. (Shaughnessy) V Ryan (1960)* below. Moreover if consent is missing in the above circumstances, then the accused is liable to the more serious charge of rape.

Consider the following cases :

The People (A. G.) V O'Connor (1949)
On a charge of unlawful carnal knowledge of a girl under the age of fifteen years or, under the age of seventeen years, there must be precise evidence of age.

The People (A. G.) V Kearns (1949)
The accused was charged with the unlawful carnal knowledge of a girl under the age of fifteen years of age, he pleaded guilty. On his plea in mitigation of sentence the trial judge refused to admit evidence that the appearance of the girl led the accused to believe that the girl was over seventeen years of age. It was held by the Court of Criminal Appeal that such evidence should have been admitted.

A. G. (Shaughnessy) V Ryan (1960)
It was held by the Supreme Court that consent is no defence to a charge of attempting to have carnal knowledge of a girl over the age of fifteen years and under the age of seventeen years.

Defilement of Idiots etc.
By section 4 of the act; any person who, in circumstances which do not amount to rape, unlawfully has carnal connection of any woman or girl who is an idiot, or an imbecile, or is feebleminded shall if the accused knew of the women's state of mind, be guilty of a misdemeanour, for which the penalty is two years imprisonment.

An idiot is a person born without a mind; an imbecile is a person deprived of the mind by disease or injury; and a feebleminded person is a person, so born or, who through disease or injury,is of impaired. mental faculties. There is an offence under the Lunacy Act 1890, section 324, which relates specifically to persons having the care or charge of any female lunatic and has the same penalty. The Mental Treatment Act 1945, section 254 provides that where a person has been convicted of an offence under section 4 and such person had the charge of the woman or girl the penalty shall be five years imprisonment.

Householder Permitting Defilement of Young Girl
The Criminal Law Amendment Act 1885 at section 6, as amended by the 1935 Act provides that; Any person who being the owner or occupier of any premises induces or knowingly suffers any girl to be in such premises for the purposes of being unlawfully and carnally known by any man, shall be liable where the girl is under fifteen years to five years imprisonment, or where the girl is under seventeen years to two years imprisonment.

Unlawful Detention with Intent
Section 8 of the 1885 Act provides that: Any person who detains any woman
(1) In or upon any premises with intent that she may be unlawfully and carnally known by any man, or
(2) In any brothel,
shall be liable to two years imprisonment.

INCEST

This offence involving sexual intercourse does not involve the consent of the woman but is dependant upon specified degrees of consanguinity between the parties. It was not a crime at common law although punishable by the ecclesiastical courts. Incest became a statutory crime by the Punishment of Incest Act 1908.

Incest by males S. 1

(1) Any male person who has carnal knowledge of a female person, who is to his knowledge his grand daughter, daughter, sister, or mother commits an offence. The penalty on conviction is seven years imprisonment. Provided that if, on indictment for this offence, it is proved that the female person is under fifteen years of age then the male will be subject to section 1 of the Criminal Law Amendment Act 1935 above.

(2) Consent of the female is no defence, in the absence of consent the male will be guilty of the more serious charge of rape.

(3) If any male person attempts to commit this offence, he shall be guilty of a misdemeanour, the penalty on conviction of this is two years imprisonment.

(4) On conviction of a male offender where female is under twenty-one years of age, the court may divest the offender of all authority over such female and remove the offender from such guardianship.

Incest by females S. 2

Amended by section 12 of the Criminal Law Amendment Act 1935 provides: that any female above the age of seventeen years who with consent permits her grandfather, father, brother, or son to have carnal knowledge of her knowing of the relationship is guilty of a misdemeanour and commits a like offence.

The knowledge of the accused person of the relationship is essential to the offence of incest. The relationship of the parties may be proved by oral evidence or by certificates of marriage and birth, together with identification. An admission as to the relationship would be sufficient evidence of such.

Additional provisions of the Act

3.   The expression "brother" and "sister" respectively, include half-brother and half-sister legitimate or illegitimate.

4.(3) If on the trial of any indictment for rape, the jury are satisfied that the defendant is guilty of this offence, but are not satisfied that the defendant is guilty of rape, the defendant may be found guilty of this offence.

5.   All proceedings under the Act are to be held in camera.

6.   No prosecutions may be commenced without the sanction of the director of public prosecutions.

ABDUCTION OF FEMALES

The Offences Against the Persons Act 1861, created most of the offences in this area.

Abduction of a girl under sixteen years of age

Section 55 : Whosoever shall unlawfully take or cause to be taken any unmarried girl, being under the age of sixteen years, out of the possession and against the will of her father or mother shall be liable on conviction to two years imprisonment. This offence does not involve carnal knowledge.

R. V Prince (1875)

Prince took an unmarried girl under sixteen years out of the possession and against the will of her father. The girl looked much older and the jury found that she had told Prince that she was eighteen, that he bona fide believed her, and that his belief was reasonable. It was held on appeal that a reasonable belief that a girl was over sixteen was no defence to the charge.

Abduction of a girl under eighteen years of age

The Criminal Law Amendment Act 1885, section 7 as amended by the Criminal Law Amendment Act 1935 provided that : Any person who, with intent that any unmarried girl under the age of eighteen years should be unlawfully and carnally known, takes or causes to be taken such girl out of the possession and against the will of her father or mother shall be liable to two years imprisonment. The former position as to a reasonable belief as to the age of the girl was a good defence, has been removed by the 1935 Act. The consent of the girl herself is no defence, not even where the proposal to go away comes from the girl and not from the man. But where the initiative and the active arrangements for the going away were taken and made by the girl this is a defence.

Abduction of heiress
Section 53 : Whosoever shall take away or detain any woman who is a heiress with intent that she be married or carnally known where it is against her will or the will of her mother or father where she is under twenty-one years of age shall be liable on conviction to fourteen years imprisonment.
An "heiress" as subsequently defined in England is; any female, who has property, or the expectation of property.

Abduction of any woman with intent to marry her
Section 54 : Whosoever shall, by force take away or detain against her will any woman of any age, with intent to marry or carnally know her shall be liable on conviction to fourteen years imprisonment.

PROSTITUTION AND BROTHEL KEEPING

Prostitution
Prostitution itself is not a criminal offence. However the offences dealt with below arise out of activities connected with prostitution.
R. V deMunck (1918)
Darling J. stated ...prostitution is proved if it is shown that a woman offers her body for purposes amounting to common lewdness for payment in return.

Procurement
The Criminal Law Amendment Act 1885 at section's 2 and 3 as amended by the Criminal Law Amendment Act 1935 makes the following provisions :
Section 2, Any person who, procures or attempts to procure any girl or woman
(1) not being a common prostitute, or of known immoral character, to have unlawful carnal connection, within or without this country, with any other person or persons, or
(2) to become, either within or without this this country a common prostitute;
(3) to leave this country with intent that she may become an inmate of or frequent a brothel elsewhere, or

70

(4) to leave her usual place of abode in this country (such place not being a brothel) with the intent that she may, for the purposes of prostitution, become an inmate or frequent a brothel, within or without this country.

shall be guilty of a misdemeanour for which the penalty is two years imprisonment.

Section 3, Any person who;

(1) by threats or intimidation procures or attempts to procure any woman or girl to have unlawful carnal connection either within or without this country; or

(2) by false pretence or false representation procures any woman or girl not being a common prostitute or of known immoral character, to have an unlawful carnal connection within or without this country; or

(3) applies, administers to, or causes to be taken by any woman or girl any alcoholic or other intoxicant, or any drug matter, or thing, with intent to stupefy or overpower so as thereby to enable any person to have unlawful carnal connection with any woman or girl.

shall be guilty of a misdemeanour, for which the penalty is two years imprisonment.

It is to be noted that the above offence may be committed by any person be they male or female and that there is no age limit in respect of the girl or woman victim, most of the offences are of an extra-territorial nature. In respect of section 3, sub-sections (1) and (3) it is not necessary that sexual intercourse should have taken place, sub-section 2 could apply to a man who procures a woman to have sexual intercourse with himself.

Soliciting

By the Criminal Law Amendment Act 1935, section 16(1) Every common prostitute who is found loitering in any street, thoroughfare, or other place and importuning or soliciting passers-by for purposes of prostitution or being otherwise offensive to passers-by shall be guilty of an offence and shall on summary conviction be liable on a first offence to a £2 fine or, in the case of a second or subsequent offence to six months imprisonment.

There is a provision contained in the Dublin Police Act 1842, section 14(11) which provides for the following offence :

Every common prostitute or night-walker loitering or being in any thoroughfare or public place for the purpose of prostitution or solicitation, to the annoyance of the inhabitants or passengers. The Town Improvement (Ireland) Act 1854, section 72 makes similar provision, the penalty in both instances being a £2 fine.

Mooney V Corporation of Dublin (1939)

A Garda arrested a woman on a charge of soliciting for the purposes of prostitution in a public thoroughfare contrary to section 14(11). It was held by the High Court, that the soliciting in question was neither a breach of the public peace nor likely to lead to a breach of the public peace, and therefore the woman in question was not a disturber of the public peace.

Male solicitation

The Vagrancy Act 1898, section 1 as amended by the Criminal Law Amendment Act 1912 provides that : Every male person who in any public place persistently solicits or importunes for immoral purposes shall be liable on summary conviction to six months imprisonment.

Living on the earnings of prostitution

The 1898 Act, as amended also provides as follows :

Every male person who knowingly lives wholly or in part on the earnings of prostitution commits an offence. Where a male person is proved to live with or be habitually in the company of a prostitute shall, unless he can satisfy the court to the contrary, be deemed to be knowingly living on the earnings of prostitution.

Every male person and every female person for the purposes of gain, who is proved to have exercised control, direction or influence over the movements of a prostitute in such a manner as to show that he or she is aiding, abetting, or compelling her prostitution with any other person or generally, shall be deemed to be living on the earnings of prostitution, and shall be guilty of an offence.

The penalty on summary conviction is six months imprisonment, or on indictment is two years imprisonment.

Brothel keeping

The Criminal Law Amendment Act 1935, section 13 provides that any person who keeps or manages or acts or assists in the management of a brothel commits an offence. Persons in charge of any premises or landlords are equally guilty if they are aware of what is happening. The penalty on first conviction is a £100 fine and or six months imprisonment and, in the case of a second or subsequent conviction to a £250 fine and or five years imprisonment.

PUBLIC OFFENCES AND ASSAULTS

Indecent exposure

At common law it is a misdemeanour to commit an act outraging public decency in public and in such a way that more than one person sees, or is at least able to see, the act. The more usual way of committing this offence is by indecently exposing the body. It is not necessary to prove any sexual motive or any intention to insult or annoy. It may be committed by a female and the exposure need not necessarily be to a person of the opposite sex.

The Vagrancy Act 1824, section 4 provides that a person may be found to be a rogue and a vagabond where such person, exposes his person in any public place, with intent to insult any female. The penalty is a £25 fine and or three months imprisonment. It has been held that "person" means penis.

Public indecency

The Criminal Law Amendment Act 1935, section 18 provides that : Every person shall commit, at or near or in sight of any place along which the public habitually pass as of right or by permission, any act in such a way as to offend modesty or cause scandal or injure the morals of the community shall be guilty of an offence and shall on summary conviction be liable to a £2 fine and or one months imprisonment.

Indecent assault upon a female

This is a physical assault upon a female combined with circumstances of indecency. Assault as used here includes a battery. This offence could be committed by a female. The Criminal Law (Rape) Act 1981 at section 10 provides that if a person is convicted on indictment of this offence he shall be liable to ten years imprisonment.

The People (A.G.) V O'Connor (1949)

It is not open to a jury to convict on a charge of indecent assault upon a female where the evidence proved shows that

73

the person assaulted consented to the act committed upon her.

However the 1935 Act at section 14, provides that ; it shall not be a defence to a charge of indecent assault upon a person under the age of fifteen years to prove that such person consented to the act alleged to constitute such indecent assault.

Indecent assault upon a male

The Offences Against the Persons Act 1861 at section 62 provides that whosoever shall be guilty of an indecent assault upon any male person shall be liable to ten years imprisonment. Given the nature of an assault, consent would be a defence to this charge, but only if the person is over fifteen years of age.

UNNATURAL OFFENCES

Buggery and Sodomy

The Offences Against the Persons Act 1861, section 61 provides that-

Whosoever shall be convicted of the abominable crime of buggery, committed either with mankind or with any animal, shall be liable to penal servitude for life.

Buggery consists of having carnal knowledge as follows :

    (a) by a man with a man *per anum,*

    (b) by a man with a woman *per anum*,

    (c) by a man with an animal *per anum* or *per vaginam*,

    (d) by a woman with an animal *per anum* or *per vaginam.*

All the above are known as sodomy, (c) and (d) are also known as bestiality. Consent is no defence, the consenting party may be guilty as a principal.

A husband and wife can be convicted of this offence. A boy under fourteen years or a girl under twelve years are deemed incapable of committing this offence or any attempt thereto. As in the case of rape, carnal knowledge shall be deemed complete upon proof of penetration only no emission of seed is required, corroboration of evidence is required in these cases.

A. G. V Troy

Troy was convicted of buggery and appealed on the ground that the medical evidence was the only evidence that the boy had been interfered with but that it was not corroboration that he had interfered with the boy and that the trial judge had failed to make this clear. It was held by the Court of Criminal Appeal

74

that the medical evidence did not corroborate the evidence of the boy.

Section 61 of the 1861 Act provides that : Whosoever shall attempt to commit buggery, or shall be guilty of an assault with intent to commit the same, shall commit an offence and be liable on conviction to ten years imprisonment

Gross indecency

The Criminal Law Amendment Act 1885, section 11 provides that any male person who, in public or in private, commits or is party to the commission of, or procures or attempts to procure the commission by any male person of, any act of gross indecency with another male person, shall be liable on conviction of such offence to two years imprisonment.

Gross indecency is not defined in the Act. It means any sexual act between male persons other than buggery and there is no need for physical contact. Consent is no defence to this offence and both parties involved may be guilty. The effect of this provision and the absence of a like provision in respect of female persons means that the practise of homosexual acts between men is a crime, whilst the practise of lesbianism is not criminal.

The People (A.G.) V McClure (1945)

The accused had pleaded guilty to a charge of gross indecency. He was thirty-three years old and this was his first offence. It was held by the Court of Criminal Appeal that given the good character of the accused, and the fact that it was a first offence, the sentence would be reduced.

Norris V A. G. (1984)

The plaintiff claimed that the above provisions infringed Article 40 of the Constitution. It was held by the High Court; that neither section 61 or 62 made any distinction between men and women or between homosexuals and heterosexuals and that accordingly, neither contravened article 40. The Supreme Court in upholding the decision of the High Court further declared, that neither the omission from the 1861 Act and the 1885 Act of offences relating to acts of gross indecency by females, nor, the omission of offences relating to the sexual activities of heterosexuals outside marriage was contrary to Article 40.

Chapter 9

Offences concerning children and young persons

There are a number of offences that are specific to children, when considering these regard should be had to offence covered elsewhere, in particular those in the chapters on Homicide, Assault and Battery, Sexual Offences and Childbirth.

The Offences Against the Persons Act 1861 makes the following provision :

Wilful neglect S. 26
Whosoever, being legally liable, either as a master or mistress, to provide for any apprentice or servant necessary food, clothing or lodging, shall wilfully and without lawful excuse refuse or neglect to provide the same, or shall unlawfully and maliciously do or cause to be done any bodily harm to such, such that life shall be endangered or life injured, shall be guilty of a misdemeanour and liable to three years imprisonment.

Exposing children whereby life endangered S. 27
Whosoever shall unlawfully abandon or expose any child being under the age of two years, whereby the life of such child shall be endangered, or the health of such child shall have been or shall be likely to be permanently injured, shall be guilty of a misdemeanour and shall be liable to three years imprisonment.

Child stealing S. 56
"Whosoever shall unlawfully, either by force or fraud, lead or take away, or decoy or entice away or detain, any child under the age of fourteen years, with intent to deprive any parent, guardian, or other person, having the lawful care or charge of such child of the possession of such child, or with intent to steal any article upon or about the person of such child,. . shall be guilty of felony,. . " and liable to seven years imprisonment.

The main provisions are contained in the Children Act 1908.

Cruelty S. 12
If any person over the age of seventeen years, who has the custody, charge, or care of any child or young person, wilfully assaults, ill-treats, neglects, abandons, or exposes such child or young person, or causes or procures such young person to be assaulted, ill-treated, neglected abandoned, or exposed, in a manner likely to cause such child or young person unnecessary suffering or injury to his health (including injury to or loss of sight, or hearing, or limb, or organ of the body, and any mental derangement) that person shall be guilty of a misdemeanour, for which the penalty on indictment is £100 and or two years imprisonment and summarily is £25 and or six months imprisonment.
"seventeen years" was substitutes for "sixteen years" by section 4 of the Children(Amendment) Act 1957.

A person shall be deemed to have neglected a child if he fails to provide adequate food, clothing, medical aid, or lodging or fails to take steps to procure the same.

A person may be convicted, notwithstanding that actual suffering or injury to health, or the likelihood of such suffering or injury to health, was obviated by the action of another person, or that the child or young person has died.

Upon the trial for the manslaughter of a child or young person of whom the accused had the custody, charge or care, the court may find an accused guilty of this offence.

Being knowingly interested, directly or indirectly, in any sum of money that is to accrue or to be paid in the event of the death of a child or young person is an aggravation of this offence.

Suffocation of infant S. 13
Where it is proved that the death of an infant under the age of three years of age was caused by suffocation (not being suffocation caused by disease or the presence of any foreign body in the throat or air-passage of the infant) whilst the infant was in bed with some other person over sixteen years of age, and that other person was at the time of going to bed under the influence of drink, that other person shall be deemed to have neglected the infant in a manner likely to cause injury to its

77

health within the meaning of the Act.

Begging S. 14
If any person causes or procures any child or young person, or having
the custody, charge or care of a child or young person, allows that child or young person to be in any street, premises, or place for the purpose of begging or receiving alms, or of inducing the giving of alms, whether or not there is any pretence of singing, playing, performing, offering anything for sale or otherwise, this is an offence for which the penalty is £25 and or six months imprisonment.

Exposure to burning S. 15
If any person over the age of sixteen years, who has the custody, charge, or care of any child under the age of seven years, allows that child to be in any room containing an open fire grate not sufficiently protected to guard against the risk of the child being burnt or scalded, without taking reasonable precautions against that risk, and by reason thereof the child is killed or suffers serious injury, this is an offence for which the penalty is a £10 fine.
This does not however affect any liability for any indictable offence.

Frequenting brothels S. 16
If any person having the custody, charge, or care of a child or young person between the ages of four and seventeen years allows that child or young person to reside in or frequent a brothel, this is an offence for which the penalty is £25 and or six months imprisonment.
Where a person is charged with an offence under section 6 of the Criminal Law Amendment Act 1885, it may be reduced to this offence.

Seduction and prostitution S. 17
If any person having the custody, charge or care of a girl under the age of seventeen years causes or encourages the seduction or prostitution or unlawful carnal knowledge of that girl, this is a misdemeanour for which the penalty is two years imprisonment.
A person shall be deemed guilty of this offence, if he has

knowingly allowed the girl to consort with, or to enter or continue in the employment of, any prostitute or person of known immoral character. See also sexual offences, chapter 8.

Sale of cigarettes   S. 39
If a person sells to a person under the age of sixteen years any cigarettes, whether for his own use or not, it is an offence for which the penalty is a £2 fine and on a second offence a £5 fine.

Sale of intoxicating liquor
The Intoxicating Liquor Act 1988, when initiated as a Bill provided in
Section 31 as follows :
(1) The holder of any licence shall not
    (a) sell or deliver intoxicating liquor to a person under the age of eighteen years,
    (b) sell or deliver intoxicating liquor to any person for consumption on his licenced premises by a person under the age of eighteen years,
    (c) permit a person under the age of eighteen years to consume intoxicating liquor on his licenced premises.
(2) The holder of a licence of any licenced premises shall not sell or deliver intoxicating liquor to any person for consumption off his licenced premises by a person under the age of eighteen years
    in any place other than a private residence.

It is to be noted that the word "knowingly" is absent from the above. It will be a good defence for a licence holder to show that he had reasonable grounds for believing that a person was over the age of eighteen years.
The penalty on summary conviction for a first offence is a £50 fine, for a second offence a £100 fine and for a third offence a £300 fine.

The Intoxicating Liquor Act 1962, at section 27 (2) provides that: Intoxicating liquor in confectionery shall not be sold to a person who is under the age of sixteen years. A person who knowingly contravenes this section is liable to a £50 fine.

Unlawful gaming
By virtue of section 14(c) of the Gaming and Lotteries Act 1956; any gaming carried on at an amusement hall or funfair is unlawful if a person under the age of sixteen years is permitted

to play. See also the consideration of gaming later.

Pawning

The Pawnbrokers Act 1964, at section 19 (1)(a) provides that: A pawnbroker shall not knowingly take anything in pawn from a person under the age of sixteen years whether offered for pawning by that person on his own behalf or on behalf of another. The penalty is a £50 fine and or six months imprisonment.

It shall be a good defence for a pawnbroker to show that he did not know and had no reason to suspect that the person was under the age of sixteen years.

Solvent abuse

The Child Care Bill 1988, currently before the Dail provides that: any retailer who knowingly sells solvents to a minor for purpose of inhalation, commits an offence. A minor is a person under the age of eighteen years. Provision is to be made for a penalty of a £1,000 fine and or twelve months imprisonment.

Chapter 10

OFFENCES CONCERNING CHILD BIRTH

INFANTICIDE

Infanticide is the murder of a young child by its mother. In order that such women would not be liable for sentence of death the Infanticide Act 1949 was passed, this act provides that a woman is guilty of infanticide if;
(a) by any wilful act or omission she causes the death of her child, being under the age of twelve months, and
(b) the circumstances are such but for the act it would be murder, and
(c) at the time the balance of her mind was disturbed by reason of her not having fully recovered from the effect of giving birth to the child or by reason of the effect of lactation consequent upon the birth of the child.

On the preliminary investigation by the District Court of a charge against a woman for the murder of her child, the Justice may alter the charge to one of Infanticide. The penalty is as for manslaughter penal servitude for life.

ABORTION

Section 58(A) Every woman, being with child, who, with intent to procure her own miscarriage, shall unlawfully administer to herself any poison or other noxious thing, or shall unlawfully use any instrument or other means whatsoever with the like intent,... shall be guilty of a felony and on conviction liable to penal servitude for life,

Section 58(B) .... whosoever with intent to procure the miscarriage of any woman, whether she be or be not with child, shall unlawfully administer to her or cause to be taken by her any poison or other noxious thing, or shall unlawfully use any instrument or other means whatsoever with the like intent, shall be guilty of felony and on conviction liable to penal servitude for life.

"Poison or other noxious thing'. The administering of a

recognized poison, even in a small harmless quantity, is an offence. Where something other than a recognized poison is used, it must be shown to be harmful.

"other means". This has been held to include the fingers of the hand.

"intent" If the substance administered is a poison or other noxious thing or if any instrument or other means is used to procure an abortion, then, provided that there was an intent to procure a miscarriage, the fact that no miscarriage was or could be produced is not relevant. These sections of the Offences Against the Person Act 1861 are entitled "attempts to procure Abortion".

If a woman is not pregnant and administers to herself any poison, etc., she is unable to commit the principle offence and therefore cannot be convicted of the crime of attempt. However not the following paragraph.

Conspiracy and aiding and abetting

It should be noted that in (A) it is essential that the woman be pregnant, whereas this is not the case in (B). It has been held that a woman, even though she is not pregnant, may be convicted of conspiring with others, or of aiding and abetting others to administer any poison, etc. to her contrary to (B)

Supply or procure

Section 59 Whosoever shall unlawfully supply or procure any poison or other noxious thing, or any instrument or thing whatsoever, knowing that the same is intended to be unlawfully or employed with intent to procure the miscarriage of any woman, whether she be be or be not with child, shall be guilty of misdemeanour and on conviction liable to three years imprisonment.

"procure". As used firstly in section 59 means getting possession from another.

Counselling and assisting abortion

Attorney General (S.P.U.C.) V Open Door Counselling and Dublin Well Women (1988)

Article 40.3.3 of the Constitution provides that the State acknowledges the right to life of the unborn and with due regard to the equal right to life of the mother guarantees in its laws to defend and vindicate that right. The defendants carried on a service to pregnant women which included non-directive counselling. Abortion might be one of the options discussed during such counselling, and where the client wished to consider such option further, the defendants arranged to refer her to a medical clinic in Britain where abortions are performed. The plaintiff claimed that the activities of the defendants were unlawful having regard to the provisions of the Constitution and an order prohibiting the defendants from carrying on the said activities. In the High Court; Hamilton P. stated " I am satisfied that the activities of both defendants, through their servants and agents amount to counselling and assisting pregnant women to travel abroad to obtain further advice on abortion and to secure an abortion." He went on to state that such activities were unlawful having regard to Article 40.3.3 . On appeal to the Supreme Court; Finlay C. J. varied the order of Hamilton P. as follows " and it is ordered that the defendants ..... be perpetually restrained from assisting pregnant women within the jurisdiction to travel abroad to obtain abortions by referral to a clinic, by the making for them of travel arrangements, or by informing them of the identity and location of and the method of communication with a specified clinic or clinics or otherwise."

Advocacy
The Censorship of Publications Act 1929 Section 16 makes the following provision:
        (i)   it shall not be lawful for any person
        (a) to print or publish
        (b) to sell
        (c) to distribute
any book which advocates   the procurement of abortion or miscarriage

CONCEALMENT OF BIRTH

Section 60; If any woman shall be delivered of a child, every person who shall, by any secret disposition of the dead body of the said child, whether such child died before, at, or after its birth, endeavour to conceal the birth thereof, shall be guilty of a misdemeanour and be liable of two years imprisonment.
The offence may be committed by any person; and any person who assists in concealing the body is a principal in the first

degree.

R V Berriman (1854)

There is no offence of concealment unless a child "had arrived at that stage of maturity at the time of birth that it might have been a living child"; per Earle J. Thus the concealment of a few months old foetus would be no offence.

If a person is acquitted of Infanticide and there is sufficient evidence, such person may be convicted of this offence.

Secret disposition

Mere denial of the birth is not sufficient without some actual and secret disposition of the body. What is a secret disposition must depend on the circumstances of each particular case. A mere abandonment of the body will not sufficient, there must have been an attempt to prevent the body being found. The concealment must be from the world at large and not from any particular individual. A mere concealment of the fact of birth would not suffice.

Body of child

In order to convict a woman of endeavouring to conceal the birth of her child a dead body must, as a rule, be found and identified as that of the child of which she is alleged to have been delivered.

Chapter 11

WHAT CONSTITUTES LARCENY

The law relating to larceny is principally contained in the Larceny Act 1861 and in the Larceny Act 1916, the later Act's purpose was described as "to consolidate and simplify the law relating to larceny triable on indictment, and similar offences.", in doing this it partly replaced and repealed the earlier Act. It is to the 1916 Act that all references in this and the following chapters are too unless otherwise stated.

THE DEFINITION OF STEALING

The Larceny Act, 1916 at section 1 (1) declares that for the purpose of the act; A person steals who, without the consent of the owner, fraudulently and without a claim of right made in good faith, takes and carries away anything capable of being stolen with intent, at the time of such taking, permanently to deprive the owner thereof;

The act further provides that a person may be guilty of stealing any such thing notwithstanding that he has lawful possession thereof, if, being a bailee or part owner thereof, he fraudulently converts the same to his own use or the use of any person other than the owner;

Takes 1.(2)(i)
The expression takes includes obtaining possession -
(a) by any trick;
(b) by intimidation;
(c) under a mistake on the part of the owner with knowledge on the part of the taker that possession has been so obtained;
(d) by finding, were at the time of the finding the finder believes that the owner can be discovered by taking reasonable steps;

Carries away 1.(2)(ii)
The expression carries away includes any removal of anything from the place which it occupies, but in the case of a thing attached, only if it has been completely detached;

85

Owner 1.(2)(iii)
The expression owner includes any part owner, or person having possession of control of, or a special property in, anything capable of being stolen;

Capable of being stolen 1(3)
Everything which has value and is the property of any person, and if adhering to the reality then after severance therefrom, shall be capable of being stolen:

(a) save as hereinafter expressly provided with respect to fixtures, growing things, and ore from mines, anything attached to or forming part of the realty shall not be capable of being stolen by the person who severs the same from the realty, unless after severance he has abandoned possession thereof; and

(b) the carcase of a creature wild by nature and not reduced into possession while living shall not be capable of being stolen by the person who has killed such creature, unless after killing it he has abandoned possession of the carcase.

The constituent parts of the definition of stealing not referred to in the act can now be considered.

Without the consent of the owner
If a person takes with the consent of the owner, then there can be no stealing. However consent on the part of the owner, must be given freely, without any duress. Given the wide definition of the owner referred to above, any consent would also be required from a person having possession , control, or a special property in anything, such as an employee of the owner.

Fraudulently and without a claim of right
There can be no stealing where a person takes something, believing that he has a right to do so. Where there is a mistake of fact or of law, or even if a person uses violence to recover what he believes to be his own property, there can be no crime. Any claim of right must be made in good faith, an open taking may be evidence of good faith
The People (A. G.) V. Grey (1944).
The appellant, an officer of a public company was charged with taking property contrary to section 20.1(ii) . It was held by the Court of Criminal Appeal that a claim by the appellant that, he

honestly believed that he was entitled to take the property should have been left to the jury with the direction that if when he took the property, he honestly believed that he was entitled to do so, he ought to be acquitted, even though his claim to be so entitled was not well founded in law or in fact.

The People (D.P.P.) V O'Loughlin (1979)

The police found stolen machinery on the land of the accused. He was convicted of larceny. During the course of the trial the judge had refused to allow evidence in support of a claim of right based on an alleged belief by the accused that he had been entitled to take the machinery from its owner because the latter owed him money. It was held by the Court of Criminal Appeal that the accused should have been allowed to introduce evidence in support of his alleged claim of right, because such, although not well founded in law or in fact may be established.

D P P V Morrissey (1982)

The defendant was charged with feloniously stealing meat contrary to section 2 of the Act. He had ordered the meat at the meat counter of a supermarket. He admitted taking the meat but explained that he did not know why he had done so as he had not got the money to pay for it. The District Justice stated a case as to whether such facts sufficed to sustain a charge. It was held by the High Court that in the absence of evidence to the contrary the only necessary inference from the giving of the meat to the defendant was that he was required to show the meat and pay the price of it before leaving and that he had accepted it with this knowledge. It follows in the absence of evidence to the contrary the only necessary inference was that on leaving the shop without his disclosing his possession of the meat and without paying for it, the defendant at the time of leaving if not at the time of receiving the meat, had the intention of depriving the owner of it and that he had obtained it fraudulently and without the consent of the owner.

With intent at the time of such taking

There must be an intention at the time of the taking, to permanently deprive the owner of his property. Where an accused intended only to temporarily deprive an owner of his property then he cannot be convicted of stealing. A person must have at the time of the time of the taking made up his mind that he was going to permanently deprive the owner of his property, this is the intention of stealing known as the *animus furandi*, it is the *mens rea* of larceny.

If a person receives goods innocently and subsequently appropriates them, he cannot be guilty of larceny.

R V Hehir (1895)
Hehir was given a £10 note in mistake for a £1 note. When Hehir discovered its true value, he fraudulently appropriated it to his own use. On this evidence he was convicted of larceny. It was held on appeal that the subsequent fraudulent misappropriation of the £10 note, innocently acquired was not larceny.

Kinds of larceny

Through the period of the development of the common law, distinction were made as to different kinds of larceny. A distinction was made according to the value of the thing stolen. If it were worth only 12d. or less, the offence was a "Petty" larceny. If the thing were worth more than 12d. the offence was "Grand" larceny. This distinction ceased to apply after 1827. Thereafter larceny was still considered to be either "Simple" or "Aggravated". See below re simple larceny. Aggravated larceny is of various kinds. The circumstances by which larceny may be aggravated are as follows :
(1) The place where it is committed, i.e. a dwelling-house.
(2) The manner in which it is committed, i.e. robbery.
(3) The person by whom it is committed, i.e. embezzlement.
(4) The nature of the thing stolen, i.e. wills, postal packets.

Simple larceny

By section 2 of the Act: Stealing for which no special punishment is provided shall be simple larceny, punishable with five years imprisonment.

The State (Foley) V Carroll (1980)
It was held by the High Court, that the offence of simple larceny in section 2, is not the creation of statute but is an offence at common law for which a statutory penalty is provided by that section.

Attempt to steal

Re Michael Woods (1970)
It was held by the Supreme Court, that an attempt to steal is an offence at common law and the punishment is either fine or imprisonment.

Accessories and abettors

By section 35 of the Act: Every person who knowingly and wilfully aids, abets, counsels, procures or commands the commission of an offence punishable under this Act shall be liable to be dealt with, indicted, tried and punished as a principal offender.

Husband or wife

At common law the possession of husband and wife was one and the same, so that neither could be convicted of stealing the other's goods. However by section 36 of the Act, every wife has the same remedies for the protection of her property as if such property belonged to her as feme sole. However it is provided that no proceedings can be taken by a wife against her husband, while they are living together, concerning property claimed by her, nor, while they are living apart, as to any act done by the husband while they were living together concerning property claimed by her, unless such property has been wrongfully taken by the husband when leaving or deserting, or about to leave or desert, his wife.

SUBJECTS OF LARCENY

Cattle etc. S.3
Every person who steals any horse, cattle, or sheep shall be guilty of a felony, and on conviction liable to fourteen year imprisonment.

Killing animals S.4
Every person who wilfully kills any animal with intent to steal the carcase, skin, or any part of the animal killed, shall be guilty of felony, and on conviction liable as if he had stolen such animal.

Dogs S.5
Every person who -
(1) steals any dog after a previous summary conviction of any such offence, or
(2) unlawfully has in his possession or on his premises any stolen dog, or the skin thereof , knowing such dog or skins to have been stolen, after a previous summary conviction of any such offence, or

(3) corruptly takes any money or reward, directly or indirectly, under pretences or upon account of aiding any person to recover any stolen dog, or any dog which is in the possession of any person not being the owner thereof;

shall be guilty of a misdemeanour, and on conviction liable to eighteen months imprisonment.

By section 18 of the Larceny Act 1861, the stealing of a dog is a summary offence, for which the penalty is up to six months imprisonment.

Wills S.6

Every person who steals any will, codicil, or other testamentary instrument, either of a dead or of a living person, shall be guilty of felony and on conviction liable to life imprisonment.

By section 29 of the 1861 Act, for any fraudulent purpose to destroy, cancel,obliterate, or conceal, either during the life or after the death of the testator, the whole or any part of any will, codicil, or other testamentary instrument, whether of real or personal property, is a like offence.

Documents S.7

Every person who steals the whole or any part of -
(1) any document of title to lands; or
(2) any record, writ, return, panel, petition, process, interrogatory, deposition, affidavit, rule, order, warrant of attorney, or any cause of matte, civil or criminal, begun, depending, or terminated in any such court; or
(3) any original document relating to the business of any office of employment under the State.

shall be guilty of felony, and on conviction liable to five years.

By section 46 of the Act the expression "document of title to lands" includes any deed., map, roll, register, paper, or parchment, written of printed., or partly written and partly printed, being or containing evidence of the title, or any part of the title, to any real estate or to any interest in or out of any real estate.

Fixtures, trees, etc. S.8

Every person who

(1) Steals, or, with intent to steal , rips cuts severs or breaks-
   (a) any glass or woodwork belonging to any building; or
   (b) any metal or utensil or fixture, fixed in or to any building; or
   (c) anything made of metal fixed in any land being private property, or in any place dedicated to public use or ornament, or in any burial-ground:
(2) Steals, or, ..cuts breaks,roots up,or destroys or damages the whole or any part of any tree, sapling, shrub, or underwood growing-...
(3) Steals,...destroys or damages any plant, root, fruit, or vegetable production growing in any garden, etc. after a previous summary conviction of any such offence;
shall be guilty of a felony and liable as in the case of simple larceny.

Goods in process of manufacture S.9
Every person who steals to the value of ten shillings, any woollen, linen, hempen, or cotton yarn or any goods ..... during any stage, process or progress of manufacture, ...fourteen years imprisonment.

Abstracting of electricity S.10
Every person who maliciously or fraudulently abstracts, causes to be wasted or diverted, consumes or uses any electricity shall be guilty of felony, and liable as in the case of simple larceny.

Ore from mines S.11
Every person who steals, or severs with intent to steal, the ore of any metal, etc. from any mine .. liable to two years imprisonment.

Postal packets S.12
Every person who -
(1) steals a mail bag ; or
(2) steals from a mail bag, post office, officer of An Post, or mail, any postal packet in course of transmission by post ; or
(3) steals any chattel, money or valuable security out of a postal packet in course of transmission by post ; or

(4) stops a mail with intent to rob the mail ;
shall be guilty of felony and liable to life imprisonment.

POACHING

The Night Poaching Act 1828 as amended by the Night Poaching Act 1844, makes provision for poaching by night.

By section 1 of the Act as amended it is provided that any person who by night (i.e. from one hour after sunset to one hour before sunrise)

(i) unlawfully takes or destroys any game or rabbits on any land, whether open or enclosed, or upon any road, highway, or path; or

(ii) unlawfully enters or is on any land, whether open or enclosed, with any gun, net or other instrument for the purpose of taking game.

shall be guilty of an offence for which the penalty on summary conviction in the case of a first offence is three months imprisonment and in the case of a second offence is six months imprisonment and on indictment in the case of a third offence it being a misdemeanour is seven years imprisonment.

By section 9 of the Act as amended; Where three or more persons by night unlawfully enter or be upon any land, open or enclosed, or any road etc. for the purpose of taking or destroying game or rabbits, and if any such person is armed with any gun, stick, club or other offensive weapon they shall be guilty of a misdemeanour for which the penalty is fourteen years imprisonment.

Chapter 12

RECEIVING STOLEN GOODS

By section 33 of the Act; Every person who receives any property knowing the same to have been stolen or obtained in any way whatsoever under circumstances which amount to felony or misdemeanour, shall be guilty of an offence of the like degree.

The ingredients of this offence are as follows :
(1) The commission of the principal offence,
(2) That the property was received by the accused,
(3) That the receipt was with felonious intent,
(4) That the goods at the time of their receipt were stolen,
(5) Knowledge that the goods were stolen.

Commission of the principal offence
The commission of the principal offence; that the goods with which the accused is charged with receiving were obtained in some way under circumstances amounting to felony or misdemeanour, see *Walters V Lunt* in chapter 4 above.

It is not necessary, to prove from whom or by whom the goods were stolen. The circumstances in which the accused received the goods may of themselves prove that they were stolen.

The People (A.G.) V Mulcahy and Carney
It was held by the Court of Criminal Appeal, that it is a necessary ingredient of the crime of receiving stolen goods that some person other than the receiver should be shown to have stolen them.

A person cannot be guilty of receiving, if he has stolen the goods himself;

O'Leary V Cunningham (1980)
It was held by the Supreme Court that, as the evidence established that the accused was guilty of robbery of money on the occasion mentioned in the charges, the accused could not be convicted of having received that money on the same occasion, knowing it to have been stolen.

At common law an indictment did not lie for receiving property stolen abroad, however this has been altered by section 33(4) of the Act.

93

Attorney General V Finegan (1933)

The applicant was convicted of having in County Louth, receiving a bicycle lamp knowing it to have been stolen. At the trial it appeared that the lamp had been taken from a bicycle just outside the boundary of the State. It was held by the Court of Criminal Appeal that the evidence that the lamp had been stolen outside the State, did not oust the jurisdiction of the court.

Property was received by the accused

That the property was received by the accused. It must be proved that the accused had possession or control of the property. It is not necessary that he should have the goods in his hands, It will be sufficient, if the goods are in the hands of an associate, or on the accused's premises, or in the hands of a servant.

Receipt was with felonious intent

It must be proved that the receipt was with felonious intent. Where there is an innocent receipt, a subsequent intention to appropriate the property does not constitute the necessary intention for the offence.

Goods at the time of their receipt were stolen

That the goods at the time of their receipt were stolen. If an owner had resumed possession of the good before they were received by an accused, then they have ceased to be stolen goods.

R V Schmidt (1866)

A stole goods from a railway company and sent them to B by the same railway company. The theft was discovered by an employee of the company, who stopped the goods and gave them to a porter to keep, but then subsequently ordered the porter to take the goods to B. It was held that, as the company had resumed possession, the goods were no longer stolen goods and that B could not be convicted of receiving.

Knowledge that the goods were stolen

That the accused at the time when he received the property knew that it was stolen. This may be proved by direct evidence or circumstantially by evidence of facts from which knowledge may be inferred. There is a presumption that an accused will, if innocent, explain his possession on oath at the earliest possible time.

The People (A.G.) V Shaw (1960)
It was held by the Court of Criminal Appeal that, the evidence of a third party that the goods were sold to him by the accused shortly after the theft can, in the absence of any explanation given by the accused of the manner in which the goods came into his possession, properly be treated by the jury as corroborative of the thief's evidence that the goods were stolen by him and received by the accused.

Evidence

By section 43(1) of the Act, where proceedings are taken against a person for receiving stolen property, evidence that other property stolen within the preceding twelve months was found or had been in his possession may be given at any stage of the proceedings for the purpose of proving his guilty knowledge.

People (Attorney-General) V. Oglesby (1966)
The accused was convicted in the Circuit Court on the charge of receiving a tape recorder the property of C.I.E. knowing it to have been stolen. The accused had told the guards that he had bought the tape recorder from a man in a pub. It was held by the Court of Criminal Appeal, that the so called doctrine of recent possession does not exist, but that it is a convenient way of referring to inferences of fact which, in the absence of any satisfactory explanation, may be drawn as a matter of common sense from other facts. It is the duty of a trial Judge to state any explanation to the jury; he may then comment on it.

The onus of proving guilty knowledge, however always remains on the prosecution.

The People (A.G.) V Lillis (1958)
It was held by the Court of Criminal appeal that, in a case of receiving stolen goods, a direction that the jury should convict if they were satisfied that the explanation given by the accused of how the goods came into his possession was a fabrication could not convey to the jury that the burden of proof had shifted in any degree from the prosecution and is a proper direction.

Penalty

If the original stealing or obtaining was a felony, the receiver is guilty of a felony and liable to fourteen years imprisonment.

If the original stealing or obtaining was a misdemeanour, the receiving is a misdemeanour and the offender is liable to seven years imprisonment.

If the original stealing was a summary offence under the Larceny Act 1861, the receiving is a similar offence with the same penalty.

Unlawful possession

The Criminal Justice Act 1951, at section 13 provides as follows ;

(1) A member of the Garda Siochana may arrest without warrant a person whom he reasonably suspects of having or conveying in any manner anything stolen or unlawfully obtained.

(2) A person who is charged before the District Court with having in his possession or on his premises with his knowledge or conveying in any manner anything which may be reasonably suspected of being stolen or unlawfully obtained and who does not give an account to the satisfaction of the Court how he came by it shall be guilty of an offence, for which the penalty is £5 and or two months imprisonment.

Attorney General V Brodigan

An accused who was suspected of being concerned in a housebreaking either as principal or receiver, was charged in the District Court with unlawful possession of a sum of money contrary to section 13 of the Criminal Justice Act, 1951. The evidence against him was that he had spent a considerable sum of money of which he gave no satisfactory account but no sum of money had been found on his person or on his premises, and none of the money spent by him was identifiable as the subject-matter of the housebreaking. It was held that the possession necessary to support such a charge, must be referable to the time when such charge was preferred, and that in the absence of evidence of possession at such time, such charge must be dismissed.

Withholding information regarding stolen property

The Criminal Justice Act 1984, at section 16(1) provides as follows:

Where a member of the Garda Siochana -

(a) has reasonable grounds for believing that an offence

consisting of the stealing, fraudulent conversion, embezzlement or unlawful obtaining or receiving of money or other property has been committed,

(b) finds any person in possession of any property,

(c) has reasonable grounds for believing that the property includes, or may include the property referred to in (a) and

(d) informs that person of his belief,

he may require that person to give him an account of how he came by the property.

Failure to give an account is an offence, for which the penalty on summary conviction is £1,000 fine and or twelve months imprisonment.

Restitution

The general rule is that the property rights in stolen goods always remain in the original owner, no matter how many times they may change hands for good consideration, whether by sale in market overt or otherwise. By section 45 of the Act, where a person is prosecuted to conviction any property affected shall be restored to it's original owner. This is done by means of a restitution order.

Chapter 13

LARCENY IN PROPERTY

Larceny in dwelling-houses S. 13
Every person who steals in any dwelling house any chattel, money, or valuable security shall-
(a) if the value of the property stolen amounts to five pounds:.. be guilty of felony and liable to fourteen years imprisonment.
No breaking or entry with intent to commit an offence need be proved, but the building must be a dwelling-house, and the goods must be under the protection of the house. Under this section an owner of a house can be prosecuted for larceny.

Larceny from ships,docks, etc. S. 15
Every person who steals-
        (1) any goods in any vessel,...
        (2) any goods from any dock,...
        (3) any part of any vessel in distress,...
shall be guilty of felony and liable for fourteen years imprisonment.

Larceny by tenants or lodgers S. 16
Every person who, being a tenant or lodger, or the husband or wife of any tenant or lodger, steals any chattel or fixture let to be used by such person in or with any house or lodging shall be guilty of felony and on conviction thereof liable-
(a) if the value exceeds five pounds, seven years imprisonment.
(b) in all other cases, two years imprisonment.

Burglary S. 23A
(1) A person is guilty of burglary if-
    (a) he enters any building or part of a building as a trespasser and with intent to commit any such offence as is mentioned in subsection (2), or
    (b) having entered any building ar part of a building as a trespasser, he steals or attempts to steal anything in the building or that part of it, or inflicts or attempts to inflict on any person therein any grievous bodily harm.
(2) The offences referred to in subsection (1)(a) are offences

of stealing anything in the building or part of a building in question,

of inflicting on any person therein any grievous bodily harm or

raping any woman therein and

of doing unlawful damage to the building or anything therein.

(4) A person guilty or burglary shall be liable to fourteen years imprisonment.

"enter"

The term "enter" is not defined in the Act, at common law there was a sufficient entry when any part of the body of the accused went over the threshold, for example a finger. If an instrument is inserted into the building for the purpose of committing the ulterior offence, there is an entry even though no part of the body is introduced into the building. On the other hand, the insertion of an instrument for the purpose of gaining entry and not for the purpose of committing the ulterior offence, is not an entry if no part of the body enters.

R V Collins (1972)

Collins had climbed a ladder to an open window through which he saw a sleeping girl, with whom he had some slight acquaintance. The girl awoke and believing that Collins was her boyfriend, welcomed him to her bed, where intercourse took place. On discovering her mistake the girl struck Collins. Collins was convicted of burglary in that he had entered a building as a trespasser with intent to commit rape. The Court of Appeal allowed an appeal on the basis that the jury were never invited to consider the question whether Collins did enter the premises as a trespasser, that is to say knowing perfectly well that he had no invitation to enter or reckless of whether or not his entry was with permission.

R V Brown (1985)

Brown had been seen partially inside a broken shop window, his feet still on the ground outside, rummaging through the goods. He was convicted of burglary and appealed on the basis that entry meant a complete entry. His appeal was dismissed, it being held that the entry had to be "effective". Whether it is so depends on the circumstances of the case, and it was obviously effective here.

"Trespass"

"Trespass" involves an entry on land without an invitation of any sort and without lawful justification. Were consent to entry is obtained by fraud, then the entry is a trespass. With regard to mistake, a defendant ought not to be guilty of burglary if he honestly believes that the owner has consented, or honestly believes that he has a right of entry even though his mistake in the circumstances is an unreasonable one. Note R V Collins above.

R V Jones; R V Smith (1976)

Smith and Jones had entered a bungalow belonging to the father of one of them and had taken two televisions. They were convicted of burglary. They appealed on the basis that a person who had a general permission to enter, such as a son, could not be a trespasser for the purposes of the offence. The Court of Appeal dismissed the appeal. James L.J. stated "..it is our view that a person is a trespasser....if he enters premises of another knowing that he is entering in excess of the permission that has been given to him, or being reckless that he is acting in excess of the permission given or that he is acting recklessly as to whether he exceeds that permission, then, that is sufficient for the jury to decide that he is in fact a trespasser.."

"intent"

The "intent" must have existed at the time of the entry, the subsequent formation of an intention to steal after an entry will not suffice. It is not relevant that the stealing was or was not possible; it is sufficient that an accused had an intent to steal.

"Building"

"Building" itself is not defined, presumably it covers not only houses, but shops and offices, however subsection 3 states that references to a building shall apply also to an inhabited vehicle or vessel at times when the the person having a habitation in it is not there as well as well as at times when he is there. Outbuildings of a house seem to be a building. To be a building, the structure must have some degree of permanence and it seems clear that it would not include a tent even though some person lived in the tent.

Aggravated burglary S. 23B

(1) A person is guilty of aggravated burglary if he commits any burglary and at the time has with him any firearm or imitation firearm, any weapon of offence or any explosive; and for this purpose-

    (a) firearm includes an airgun or airpistol, and imitation firearm means anything that has the appearance of being a firearm, whether capable of being discharged or not;

    (b) weapon of offence means any article made or adopted for use for causing injury to or incapacitating a person or intended by the person having it with him for that purpose.

    (c) explosive means any article manufactured for the purpose of producing a practical effect by explosion, or intend by the person having it with him fir that purpose.

(2) A person guilty of aggravated burglary shall be liable on conviction on indictment to imprisonment for life.

<u>"at the time"</u>

"at the time" for a person to be convicted, it is necessary to show that he had the firearm etc. with him at the time he committed the burglary.

R. V Francis (1982)

The accused gained entry to a house, armed with sticks. After throwing away the sticks he stole property. The Court of Appeal substituted a conviction for burglary for one of aggravated burglary. Unless the accused intended to steal when he entered the house, he was only guilty of aggravated burglary if he had a weapon with him at the time when he stole.

R V O'Leary (1986)

The accused armed himself after entering a house. It was held by the Court of Appeal that the material time for the possession of a weapon is the point at which the accused actually stole.

Being found by night S. 28

Every person who shall be found by night -

(1) armed with any dangerous or offensive weapon or instrument, with intent to break or enter into any building and to commit any felony therein; or

(2) having in his possession without lawful excuse (the proof

whereof shall lie on such person) any key, picklock, crow, jack, bit or other implement of housebreaking; or

(3) having his face blackened or disguised with intent to commit any felony; or

(4) in any building with intent to commit any felony therein;

shall be guilty of a misdemeanour and liable -

(a) if previously convicted : ten years imprisonment.

(b) in all other cases : five years imprisonment.

By virtue of section 41 of the Act, any person may arrest without warrant anyone who is, or whom he, with reasonable cause, suspects to be, committing this offence.

By virtue of section 46 the expression "night" means the interval between nine o'clock in the evening and six o'clock in the morning of the next succeeding day.

There is similar provision, regarding the possession of implements contained in the Vagrancy Act 1824, at section 4 which is not confined to possession at night, see chapter 20 on public peace.

Chapter 14

LARCENY FROM PEOPLE

In dwelling-houses   S. 13
Every person who steals in any dwelling-house any chattel, money, or valuable security shall-
(b) if he by any menace or threat puts any person being in such dwelling-be liable to fourteen years imprisonment.

From the person   S. 14
Every person who steals any chattel, money or valuable security from the person of another shall be guilty of felony and liable to fourteen years imprisonment.

Robbery S. 23
(1) A person is guilty of robbery if he steals, and immediately before or at the time of doing so, and in order to do so, he uses force on any person or puts or seeks to put any person in fear of being then and there subjected to force.
(2) A person guilty of robbery, or of an assault with intent to rob shall be liable on conviction on indictment to imprisonment for life.

"If he steals"
The force, or threat of force, if it is to amount to robbery, must be used in order that the accused might steal; therefore, where a person does not steal, he cannot be convicted of robbery.

"Immediately before or at the time"
Where force is used in order to steal, it will constitute the offence only where it is used at the very time of stealing, or immediately before.
R V Hale (1978)
The defendant entered the house of a woman. He put his hand over her mouth to stop her screaming, went upstairs, took her jewellery and then tied her up and gagged her before making off. He was convicted of robbery. The Court of Appeal dismissed his appeal and held that the jury were entitled to convict, relying on the force used at the start when the accused

put his hand over the woman's mouth; further the force used in tying her up also occurred "immediately before or at the time of stealing" as is required since the act of appropriation was a continuing one and the stealing was not over when she was tied up.

"Uses force or seeks to put any person in fear"
The actual or threatened use of force against a person will suffice.
(a) The force may be minimal but must be more than a slight physical contact. A mere accidental use of force will not suffice.
(b) The force or threat of force must be against a person, a threat to damage property will not suffice.
(c) The actual or threatened force can be against any person and need not be against the person whose property is stolen.
(d) The question of whether or not force, has been used in an alleged robbery is for the jury.
R V Dawson (1976)
The Court of Appeal held in upholding a conviction, that it was open to a jury to decide that nudging the victim so as to cause him to lose his balance (thereby enabling an accomplice to steal his wallet) was sufficient "force" to justify a conviction for robbery.

Blackmail

Demanding with menaces   S. 29
(1) Every person who -
   (i) utters, knowing the contents thereof, any letter or writing demanding of any person with menaces, and without any reasonable or probable cause, any property or valuable thing;
   (ii) utters, knowing the contents therof, any letter or writing accusing or threatening to accuse any other person of any crime . with intent to extort or gain thereby any property or valuable thing from any person;
   (iii) with intent to extort or gain any property or valuable thing from any person accuses or threatens to accuse either that person or any other person (whether living or dead) of any . crime;

shall be guilty of felony and liable to life imprisonment.

(2) Every person who with intent to defraud or injure any other person -

    (a) by any unlawful violence to or restraint of the person of another, or

    (b) by accusing or threatening to accuse any person (whether living or dead) of any crime.

    compels . any person to execute, make, accept, endorse, alter, or destroy . any valuable security

shall be guilty of felony and liable to life imprisonment.

(3) This section applies to any crime punishable with death or imprisonment for not less than seven years, or any assault with intent to commit any rape, or any attempt to commit any rape, or any solicitation, persuasion, promise or threat offered or made to any person, whereby to move or induce such person to commit or permit the crime of buggery.

(4) It is immaterial whether any menaces or threats be of violence, injury, or accusation to be caused or made by the offender or by any other person.

Demanding with menaces with intent to steal S. 30
Every person who with menaces or by force demands of any person anything capable of being stolen with intent to steal the same shall be guilty of felony and on conviction thereof liable to five years imprisonment.

Menaces
Thorne V Motor Trade Association (1937)
Lord Wright said " I think the word 'menace' is to be liberally construed and not as limited to threats of violence but as including threats of any action detrimental to or unpleasant to the person addressed."

Threatening to publish with intent to exhort S. 31
Every person who with intent -
(a) to extort any valuable thing from any person, or
(b) to induce any person to confer or procure for any person any appointment or office of profit or trust,
(1) publishes or threatens to publish any libel upon any other person (whether living or dead);

(2) directly or indirectly threatens to print or publish, or directly or indirectly proposes to abstain from or offers to prevent the printing or publishing of any matter or thing touching any other person (whether living or dead).

shall guilty of a misdemeanour and be liable to two years imprisonment.

Obtaining by false pretences   S. 32

Every person who, by any false pretence, with intent to defraud, obtains from any other person any chattel, money, or valuable security or causes or procures any money to be paid, or any chattel or valuable security to be delivered to himself or to any other person for the use or benefit or on account of himself or any other person is guilty of a misdemeanour, for which the penalty is five years imprisonment.

The Criminal Justice Act 1951, at section 10 makes provision for a like offence, with the inclusion of the words "anything capable of being stolen", which has the effect of broadening the offence.

To constitute this offence, it is necessary that :

(1) A pretence or representation must be made.
(2) The pretence must be made to the person from whom the property was obtained or his agent.
(3) The pretence must be to a matter of fact and not opinion.
(4) The pretence must have relation to past or present facts.
(5) The pretence must be false to the knowledge of the accused.
(6) The pretence must be the cause of the obtaining.
(7) The obtaining must be with intent to defraud.
(8) The intent must be to deprive the owner wholly of his property.

Attorney-General V. Sullivan (1964)

S. a registered midwife was charged with unlawfully attempting to obtain money by false pretences with intent to defraud. It was alleged that she had prepared certain prescribed forms which, if genuine, would have signified her professional attendance on the patients named on the said forms, and had them signed by the said patients. S. did not attend any of these patients and the forms submitted by her were fictitious and, it was alleged were presented with fraudulent intent. It was held by the Supreme Court that each false "claim" was an act sufficiently proximate to constitute an attempt to commit the offence of obtaining by false pretences. It was held further that the offences in question are quiet clearly common law offences.

The People (Attorney General) V Heald (1954)

The applicant was the matron of a convalescent home run by an order of nuns and had authority to collect and expend fees and charges from patients in her discretion. She received into the home two elderly ladies on their paying her £2,000, which she placed in her own personal bank account, concealing this from the nuns. The nuns had discontinued their practice of receiving patients on a lump sum basis. The applicant was charged with 1, larceny and 2, fraudulent conversion contrary to section 20.1(IV)(b) of the Larceny Act 1916, she was acquitted of larceny and acquitted of fraudulent conversion. It was held by the Court of Criminal Appeal, that, in order to sustain the conviction it must be shown that the applicant had authority to receive the sum of money on behalf of the nuns and the onus of proving such authority lay on the prosecution. It was also held that, as there was a count of larceny in the indictment the jury could have been told that they could convict of obtaining money by false pretences on that count, the applicant had been in peril on a charge of false pretences and her acquittal of larceny precluded her from being now tried upon a charge of false pretences. The court accordingly ordered that the conviction should be quashed.

Cheating

Cheating is a misdemeanour at common law for which the penalty is imprisonment, it has been defined as "...deceitful practices, in defrauding or endeavouring to defraud another of his own right by means of some artful device, contrary to the plain rules of common honesty."

Chapter 15

EMBEZZLEMENT and FRAUDULENT CONVERSION
(LARCENY BY PEOPLE)

EMBEZZLEMENT

At common law a servant could not be convicted of larceny, as he had properly acquired the legal possession of his master's goods. Accordingly it was necessary that an offence of embezzlement be created by statute. The distinction between embezzlement and larceny as regards clerks and servants is; In larceny the thing stolen is taken out of the possession of the master, whereas in embezzlement the thing is appropriated before it has come into the possession of the master, in breach of the duty to hand over that thing to the master.

Embezzlement by clerks or servants   S. 17

Every person who -

(1) being a clerk or servant or person employed in the capacity of a clerk or servant -
   (a) steals any chattel, money or valuable security belonging to or in the possession or power of his master or employer; or
   (b) fraudulently embezzles the whole or any part of any chattel, money or valuable security delivered to or received or taken into possession by him for or in the name or on the account of his master or employer :
(2) being employed in the public service or in the police -
   (a) steals any chattel, money or valuable security belonging to or in the possession the State or entrusted to or received or taken into possession by such person by virtue of his employment; or
   (b) embezzles or in any manner fraudulently applies or disposes of for any purpose whatsoever except for the public service any chattel, money or valuable security entrusted to or received or taken into possession by him by virtue of his employment :

shall be liable to fourteen years imprisonment.

The essentials to be proved in this offence are :

   (1) Clerk or servant.

(2) For or on account of.
(3) The appropriation.

Clerk or servant.
This section does not apply where a man is an agent, but only where the relationship of master and servant exists. Whether such relationship exists is a question of fact for the jury. An agent is a person employed to act and contract as the representative of another person, who is his principal. A servant is a person who, as an instrument for the performance of work, gives his time and labour to and under the control and bound to obey the orders of his master.
The People (Attorney-General) V Warren (1945)
A rate collector appointed by Dublin Corporation was convicted on the Circuit Court of embezzlement contrary to Section 17(1) of the Larceny Act 1916. It was held by the Court of Criminal Appeal that the appellant, was not a servant of the Corporation and the conviction was set aside.

For or on account of.
The money must have been received by the accused for, or in the name of, or on account of, his master or employer.
This requirement will be satisfied:
(1) Where a third part delivers something to the servant so that upon receipt of it by him the master becomes the owner of it and the servant misappropriates it.
(2) Where a third party delivers something to the servant intending thereby to deliver possession of that thing to the master, and the servant misappropriates it.
(3) Where a servant steals or embezzles things belonging to his master and sells them to a third party from whom he receives money. If he has received money in some other way, then that is not embezzlement.

The appropriation.
This may be proved by showing that the accused failed to account for or denied the receipt of the money or thing embezzled.It is not sufficient to prove a general deficiency in account, some specific sum must be proved to be embezzled.
Attorney General V Gleeson.
A clerk was indicted under Section 17(1)b of the Larceny Act

1916. It was held by the Court of Criminal Appeal, that the case of false entries and general deficiencies in tots made by the prosecution, if proved to the satisfaction of the jury, exhibited all the essential ingredients of the crime of embezzlement.

The doctrine of possession is so technical that it is not always clear whether it is larceny or embezzlement that a servant is guilty of. The absolute necessity for accuracy as far as the indictment is concerned is removed by section 44(2) which provides that; if on the trial of any indictment for embezzlement it is proved that the defendant stole the property in question, the jury may find him guilty of stealing; and on the trial of any indictment for stealing the jury may in like manner find the defendant guilty of embezzlement.

Embezzlement by officers of An Post   S. 18
Every person who being an officer of An Post steals or embezzles a postal packet in course of transmission by post . shall be liable
(a) if the postal packet contains any chattel, money or valuable security, to penal servitude for life.
(b) in all other cases . seven years imprisonment.
See also postal and telecommunications offences in chapter 23.

Embezzlement by officers of Bank of Ireland S.19
Every person who being an officer or servant of the Bank of Ireland and guilty of embezzlement shall be liable to life imprisonment. This was formulated when it was perceived that the Bank of Ireland would become the central bank, as the Bank of England is at the present time.

FRAUDULENT CONVERSION
Fraudulent conversion deals with the person who has obtained ownership on behalf of someone else. Although fraudulent conversion, unlike larceny and embezzlement, catches a person who is the owner of the goods, the definition of the offence is phrased widely enough to catch a person who has possession or, even only custody of the goods. Those who are not clerks or servants, such as agents could not be convicted of embezzlement and had a similar exemption under the common law. A trustee, since he has possession and even legal ownership of the things he holds for his cestui que trust, could

not by appropriating them commit any offence against the common law.

Conversion S. 20

(1) Every person who -

    (i) being entrusted either solely or jointly with any other person with any power of attorney for the sale or transfer of any property, fraudulently sells, transfers, or otherwise converts the property or any part thereof to his own use or benefit, or the use or benefit of any person other than the person by whom he was so entrusted; or

    (ii) being a director, member or officer of any body corporate or public company, fraudulently takes or applies for his own use or benefit, or for nay use or purpose other than the use or purpose of such body corporate or public company, any of the property of such body corporate or public company: or

    (iii) being authorized to receive money to arise from the sale of annuities or securities ....; or

    (iv)(a) being entrusted either solely or jointly with any other person with any property in order that he may retain in safe custody or apply, pay, or deliver, for any purpose or to any person, the property or any part thereof or any proceeds thereof; or

    (b) having either solely or jointly with any other person received any property for or on account of any other person;

    fraudulently converts to his own use or benefit, or the use or benefit of any other person, the property or any part thereof or any proceeds thereof;

shall be guilty of a misdemeanour and be liable to seven years imprisonment.

The essential to be proved in this offence are:

    (1) That the money, property, etc. was entrusted to the defendant for a particular purpose.

    (2) That he used it for some other purpose.

    (3) That the misuse was fraudulent and dishonest.

See *The People(A.G.) V Grey (1944)* above chapter 11.

It is for a jury to decide the question whether a person has been "entrusted" with property or has received it "for or on account of" another person.

Attorney General V Lawless (1930)

It was held by the courts of Criminal Appeal that on a charge of fraudulent conversion under section 20(1)(iv)(b), the question of whether money has been received by the accused "for on account of" other persons is in fact to be decided by the jury, and they must be expressly directed to find on the point.

The People (Attorney-General) V Cowan

The appellant a solicitor, was convicted of having fraudulently coveted to his own use a sum of money received by him for and on behalf of a client who had instructed him to obtain a grant of administration on his behalf to the estate of his infant son, to which he was entitled. A bank draft of the proceeds of the estate, made out to the client was at the applicants requests signed by him. The applicant lodged the bank draft to his own account. The client was not informed nor was he aware of the nature of the document he signed. Despite several demands he did not receive the money due to him. It was held by the Court of Criminal Appeal that the appellant when he received the money did so on his client's account. The appeal was dismissed and dismissed again by Supreme Court.

Conversion by trustee S. 21

Every person who, being a trustee, of any property for the use or benefit either wholly or partially of some other person, or for any public or charitable purpose, with intent to defraud converts or appropriates the same or any part thereof to or for his own use or benefit, or the use or benefit of any person other than such person as aforesaid, or for any purpose other than such public or charitable purpose as aforesaid, or otherwise disposes of or destroys such property or any part thereof, shall be guilty of a misdemeanour and liable to seven years imprisonment.

No prosecution shall be commenced-

(a) by any person without the sanction of the Attorney General;

(b) by any person who has taken any civil proceedings against such trustee, without the sanction also of the court.

By section 46, "trustee" means a trustee on some express trust created by some deed, will, or instrument in writing, and includes the heir or personal representative of any such trustee, and any other person upon or to whom the duty of such trust shall have devolved or come.

Factors obtaining advances S. 22

(1) Every person who, being a factor or agent entrusted either solely or jointly with any other person for the purpose of sale or otherwise, with the possession of any goods or of any documents of title to goods contrary to or without the authority of his principal in that behalf for his own use or benefit, or for the use or benefit of any person other than the person by whom he was so entrusted, and in violation of good faith-.

   (i) Consigns, deposits, transfers, or delivers any goods or documents of title so entrusted to him as and by way of a pledge, lien, or security for any money or valuable security borrowed or received, or intended to be borrowed or received by him; or

   (ii) Accepts any advances of any money or valuable security on the faith of any contract or agreement to consign, deposit, transfer, or deliver any such goods or documents of title;

shall be guilty of a misdemeanour and liable to seven years imprisonment. Provided that no such factor or agent shall be liable to prosecution, for consigning, etc. any such goods, etc. if they are not made a security for or subject to the payment of any greater sum of money than, at the time of such consignment,etc. justly due and owing to such agent from his principal, together with the amount of any bill of exchange drawn by or on account of such principal and accepted by such factor or agent.

RELATED OFFENCES

Corruptly taking a reward   S. 34

Every person who corruptly takes any money or reward, directly or indirectly, under pretence or upon account of helping any person to recover any property which has, under circumstances which amount to felony or misdemeanour, been stolen or obtained in any way whatsoever, or received, shall(unless he has used all due diligence to cause the offender to be brought to trial for the same) shall be guilty of felony and on conviction liable to seven years imprisonment.

113

False personation

The False personation Act 1874, at section 1 provides that ;
Any person who shall falsely and deceitfully personate any person, or the heir, executor, or administrator, wife, widow, next of kin, or relation of any person, with intent fraudulently to obtain any land, estate, chattel, money, valuable security, or property shall be guilty of a felony for which the penalty is two years imprisonment.

Falsification of accounts

The Falsification of accounts Act 1875 at section 1, provides that it is a misdemeanour, the penalty for which is seven years imprisonment, for a clerk, officer, or servant, or person employed in any such capacities, wilfully and with intent to defraud, to destroy, alter, falsify, or omit to make any entry in any book, papers, accounts, etc., in the possession of or received by him for his employer.

The falsification of a mechanical means of accounting is within this section.
R V Solomons (1909)
A taxi-driver put his meter out of action and appropriated the fares to himself. It was held that he could be convicted of falsifying an account.

Fraud by moneylenders

The Moneylenders Act 1900, at section 4 provides that any moneylender, or any manager, agent, or clerk of a moneylender, or any director, manager, or other officer of any corporation carrying on the business of a moneylender, who by any false, misleading, or deceptive statement, representation or promise, or by any dishonest concealment of material facts, fraudulently induces or attempts to induce any person to borrow money or to agree to the terms on which money is or is to be borrowed, shall be guilty of a misdemeanour, for which the penalty is £500 and or two years imprisonment.

Chapter 16

OFFENCES OF DAMAGE TO PROPERTY

ARSON

At common law arson was the malicious and wilful burning of the house or outhouse of another man. Arson seems to have been one of the earliest crimes in which the mental element was emphasized. The common law position is no longer of great importance as it has been greatly supplemented by statute.

The statute law is contained in the Malicious Damage Act 1861. By the Act, arson is the felony of unlawfully and maliciously setting fire to buildings or to certain peculiarly inflammable kinds of other property.

It is a felony punishable with life imprisonment where a person unlawfully and maliciously sets fire to :
(1) Any church, chapel, meeting-house, or other place of divine worship (section 1).
(2) Any dwelling house, any person being therein (section 2) The words "....any person being therein..." refer to a person other than the accused.
(3) Any house, stable, coach-house, outhouse, warehouse, office, shop, mill, malt-house, hop-oast, barn, storehouse, granary, hovel, shed, or fold, or to any farm building, etc. (section 3).
(4) Any station, engine-house, warehouse, or other building belonging to or appertaining to any railway, port, dock or harbour, or to any canal or other navigation (section 4).
(5) Any public building, which shall include any building belonging to the State, to a State authority or to any other state, (section 5, as amended by the Criminal Law(Jurisdiction) Act 1976).
(6) Any mine of coal, cannel coal, anthracite, or other mineral fuel (section 26).
(7) Any stack of corn, grain. pulse, tares, hay, straw, haulm, stubble, or of any cultivated vegetable produce, or of furze, gorse, heath, fern, turf, peat, coals, charcoal, wood or bark, or any steer of wood or bark (section 17).

(8) Any ship or vessel (section 42).

(9) with intent (section 43).

It is a felony punishable with fourteen years imprisonment where a person unlawfully and maliciously sets fire to;

  (1) any buildings not already mentioned in the Act (section6),

  (2) any matter or thing being in any building (section 7),

  (3) any crops, etc whether standing or cut down (section16).

Attempts

An attempt to commit arson is an exception to the general rule that attempts to commit crimes are misdemeanours. The Act makes particular provision with regard to attempts at various offences

It is a felony punishable with fourteen years imprisonment where a person attempts;

  (1) to commit an offence, such as in section 1,2,3,4,5,6, and 7 (section 8).

  (2) to commit an offence, such as in section 26 (section 27).

  (3) to commit an offence, such as in section 42 and 43 (section44)

It is a felony punishable with seven years imprisonment where a person attempts;

  (4) to commit an offence, such as in section 16 and 17 (section18).

Ownership

In arson the question of ownership of the building does not arise. In an indictment it is unnecessary to allege the ownership of the house, nor need the ownership be proved. Neither is it necessary that there should have been an intention to injure or defraud any particular person, though it is necessary that there should have been an intention to injure or defraud.

Malice

Malice is essential, negligence as to burning is not arson. Negligence, that results in a fire is not criminal even where done in the commission of a felonious act unless the felonious act was one likely to result in the other. Setting fire to means that the building must go on fire, there need not be a visible flame. A scorching of a surface is not sufficient, a charring however would be adequate. An owner of a building may be charged with arson, if there is an intention to injure or defraud.

MALICIOUS DAMAGE

The law relating to malicious damage is also contained in the Malicious Damage Act 1861. This offence is the unlawful and malicious damage to property with intent. The mode of causing the damage is not relevant as long as the intention to damage is present.

Type of offences

The offences under the Act are numerous and the type of damage that is prohibited varies. Thus a detailed consideration of the offences is not possible here. The damage includes injury to buildings, machinery and goods, bridges and railways, trees, plants and fences, but also the drowning of mines by water, the opening of flood gates, the casting away of ship at sea, the altering of signals and the maiming of animals.

Penalties and classes of offences

The malicious injuries to various specified classes of property are rendered criminal offences of various degrees of guilt under the Act. They range from felonies punishable with life imprisonment, down to offences punishable as summary offences under the Criminal Justice Act 1951.

It is a felony punishable with life imprisonment under section 11 to riotously demolish buildings.

It is a felony punishable with fourteen years imprisonment under section 49 to damage parts of a ship in distress.

It is a felony punishable with seven years imprisonment under section 15 to destroy any machine used in agricultural operations or in the manufacture of goods.

It is a felony punishable with five years imprisonment under section 20 to damage trees and shrubs in gardens, pleasure grounds etc.

It is a misdemeanour punishable with seven years imprisonment under section 32 to destroy the dam, sluice or floodgate of any fishpond.

It is a misdemeanour punishable with two years imprisonment under section 13 for tenants to destroy buildings and sever fixtures.

It is a misdemeanour punishable with six months imprisonment under section 39 to damage works of art.

All minor cases of damage for which no punishment is provided by the Act are by virtue of section 52 summary offences. In addition to a £50 fine and or six months imprisonment, a Justice of the District Court may award compensation of up to £50.

Ownership and possession of property

At common law a person in possession of property could not be convicted of an offence of damaging that property. By section 59 of the Act, it is no defence that the defendant was in possession of the property against which or in respect of which the alleged act was done.

Malice

The offences under the Act include the expression "maliciously". This expression imports mens rea, i.e. it must be proved that the defendant foresaw that his conduct was likely to result in damage to property. Section 58 of the Act provides that every punishment imposed by the Act on any person maliciously committing any offence shall apply whether the offence shall be committed from malice conceived against the owner of the property in respect of which it shall be committed or otherwise.

Fitzgerald V Limerick Corporations (1985)

The applicant's motor car was taken without his permission by a person unknown and was later found, abandoned and crashed. It was held by the Supreme Court that; since the act of taking the car constituted a criminal offence (s.112 R.T.A.1961), and since the driver of the car at the time off the crash was committing the continuing offence of using the car without the owner's permission, the damage caused by the crash was caused in the course of the committing of a crime against the property damaged within the extended meaning of "maliciously" in section 5 of the Malicious Injuries Act 1981.

Shennick Lodge V Monaghan County Council (1986)

It was held by the Supreme Court that; The test to be applied in deciding whether a crime is a crime against property damaged is firstly to ascertain whether the crime is in general against a person, and secondly, in the light of the

118

particular penal section, what property it is intended to protect, and in applying this test to section 23A of the Larceny Act 1916, its provisions are intended to protect buildings, persons and goods therein.

Unlawfully

In certain circumstances a person is entitled to damage or destroy property belonging to another, as for example: a person is entitled to kill a dog attacking him or his animals, a person may dismantle and remove a building unlawfully put up on his premises, a person carrying out a lawful arrest or executing a search warrant may break down doors after admittance has been demanded and refused.

Claim of right

If a person honestly but erroneously believes that he is damaging his own property, or the property of the person who has instructed him to damage it, he has a good defence.

Damage

The expression "damage" means perceptible damage. To walk across a lawn will not normally cause any perceptible damage and thus not be an offence, to trample down long grass has, been held to be sufficient. Where a person is entitled to damage property, or where he thinks that he is entitled to damage property, there is still a limitation on the amount of damage that he may inflict.

R V Clemens (1898)

The defendants honestly but erroneously believed that they were entitled to demolish a hut on land over which they thought they had a right to wander at pleasure. They were not content with demolishing the hut, they threw over a cliff into the sea. On appeal the Court of Crown Cases Reserved agreed that the jury might properly have found that the defendants did more damage than was reasonably necessary (accepting for this purpose that they had a right to demolish it) and affirmed the conviction.

Other malicious damage to property

The Electricity Supply Act 1927 at section 11 provides that to unlawfully and maliciously damage any electric wires or works

119

with intent to cut off or diminish the supply of electricity is a felony for which the penalty is five years imprisonment. The Larceny Act 1861 makes it a felony to destroy or damage; a valuable security(five years imprisonment), documents of title(five years imprisonment), wills(life imprisonment), and records(five years imprisonment). Malicious damage to property can also be caused by explosives and provision is made for such in the Act, see the chapter on firearms and explosives below.

FORCIBLE ENTRY

The Forcible Entry Act 1381 and Forcible Entry Act 1786 both create offences in relation to forcible entry on to lands of another.
The modern law is contained in the Prohibition of Forcible Entry and Occupation Act 1971.

Forcible entry
Section 2 of the Act provides that a person who forcibly enters land or a vehicle shall be guilty of an offence unless:-
(a) he is the owner of the land or vehicle, or
(b) if he is not the owner, he does nor interfere with the use and enjoyment of the land or vehicle by the owner and, if requested to leave, by the owner or by a member of the Garda Siochana in uniform, he does so with all reasonable speed and in a peaceable manner, or
(c) he enters in pursuance of a *bona fide* claim of right.
"forcibly" means using or threatening to use force in relation to person or property, and for this purpose participation in action or conduct with others in numbers or circumstances calculated to prevent by intimidation the exercise by any person of his rights in relation to any property shall constitute a threat to use force, and "forcible" shall be construed accordingly.
"land" includes-
(a) messuages and tenements of any tenure,
(b) land covered by water,
(c) houses or other buildings or structures whatsoever,
(d) incorporeal hereditaments of any tenure.
"owner", in relation to land, includes the lawful occupier,

every person lawfully entitled to the immediate use and enjoyment of unoccupied land, any person having an estate or interest in land, and any person acting on behalf of the owner.
"vehicle" means an aircraft not in flight, a train, an omnibus or a boat, ship or other vessel in any port or harbour, or any river or lake, in the State or anywhere in territorial waters.

Remaining in forcible occupation
Section 3 of the Act provides that a person who remains in forcible occupation of land or a vehicle shall be guilty of an offence unless he is the owner or so remains thereon in pursuance of a bona fide claim of right.
"forcible occupation of land or a vehicle" includes-
(a) the act of locking, obstructing or barring any window, door or other entry to or means of exit from land or a vehicle with a view to preventing or resisting a lawful attempt to enter the land or vehicle,
(b) the act of erecting a physical obstacle to an entry to or means of exit from land or a vehicle with a view to preventing or resisting a lawful attempt to enter the land or vehicle,
(c) the act of physically resisting a lawful attempt at ejection from land or a vehicle.

Encouragement and advocacy
Section 4 of the Act provides that; a person who encourages or advocates the commission of an offence under section 2 or 3 of the Act shall be guilty of an offence. Where a statement is made in contravention of this by or on behalf of a group of persons, every person who is a member of the group and consented to the making of the statement shall be guilty of an offence.

Penalties
By section 7 every person who commits an offence under the Act shall be liable-
On summary conviction in this case of a first offence £50 and or six months imprisonment,
On summary conviction in the case of a second or subsequent offence £100 fine and or twelve months imprisonment.
On conviction on indictment £500 fine and or three years imprisonment.

Power of arrest

By section 9 of the Act a member of the Garda Siochana may arrest a person without warrant where-

(a) the member knows or has reasonable cause for suspecting that the person is committing and offence under section 3, and

(b) the owner of the land or vehicle to which the offence relates represents to any member of the Garda Siochana, and the member proposing to make the arrest reasonably believes, that, as a result of the continuance of the offence, serious damage to the land or vehicle or serious interference with the lawful rights of the owner in relation thereto, or serious inconvenience to the public or a section thereof, is being or will be caused, and

(c) the member proposing to make the arrest reasonably believes that the arrest is necessary to prevent the damage, interference or inconvenience, and

(d) it is not reasonably practicable to apply for a warrant.

Trade disputes

Nothing in the Act affects the law relating to acts done in contemplation or furtherance of a trade dispute within the meaning of the Trade Disputes Act, 1906.

Chapter 17

FORGERY

The Forgery Act 1913, was passed to consolidate, simplify and amend the law relating to forgery and kindred offences.

Definition
By section 1(1); forgery is the making of a false document in order that it may be used as genuine, with intent to defraud or deceive.

Making
Forgery is the making of a false document, using such a document is the separate offence of uttering.

Documents
Private documents : Documents of a private character where the intent must be to defraud, such documents are wills, codicils and other testamentary documents, deeds, bonds, bank notes, valuable securities, documents of title to land or goods, powers of attorney, policies of insurance, endorsements and assignments (all felonies) and forgeries of any other document of a like character.

Public documents : Documents of a public official character where the intent must be to defraud or deceive, this would include forgeries of all public and judicial documents, records, registers, and licences.

The penalty for forgery where it is a felony is either life imprisonment or fourteen years imprisonment, depending on the particular document forged, in the case of a misdemeanour it is two years imprisonment. The Hallmarking Act 1981 provides that in the case of hallmark dies the penalty on summary conviction is a £500 fine and or twelve months imprisonment and on conviction on indictment is a £5,000 fine and or five years imprisonment.

False
By section 1(2); False is "...if the whole ..or part (of a document) purports to be made ...by a person who did not make

123

it ..or, if though made by ..the person..the time or place..or..number or mark ..is falsely stated therein.

Mens rea
The mens rea of forgery is the " intent to defraud or deceive " . To deceive means to knowingly induce a person to believe that a thing is true which is false.To defraud is to deprive by deceit. Thus knowledge of the forgery is essential.

Uttering
By section 6; Uttering is an offence, "A person utters a forged document, seal or die, who knowing the same to be forged,....uses, offers, publishes, delivers, disposes of , tenders in evidence, or puts off the said forged document, seal or die". The penalty is as above depending upon the document uttered.

Demanding and obtaining
By section 7; It is an offence for a person who, with intent to defraud, demands, receives, obtains or causes or procures to be delivered, any property under or by virtue of a forged instrument. The penalty is fourteen years imprisonment

Possession
By section 8; It is a felony to be in possession of or to purchase or receive any forged bank note, die for making gold or silver, or a stamp die. The penalty is fourteen years imprisonment.
The penalty for the possession of hall-marking and stamp dies on summary conviction is a £500 fine and or twelve months imprisonment and on indictment is a £5,000 fine and or five years imprisonment.
By section 9; It is a felony to make or have in possession implements for forgery. The penalty is seven years imprisonment
The onus is on the accused to show that he is in lawful possession.

OTHER OFFENCES

Bank notes
The Central Bank Act 1942 at section 55(1) provides that; If

any person makes, or causes to be made, or uses for any purpose whatsoever, or utters any document purporting to be, or in any way resembling, or so nearly resembling as to be calculated to deceive, a bank note, he shall be guilty of an offence for which the penalty on summary conviction is a £5 fine.

Counterfeiting copper coins

The Decimal Currency Act 1969 at section 14 provides that the making or issuing of any piece of metal or mixed metal of any value whatsoever in the State as a coin or token for money or purporting that the holder thereof is entitled to demand any value denoted thereon is a felony for which the penalty is seven years imprisonment.

Chapter 18

ROAD TRAFFIC OFFENCES

The coming of the motor vehicle created a legal vacuum, for there was no proper provision under the common law or under statute to deal with the many legal problems that arose with the rapid development of the motor vehicle, there was minor provision in a number of statutes; The Highway Act 1835 section 72 made it an offence to drive any carriage on the pavement, The Dublin Police Act 1842 provided at section 14(5): Every Person who shall ride or drive furiously, or so as to endanger the life of limb of any person, or to the common Danger of the Passengers in any Thoroughfare shall be liable to a penalty of forty shillings. It is an offence under the Offences against the Person Act 1861 section 35 for a person having charge of a carriage or vehicle, to cause bodily harm by wanton or furious driving, which the penalty is two years imprisonment:

Attorney General V Joyce

The accused while driving a horse-drawn vehicle came into collision with a motor cycle. The driver and pillion passenger of the motor cycle were killed. The vehicle of the accused was unlighted and he was charged under section 35. It was held by the Circuit Court, that the failure to have a light was sufficient evidence, for a jury to find "wilful neglect".

The result is that today, the law in this area is statutory and of recent origin. The principal Act is the Road Traffic Act 1961, which has been updated and amended by the Road Traffic Act 1968, the Road Traffic(Amendment) Act 1978 and by the Road Traffic (Amendment) Act 1984 which greatly increases penalties.

There are other statutes relating to specific areas and there are in addition regulations made by the Minister under the principal act, such as the Road Traffic General Bye Laws 1964 and the Road Traffic (Insurance Disc) Regulations 1984.

A number of basic definitions are of particular importance :

Driving S.3 Includes managing and controlling.

Mechanically propelled vehicle S.3 Means a vehicle intended or adapted for propulsion by mechanical means, including -

(a) a bicycle or tricycle with an attachment for propelling it by mechanical power, whether or not the attachment is being used,

(b) a vehicle the means of propulsion of which is electrical or partly electrical and partly mechanical.

Public place S.3 means any street, road or other place to which the public have access with vehicles whether as of right or by permission and whether subject to or free of charge.

Public road S.3 means a road the responsibility for the maintenance of which lies on a road authority.

Attorney-General (McLaughlin) V Rhatigan

R. was charged under Section 49 and 52 of the Road Traffic Act, 1961. The only evidence adduced by the State as to the place where the offences were said to have happened was that it was described as a private car park near a licensed premises. It was held in the High Court by Davitt P. That the onus is on the prosecution to establish by proper evidence that the offences were committed in a public place and that the prosecution had not proved that the place in question was one to which the public had access and thus failed to prove an essential element of each offence.

Stanbridge V Healy (1985)

It was held by the High Court that; "public" means the public generally and not any particular class of the public.

In charge :

Haines V Roberts (1953)

It was held that a person who takes out a vehicle on the road remains in charge of it until he puts someone else in charge.

Leach V Evans (1952) 2 A.E.R. 264

It was held that an intending driver may be in charge of his vehicle before he enters it to drive it.

DRIVING OFFENCES

Driving when unfit

The Act at section 48(1) provides; A person shall not drive a mechanically propelled vehicle in a public place when he is to his knowledge suffering from any disease or physical or mental disability which would be likely to cause the driving of the vehicle by him in a public place to be a source of danger to the public. The penalty on summary conviction for a first offence is a £150 fine and or three months imprisonment. In addition there is a mandatory endorsement of a person's license.

Driving without reasonable consideration
The Act at section 51A(1) provides; A person shall not drive a mechanically propelled vehicle in a public place without reasonable consideration for, other person's using that place.

Careless driving
The Act at section 52(1) provides; A person shall not drive a mechanically propelled vehicle in a public place without due care and attention for other persons using that place. The penalty on summary conviction is £350.00 and or three months imprisonment.

"without due care and attention" The standard of driving has been considered in;

McCrone V Riding (1938)

"That standard is an objective standard, impersonal and universal, fixed in relation to the safety of other users of the highway. It is in no way related to the degree of proficiency or degree of experience attained by the individual driver."

"other persons" :

Pawley V Wharldall (1966)

This phrase includes a passenger in the vehicle driven by the accused person.

Where a person is charged of the offence of Dangerous Driving below, it may be reduced to a charge of Careless Driving.

Dangerous driving
The Act at s. 53(1) provides; A person shall not drive a vehicle in a public place in a manner (including speed) which having regard to all the circumstances of the case (including the condition of the vehicle, the nature, condition and use of the place and the amount of traffic, which then actually is, or might reasonably be expected then to be therein is dangerous to the public. The penalty on summary conviction is a £1,000 fine and or six months imprisonment.

Dangerous driving causing death or serious bodily harm
This is the same offence as Dangerous Driving above, with the provision that either death or serious bodily harm has been caused. It creates a specific offence, of what would otherwise

128

be manslaughter. The penalty for conviction on indictment is a £3,500 fine and or five years imprisonment.

The People (A.G.) V. Gallagher (1972)

It was held by the Court of Criminal Appeal that proof that the dangerous driving of a motor vehicle by an accused is one of the causes of the death of another person is sufficient to support the conviction of an accused.

By sub-section 6, Where a Garda is of the opinion that a person has committed an offence under section 53, he may arrest the person without a warrant.

Driving of dangerously defective vehicle

The Act at section 54 (1). A person who drives a mechanically propelled vehicle in a public place while there is a default affecting the vehicle which he knows of or could have discovered by the exercise of ordinary care and which is such that the vehicle is, when in motion a danger to the public shall be guilty of an offence, for which the penalty is a £350 fine and or three months imprisonment.

DRIVING OFFENCES WHILE UNDER THE INFLUENCE OF ALCOHOL OR DRUGS

The law governing the driving or being in charge of a vehicle while under the influence of an intoxicant, and the breath / blood / urine tests and procedure relating to same is to be found in Part V of the Road Traffic (Amendment) Act 1978, all references below are to the Road Traffic Acts.

Driving or attempting to drive

Section 49 1. (a) (1978) A person shall not drive or attempt to drive a mechanically propelled vehicle in a public place while he is under the influence of an intoxicant (which includes alcohol and drugs and any combination of drugs or of drugs and alcohol) to such an extent as to be incapable of having proper control of the vehicle.

This requires proof based on observation.

A. G. (Ruddy) V Kenny

The Supreme Court held that a Garda may give evidence of his opinion that the driver of a vehicle was drunk.

The State(Prendergast) V Porter (1961)

The accused was charged with attempting to drive while drunk.

He had attempted to turn the starting handle of the vehicle, then seemed to touch the dashboard. Having again turned the starting handle, he sat on the driving seat and the engine turned over but did not start. On a case stated it was held that these actions amounted to an attempt to drive.

Section 49 2. A person shall not drive or attempt to drive a mechanically propelled vehicle in a public place while there is present in his body a quantity of alcohol such that, within three hours of so driving or attempting to drive the concentration of alcohol in his blood will exceed a concentration of 100 milligrammes of alcohol per 100 millilitres of blood.

Section 49 3. A person shall not drive or attempt to drive a mechanically propelled vehicle in a public place while there is present in his body a quantity of alcohol such that, within three hours of so driving or attempting to drive the concentration of alcohol in his urine will exceed a concentration of 135 milligrammes of alcohol per 100 millilitres of urine.

This section creates a number of separate offences :
To drive, or to attempt to drive
    (1) under the influence of an intoxicant.
    (2) with a certain concentration of alcohol in the blood.
    (3) with a certain concentration of alcohol in the urine.

The State (McGroddy) V Carr (1975)
It was held by the Supreme Court that in section 49, the reference to intoxicating liquor or a drug creates a single offence.

The State (Collins) V Kelleher (1983)
It was held by the Supreme Court that, a charge brought under 1(a) of section 49 and one brought under 3. of that section are alternative charges.

The penalty on summary conviction is £1,000 fine and or six months imprisonment. Where a person is charged with an offence under section 49, he may be found guilty of an offence under section 50 below.

A member of the Garda Siochana may arrest without warrant a person who in the member's opinion is committing or has committed an offence under this section.

D.P.P. V O'Connor (1985)
These offences require proof based entirely on chemical analysis showing a concentration, beyond a permitted level, of alcohol in the blood or urine (as the case may be).

D. P. P. V Gilmore 1981
The Supreme court held that a positive result on the breath

130

testing apparatus referred to in Section 12 of the Act of 1978 is sufficient to justify the forming of an opinion of the Garda that a person is in breach of Section 49 2. or 3..

Being in charge while drunk

Section 50 1 (a) 1978 a person shall be guilty of an offence who, when in charge of a mechanically propelled vehicle in a public place with interest to drive or attempt to drive the vehicle (but not driving or attempting to drive it), is under the influence of an intoxicant to such an extent as to be incapable of having proper control of the vehicle.

Section 50 2. & 3. a person shall be guilty of an offence who is in charge of a mechanically propelled vehicle (but not driving or attempting to drive it) and in whose body there is present a quantity of alcohol such that, within three hours after having been so in charge of the vehicle, the concentration of alcohol in his blood or urine is as referred to in Section 49 above.

The penalty on summary conviction, in the case of a first offence is a £350 fine and or three months imprisonment or in the case of a second or subsequent offence is £1,000 fine and or six months imprisonment.

Where a person is charged with an offence under Section 50, he may be found guilty of an offence under Section 49 above.

Driving of animal drawn vehicle or pedal cycle

Section 51 1 A person shall not in public place;

(a) drive or attempt to drive, or be in charge of an animal drawn vehicle, or

(b) drive or attempt to drive a pedal cycle.

While he is under the influence of intoxicating liquor or a drug to such an extent as to be incapable of having proper control of the vehicle or cycle.

The penalty on summary conviction in the case of a first offence which relates to an animal drawn vehicle is a £150 fine and or one months imprisonment, in the case of any other offence under this Section the penalty is £350 fine and or three months imprisonment.

Breath test

Section 12(1) 1978 Whenever a member of the Garda Siochana is of the opinion that a person in charge of a mechanically propelled vehicle in a public place has consumed intoxicating liquor, he may require the person to provide, by exhaling into an apparatus for indicating the presence of alcohol in the breath a specimen of his breath and may indicate the manner in which he is to comply with the requirement.

Refusal to comply is an offence the penalty on summary conviction of which if £1,000 fine and or six months imprisonment.

The D.P.P. V Joyce (1985)

It was held by the Supreme Court that a request by a Garda to require any person to provide a specimen of his breath must be in a public place and that person must then be in charge of a mechanically propelled vehicle in such public place. Section 12 is limited to these powers.

Blood and urine tests

Section 13(1) 1978; Where a person arrested under Section 49(c) for driving while drunk or under Section 12(3) above has been brought to a Garda Station, a member of the Garda Siochana may at his discretion do either or both of the following:

(a) require the person to provide, by exhaling into an apparatus for indicating the concentration of alcohol in breath or blood, a specimen of his breath,

(b) require the person either to permit a designated registered medical practitioner to take from the person a specimen of his blood or, at the option of the person, to provide for the designated registered medical practitioner a specimen of the the persons urine.

Refusal to comply is an offence, the penalty on summary conviction of which is a £1,000 fine and or six months imprisonment.

Section 14 1978 makes similar provisions in respect of Section 50 above.

OTHER DRIVING OFFENCES

Prohibition of driving without a driving licence

Section 36 A person shall not drive a mechanically propelled vehicle in a public place unless he holds a driving licence for the time being having effect and licensing him to drive the vehicle.

A contravention of this section is subject to the general penalty outlined in section 102, however if a person who is summarily convicted was either disqualified or subject to a certificate of competency/fitness, he shall be liable to a £1,000 fine and or six months imprisonment. By section 39; A person may not apply for a driving licence if he is disqualified.

Compulsory insurance

Section 56 A person shall not use in a public place a mechanically propelled vehicle unless. there is an approved policy of insurance whereby the user or some other person who would be liable for injury caused by the negligent use of the vehicle at that time by the user, is insured against all sums without limit. The penalty on summary conviction is a £1,000 fine and or six months imprisonment.

The Road Traffic (Insurance Disc) Regulations 1984, which are made under the provisions of sections 5 and 11 of the Act, provide at 3(1) Where a certificate of insurance is issued to a person the vehicle insurer shall issue to such person one insurance disc for each vehicle to which the certificate relates. Which disc must be displayed on the vehicle. By section 11 of the Act, the non-compliance by a person using a vehicle in a public place of regulations made by the Minister is an offence and is liable to the general penalty provided for in the Act.

Motor tax

The Finance (Excise Duties)(Vehicles) Act 1952 at section 1 requires that vehicle excise duty be paid on motor vehicles, "vehicle excise duty " means the duty of excise charged and levied under that Act. Where vehicle excise duty is chargeable and is unpaid, then any person, who at any time while the duty remains unpaid, uses parks or otherwise keeps the vehicle in a public place or causes another person to do such, shall be guilty of an offence. The word "use" includes keeping or leaving a vehicle stationary.

The Roads Act 1920, section 13(1) provides that if a person uses a vehicle for which a license is not in force, he shall be liable to an excise penalty of £20 or an excise penalty equal to three times the amount of duty payable in respect of the vehicle, whichever is the greater. This excise penalty may be recovered and enforced upon an information by any member of the Garda Siochana before a court of summary jurisdiction.

OTHER MOTOR VEHICLE OFFENCES

Speed
Section 47   A person shall not drive a mechanically propelled vehicle at a speed exceeding a speed limit applying in relation to the vehicle and to do so shall be an offence. In this section "speed limit" means a limit which is: (a) an ordinary speed limit, (b) a general speed limit, (c) the built-up area speed limit, or (d)   a special speed limit.

Dangerous parking
Section 55 (1) A person shall not park a vehicle in a public place if, when so parked, the vehicle would be likely to cause danger to other persons using that place.   On summary conviction the penalty for a first offence during lighting-up hours, or for a second or subsequent offence is a £350 fine and or three months imprisonment, or in any other case a £150 fine and or one months imprisonment.

Taking vehicle without authority
Section 112 A person shall not use or take possession of a mechanically propelled vehicle without the consent of the owner thereof or other lawful authority. The penalty on summary conviction is a £1,000 fine and or twelve months imprisonment, and on Indictment a £2,000 fine and or five years imprisonment.

Unauthorized interference with vehicle
Section 113; A person shall not, without lawful authority or reasonable cause, interfere or attempt to interfere with the mechanism of a mechanically propelled vehicle while it is stationary in a public place, or get on or into or attempt to get on or into the vehicle while it is so stationary. The penalty is a £350 fine and or three months imprisonment.

Unlawful seizure of vehicles
By the Criminal Law (Jurisdiction) Act 1976 section 10, a person who unlawfully by force,or by any other form of intimidation, seizes or exercises control of any vehicle shall be

guilty of an offence, for which the penalty is fifteen years imprisonment.

Giving false particulars
Section 115 Where a person is required by the Act or regulations made thereunder to furnish particulars and does so with the knowledge that they are false or misleading, he commits an offence. On summary conviction the penalty is £50 fine and or six months imprisonment.

Safety belts
The Road Traffic (Construction, Equipment and Use of Vehicles)(Amendment) (No. 2) Regulations, 1978, made under the provisions of sections 5 and 11 of the Act; make it obligatory for the driver and front seat passengers in cars, station wagons and light goods vehicles first registered on or after the 1st June 1971, to wear safety belts of prescribed standards.

Where a person has been found not to have complied with the regulations, if they produce within one month of being so found, a certificate of a registered medical practitioner that, because of physical or mental disability or for medical or psychological reasons, it was undesirable or inadvisable for the person to wear a safety belt on the occasion in question, the person shall not be regarded as being in breach of the regulations.

Crash helmets
The above regulations also provide for the obligatory wearing of crash helmets of prescribed standards by the drivers of motor cycles and their passengers. Here and in the case of the above the general penalty applies

OTHER PROVISIONS

Consequential disqualification order
Section 26 of the Act provides :
(1) where a person is convicted of an offence specified in the Second Schedule to this Act, the court shall make an order (in this act referred to as a consequential disqualification order) declaring him to be disqualified from holding a driving licence.
(2) A disqualification under this section shall disqualify the

135

convicted person for holding any driving licence whatsoever during a specified period or during a specified period and thereafter until he has produced to the appropriate licensing authority a certificate of competency or a certificate of fitness or both.

(3) (a) The period of a disqualification specified in a consequential disqualification order shall, where the person to whom the order relates is convicted of-

(i) an offence under section 49 of this Act,

(ii) an offence under section 53 of this Act where the contravention caused death or serious bodily harm to another person,

(iii) an offence under section 13 (2) or (3) (1978)

be not less than one year in the case of a first offence and not less than three years in the case of a second or any subsequent offence.

(4) The period of disqualification specified in a consequential disqualification order shall, in a case not coming within subsection(3) of this section, be not less than six months on a conviction of an offence

Competency
Section 32 of the Act provides; that persons suffering from certain diseases or physical or mental disability are disqualified from holding a driving licence. However section 33 makes provision for the issue of certificates of competency.

Endorsement
Section 36 of the Act provides that: Where a person is convicted of an offence under the Act or otherwise in relation to a mechanically propelled vehicle or the driving of any such vehicle or of a crime or offence in the commission of which a mechanically propelled vehicle was used, the court, if it does not make a consequential or ancillary disqualification order, may in the case of certain offence direct that particulars of the conviction be endorsed on the driving licence held by such a person or, if he is not the holder of a driving licence but subsequently a driving licence is granted to him, on that driving licence.

General penalty
Section 102 makes provision for a general penalty on summary conviction;

(a) In the case of a first offence a £150 fine,
(b) In the case of a second, third, or subsequent offence a £350 fine,
(c) In the case of a third or subsequent offence (being so in any period of twelve consecutive months) to a £350 fine and or three month imprisonment

Notice of offence
Section 104 Where a person is charged with an offence under section's 47, 51A, 52, or 53, ... he shall not be convicted unless;
(a) He was warned at the time, or within twenty four hours thereafter, that the question of prosecuting him would be considered, or
(b) Within fourteen days . a summons . was served on him, or
(c) Within fourteen days . a detailed statement was served personally or by registered post on him.

Duties on occurrence of an accident
Section 106 makes provision where injury is caused to person or property in a public place and a vehicle is involved in the occurrence of the injury, breach of the provisions is an offence.

Duty to give information
Section 107 provides that; Where a member of the Garda Siochana alleges to a person using a mechanically propelled vehicle, that he suspects him a name and address may be demanded. A refusal to comply is an offence.

Obligation to stop
Section 109 provides the; A person driving a vehicle in a public place shall stop the vehicle on being so required by a member of the Garda Siochana, failure to do so is an offence.

Chapter 19

MISUSE OF DRUGS

The law relating to the misuse of dangerous or harmful drugs and the regulation of such drugs is contained in the Misuse of Drugs Act 1977 as amended by the Misuse of Drugs Act 1984.

Controlled Drugs S.2
A controlled drug means any substance, product or preparation which is either specified in the Schedule to the Act or has been declared by the Government to be such. The Government may by order remove or vary substances, product or preparation within the classification of controlled drugs. The substances set out in the schedule to the 1977 Act include: amphetamine, cannabis and cannabis resin, cocaine, diamorphine(heroin), lysergide (L.S.D.) and opium, whether raw, prepared or medicinal.

Regulations by Minister for Health S.4. S.5.
The Minister may make regulations enabling any person or persons, to possess a controlled drug, subject to such conditions as may be prescribed. The Minister may for the purpose of preventing the misuse of controlled drugs make regulations prohibiting absolutely, or otherwise:
(i) the manufacture, production or preparation of controlled drugs,
(ii) the importation or exportation of controlled drugs,
(iii) the supply or the distribution of controlled drugs,
(iv) the transportation of controlled drugs,
The Minister for Health, in exercise of the powers conferred on him by the 1977 Act, has issued the Misuse of Drugs Regulations 1979, which regulate the production, supply, importation, exportation, possession of, and documentation and record keeping of controlled drugs.

POSSESSION

The possession of controlled drugs is the fundamental offence under the Acts. It is not possible for a person or persons, who are not in possession to manufacture, import, export, supply, distribute or transport controlled drugs.

Possession S.3.

Subject to exceptions permitted by the Minister for Health, it shall be an offence for a person to have a controlled drug in his possession. This is an offence of strict liability, however note the defence available under section 29(2) below.

What is "Possession" has been considered in:

Warner V Metropolitan Police Commissioner (1968)

The defendant was charged with being in possession. He had been given two boxes, one containing perfume and the other the drug. He said that he thought they both contained perfume. The House of Lords held that mens rea was necessary regarding the possession, but not regarding the knowledge that what he possessed was a dangerous drug; as long as the defendant knew he possessed the container with something in it, it did not matter that he did not know, and could not reasonably have known, that the contents was a prohibited drug. Lord Pearce stated: "One may, therefore, exclude from the "possession" intended by the act....... the physical control of articles which have been 'planted' on him without his knowledge; but how much further is one to go? If one goes to the extreme length of requiring the prosecution to prove that 'possession' implies a full knowledge of the name and nature of the drug concerned, the efficacy of the Act is seriously impaired, since many drug pedlars may in truth be unaware of this. I think the term "possession" is satisfied by a knowledge only of the existence of the thing itself and not its qualities, and that ignorance or mistake as to its qualities is not an excuse."

An accused person is not in "possession" of a controlled drug, if he has consumed it, even though traces are discovered in his urine after arrest. This arose in:

Hambleton V Callinan (1968)

Lord Parker C.J. stated: '..... once one had consumed something and its whole character had alerted and no further use could be made of it, as in this case, a man could not be said to be in possession of a prohibited substance....'

R. V. Peaston (1979)

It was held that where a controlled drug was delivered to an accused by post at his request, he became the possessor as soon as it was put through the letter box, even though he was not aware of its arrival. The possession of a small quantity of a controlled drug, though it may be too small for use, does not

139

rule out the possibility of a conviction.

R. V. Boyesen (1982)
Lord Scarman stated : "It is a perfectly sensible view that the possession of any quantity, which is visible, tangible, measurable and 'capable of manipulation'...... is a serious matter to be prohibited...."

R V Lewis (1988)
The defendant was convicted of possessing controlled drugs. He was the sole tenant of a house where the police had discovered the drugs. He claimed that the tenancy was a device to obtain social security and he had never spent any time in the house. The Court of Appeal held that the jury should decide whether the defendant had possession rather than mere control by considering all the circumstances in which the custody commenced and what knowledge as to the presence of the substance the defendant had up to the time he was found with it. The question to be determined was whether the defendant had been proved to have, or ought to have imputed to him, the intention to possess, or the knowledge that he did possess, what was in fact a prohibited substance. It is not necessary that he should also know the nature of the substance.

Onus of Proof S.22
In any proceedings for an offence under the Act, where a defendant claims that he is in lawful possession of a controlled drug, the onus of proving such lawful possession, shall be on the defendant. However note defences generally below.

Possession for unlawful sale or supply S.15.
Any person who has in his possession, whether lawfully or not, a controlled drug for the purpose of selling or otherwise supplying it to another in contravention of regulations made by the Minister, shall be guilty of an offence. This offence is distinguished from the offence of possession under section 3, in that it is not relevant whether the possession is lawful or not, and possession must be for the purpose of selling or otherwise supplying to another.   A court until it is satisfied to the contrary, will assume having regard to the quantity of a controlled drug in the possession of an accused, that it was not intended for the immediate personal use of the accused, but that it was for the purpose of selling or otherwise supplying to another. This was considered in :

140

The People (D.P.P.) V. Lawless (1985)
The applicant was convicted of possession, contrary to section 15. A premises was forcibly entered by the Gardai. At the time of the entry the applicant was in the toilet, the sound of flushing was heard. A detective found seventeen packets of heroin at the manhole. Held by the Court of Criminal Appeal having regard to the presumption in section 15(2), there was no evidence that the applicant was a drug addict, or a person who required it "for immediate personal use" and further with the incriminating circumstances of the attempted destruction. There was clearly evidence of guilt.

R V Adepoju and R V Lubren (1988)
The question of what was meant by "another" was considered. Two defendants were charged with supplying to another. They appealed on the basis that the third defendant could not be charged with supplying drugs to herself. The Court of Appeal held that "another" could not be a person included in the indictment.

Penalties
The penalties for offences are contained in section 27 of the 1977 Act as amended. Every person guilty of an offence under section 3 shall be liable -
(a) where the controlled drug is cannabis or cannabis resin and the court is satisfied that the person was in possession of such drug for his personal use.
    (I) first offence: on summary conviction, a £300 fine, on conviction on indictment, a £500 fine
    (II) second offence: on summary conviction, a £400 fine, on conviction on indictment, a £1000 fine
(b) in any other case -
    on summary conviction, a £1000 fine and or twelve months imprisonment, on conviction on indictment, an unlimited fine and or seven years imprisonment.

The distinction between the possession of cannabis or cannabis resin for personal use and possession in any other case was considered in:
The State (Bloomfield) V. Nelyon & D.P.P. (1985)
It was held in the High Court by O'Hanlon J. that; The combined effect of sections 3 and 27 of the Act was to create a summary offence of unlawful possession of controlled drugs where

possession was for personal use, and a further offence which may be prosecuted as a summary or indictable offence at the option of the D.P.P. where possession was for other than personal use.

Every person guilty of an offence under section 15 shall be liable;
on summary conviction, £1000 fine and or twelve months imprisonment, on conviction on indictment, unlimited fine and or life imprisonment.

OTHER OFFENCES

Opium S.16
A person shall not, and if he does shall be guilty of an offence:
(a) smoke or otherwise use prepared opium,
(b) frequent a place used for the purpose of opium,
(c) have in his possession any pipes or other utensils made or adopted for use in connection with the smoking of opium.
It will be noted that the "use" of opium, unlike the use of most controlled drugs, is a criminal offence.

Cultivation of opium poppy or cannabis plant S.17
Every person who cultivates opium poppy or a plant of the genus Cannabis, or any plant of the genus Erythroxylon, without a licence issued by the Minister shall be guilty of an offence.

Forged or fraudulently altered prescriptions S. 18
A person shall not, and if he does so shall be guilty of an offence :
(1) forge a document purporting to be a prescription issued by a practitioner,
(2) with intent to deceive either alter or use a prescription which has been issued by a practitioner,
(3) have in his possession either a forged or altered prescription.

Occupiers permitting certain activities S. 19
A person who is the occupier or is in control or is concerned in the management of any land, vehicle or vessel and who knowingly permits any of the following to take place, shall be

guilty of an offence;

(1) the cultivation of opium poppy or cannabis,
(2) the preparation of opium or cannabis resin or prepared opium,
(3) the smoking of cannabis, cannabis resin or prepared opium,
(4) the manufacture, production or preparation of a controlled drug in contravention of regulations made by the minister,
(5) the importation or exportation of a controlled drug,
(6) the sale, distribution or supply of a controlled drug,
(7) any attempt to contravene Ministerial regulations,
(8) the possession of a controlled drug.

Sweet V Parsley (1969)
The defendant was a landlady who did not live on the premises, but only visited occasionally. Her lodgers smoked cannabis and she was charged with being concerned in the management of premises which were used for the purpose of smoking cannabis. It was not proved that she knew of the smoking, she was nevertheless found guilty, it being held that no mens rea was necessary. The House of Lords quashed the conviction and said that this was not an offence of strict liability. In relation to "knowingly permits" Lord Diplock stated : "The word 'permit', used to define the prohibited act, in itself connotes as a mental element of the prohibited conduct knowledge or grounds for reasonable suspicion on the part of the occupier that the premises will be used by someone for that purpose and an unwillingness on his part to take means available to him to prevent it"

Offences relating to acts outside the State S.20
It is an offence for any person to aid, abet, counsel or induce the commission outside the state of an offence punishable under a corresponding law.

Every person guilty of any of the above offences shall be liable, on summary conviction, £1,000 fine and or twelve months imprisonment, and on conviction on indictment an unlimited fine and or fourteen years imprisonment

Printing   S. 5/1984
A person shall not, and if he does so shall be guilty of an offence : print, publish, cause or procure to be printed or published, sell or expose or offer or keep for sale, distribute or

offer or keep for distribution, any book, periodical or other publication which either -

(1) advocates or encourages,..........the use of any controlled drug,

(2) contains any advertisement advertising any use of a pipe, utensil or other thing for use in connection with a controlled drug..

Every person guilty of this offence is liable on summary conviction to a £1,000 fine.

Attempts S.21

The Misuse of Drugs Act 1977 also creates the following offences:

(l) A person who attempts to commit an offence under the Act, or who aids, abets, counsels or procures the commission of an offence under the Act, or who solicits or incites any other person to commit an offence under the Act, shall be guilty of an offence.

Every person guilty of this offence shall be liable to be punished, on summary conviction, and on conviction on indictment, as if he were guilty of the substantive offence.

Contravening regulations and other offences S.21

(2) Any person who, whether by act or omission, contravenes or fails to comply with regulations under the Act.

(3) A person who, in purported compliance with any obligation, gives any information which he knows to be false.

(4) Any person who impedes or obstructs a member of the Garda Siochana or an authorized person in the lawful exercise of a power conferred by the Act.

(5) Any person who conceals from an authorized person any controlled drug or, who fails to produce any required book, record or other document.

(6) Any person who contravenes a condition attached to a licence, permit or authorization, or under regulations.

(7) Any person who, for the purpose of obtaining a licence, permit or authorization, makes any statement or gives information which he knows to be false, or produces any book, record or other document which he knows to be false.

144

POWERS OF GARDA SIOCHANA

Power to Search S. 23A

A member of the Garda Siochana who with reasonable cause suspects that a person is in possession in contravention of the Act of a controlled drug, may without warrant:

(a) search the person and if he considers it necessary for that purpose, detain the person for such time as is reasonably necessary for making the search. He may also require a person to accompany him to a Garda Station for the purpose of being searched. If there is a failure to comply, he may arrest the person without warrant such failure to comply is an offence.

(b) search any vehicle, vessel or aircraft in which he suspects that a controlled drug may be found and if necessary take charge of such vehicle etc. .

(c) examine and search and detain anything found in the course of a search.

Powers to Inspect S. 24

For the purpose of enforcing the Act and regulations made thereunder, a member of the Garda Siochana or a person authorized by the Minister may at all reasonable times enter any building, require any person to produce any controlled drugs or, books records or other documents and inspect the same.

Power of Arrest S. 25

In addition to the power of a member of the Garda Siochana to arrest a person without warrant in respect of a search above, there are additional powers of arrest under section 25. Where with reasonable cause a member of the Garda Siochana suspects that an offence under section 15 (Possession of controlled drugs for unlawful sales or supply) has been committed and so suspected a person having committed the offence, he may arrest the person without a warrant.

Where with reasonable cause a member of the Garda Siochana suspects that any other offence under the act has been committed or attempted, and suspects a person of having committed the offence or having made the attempt, then if he

(a) with reasonable cause suspects that the person will abscond or

(b) has reasonable doubts as to the persons identity or place of abode or

(c) knows that the person does not ordinarily reside in the State, or has reasonable doubts as to whether the person so resides

he may arrest the person without a warrant.

Search warrant   S. 26
If a   District Justice or a Peace Commissioner is satisfied by information on oath of a member of the Garda Siochana that there is reasonable grounds for suspecting that -

(a) a person is in possession unlawfully of a controlled drug or forged prescription on a particular or other land, or

(b) opium poppy , a plant of the genus cannabis or a plant of the genus erythroxylon is being cultivated contrary to section 17 of the Act or in any premises or other land, or

(c) documents dealing with an offence under the Act or under a corresponding law outside the State, is in the possession of a person on any premises,

he may issue a   search warrant.

GENERAL

Remand   S. 28
A court has power to remand persons convicted under section 3,15,16,17, or 18 of the Act and to obtain a report and in certain cases to arrange for the medical treatment or for the care of such persons.

Defences generally   S. 29
(1) Where it is proved that a defendant had in his possession or supplied a controlled drug, he shall not be acquitted by reason only of proving that he neither knew or suspected that the substance was a particular controlled drug alleged.

(2) Where it is proved that a defendant had in his possession a controlled drug or a forged or altered prescription, it shall be a defence to prove that -

    (a) he did not know and had no reasonable grounds for suspecting -

        (i) that what he had in his possession was a controlled

146

drug or such a prescription, or

    (ii) that he was in possession of a controlled drug or such a prescription, or

(b) he believed the substance, product or preparation to be a controlled drug of a particular class, and that, if it had been of that class he would not have been committing an offence, or

(c) knowing or suspecting it to be such a drug or prescription, he took or retained possession of it for the purpose of -

    (i) preventing another from committing an offence, or

    (ii) delivering it into custody

and that as soon as practicable he took steps to destroy the drug or document or to deliver it into custody.

(3) A defendant charged under section 15 may rebut any presumption, by showing that he was in lawful possession of a controlled drug.

(4) An occupier where charged under section 19 may show that he took steps to prevent any activities.

(5) In any proceedings for an offence under section 16, 17, or 21(a) or for an attempt to commit an offence, the defendant may prove that he neither knew of nor suspected the existence of some fact alleged by the prosecutor which it is necessary for the prosecutor to prove.

(6) In any proceedings for an attempt to commit an offence under the Act, the above defences shall be open to the defendant.

(7) Nothing shall prevent a person from raising a defence which, would be open to him to raise in proceedings for an offence under the Act.

Forfeiture   S. 30

A court by which a person is convicted under the Act may order anything shown to it's satisfaction to relate to the offence to be forfeited and either destroyed or dealt with in such manner as the court thinks fit.

Chapter 20

OFFENCES AGAINST THE PUBLIC PEACE

Affray

Affray is a misdemeanour at common law it consists of fighting by one or more persons, or a display of force by one or more persons, but with any violence, in such a manner as to frighten reasonable people. Fighting in a private place, or at some distance from the public road where no one else is present other than those who are aiding and abetting, does not amount to an affray, but an assembly for such a purpose is unlawful, and the parties concerned may be convicted of an assault, or of taking part in an unlawful assembly. A person acting in self-defence cannot be guilty of an affray by fighting. Before a person can be convicted of an affray, even as an aider and abettor, it must be proved that he was at least encouraging the participants in a fight, his presence even if he intended to participate is not enough.

Attorney General V Cunningham (1932)

It was held by the Court of Criminal Appeal that in order to constitute a breach of the peace, an act must be such as to cause reasonable alarm and apprehension to members of the public.

Challenges

It is a misdemeanour at common law punishable by fine and imprisonment to either verbally or in writing to challenge a person to fight or to attempt to provoke a person to give such a challenge.

Public nuisance

Public nuisance is a misdemeanour at common law, It consists of an unlawful act or omission which obstructs or causes inconvenience or damage to the public. An example would be the emission of noise or smells from a factory in such a way as to cause serious inconvenience. Where special damage is caused as the result of a public nuisance, a civil action for damages can be brought. Public Nuisance is an exception to the general rule that a master is not vicariously liable for crimes committed by his servants.

148

Nuisances in public thoroughfares

The Dublin Police Act 1842, which applies in the Dublin Metropolitan District of the Garda Siochana makes the following provision.

XIV.   And be it enacted, that every person shall be liable to a penalty not exceeding Forty Shillings who, within the Limits of the Police District, shall in any Thoroughfare of Public Place commit any of the following Offences; (that is to say,)

2. Every person who shall turn loose any horses or cattle.

3. Every person who by negligence or ill-usage in driving cattle shall cause any mischief to be done by such cattle or who shall in anyway misbehave himself in the driving, care or management of such cattle ; and also every person, not being hired or employed to drive such cattle who shall wantonly and unlawfully drive or hunt any such cattle.

5. Every Person who shall ride or drive furiously, or so as to endanger the life of limb of any person, or to the common Danger of the Passengers in any Thoroughfare:

10. Every Person who, without the Consent of the Owner or Occupier, shall affix any Posting Bill or other Paper against or upon any Building, Wall, Fence, or Pale, or write upon, soil, deface, or mark any such Building, Wall, Fence, or Pale with Chalk or Paint or in any other way whatsoever, or wilfully break, destroy or damage any Part of any such Building, Wall, Fence, or Pale or any Fixture of Appendage there unto, or any Tree, Shrub, or Seat, in any public Walk, Park or Garden.

11. Every common Prostitute or Night-Walker loitering or being in any Thoroughfare or Public Place for the Purpose of Prostitution or Solicitation, to the annoyance of the Inhabitants or Passengers.

12. Every person who shall sell, or distribute, or offer for sale or Distribution, of exhibit to public view, any profane, indecent, or obscene book, paper, print, drawing, painting, or representation, or sing any profane, indecent, or obscene song or ballad,or write or draw any indecent or obscene word, figure or representation, or use any profane, indecent or obscene language, to the annoyance of the inhabitants or passengers.

13. Every person who shall use any threatening, abusive, or insulting words or behaviour, with intent to provoke a

breach of the peace, or whereby a breach of the peace may be occasioned.

15. Every person who shall wantonly discharge any firearm or throw or discharge any stone or other missile, to the damage or danger of any person, or make any bonfire or throw or set fire to any fireworks.
16. Every person who shall wilfully and wantonly disturb any inhabitant by ringing any doorbell or knocking at any door without lawful excuse, or unlawfully extinguish any public light.
17. Every person who shall play at any game to the annoyance of the inhabitants or passengers, or who shall make or use any slide on ice or snow in any street or other thoroughfare to the common danger of passengers.

Any Garda may arrest without warrant any person who shall commit any such offence within his view. The Towns Improvement Act (Ireland) 1854, which applies in a large number of urban areas outside of Dublin, makes similar provision.

Nuisance by barking dogs

The Control of Dogs Act 1986 at section 2; prohibits the keeping of a dog without a licence, and section 27; makes it an offence to keep a barking dog for which the penalty on summary conviction is a £100 fine.

Littering a public place

The Litter Act 1982 at section 3 provides that a person shall not-

(a) deposit anywhere, whether in a receptacle or not, any substance, material or thing for collection by or on behalf of a local authority, or
(b) (i) otherwise place or leave anywhere or
    (ii) throw down anywhere,

any substance, material or thing so as to create or tend to create litter in a public place or litter that is visible from a public place.

To do so is an offence for which the penalty on summary conviction is an £800 fine. By section 5 of the Act where a litter warden with reasonable grounds suspects that an offence has been committed, he can levy a £5 fine.

Obstruction at General Post Office

The Post Office Act 1908 at section 68 provides that;

(1) A hackney carriage shall not stand or ply for hire opposite the G.P.O. in Dublin and if any driver or person having the management of any hackney carriage, permits that same to stand or ply for hire opposite the G.P.O. he shall be guilty of an offence,

(3) In any hawker, newsvendor, or idle or disorderly person stops or loiters on the flagway or pavement opposite the G.P.O., he shall be guilty of an offence.

The penalty on summary conviction is a £5 fine.

VAGRANCY

The Vagrancy Act 1824 was extended to Ireland by section 15 of the Prevention of Crimes Act 1871. The Act creates three classes of vagrants :

Idle and disorderly person   S. 3

A person shall be deemed to be an idle and disorderly person where such person :

(1)   Causes his family to become a charge on the parish,

(2)   Hawks goods without a pedlars licence,

(3)   is a common prostitute,

(4)   Begs in a public place.

An idle and disorderly person is liable to a £5 fine and or one months imprisonment.

A rogue and a vagabond   S. 4

A person shall be deemed to be a rogue and a vagabond where such person :

(1)   Tells fortunes,

(2)   Wanders abroad, *

(3)   Exposes to public view any obscene print or picture,

(4)   Exposes his person with intent to insult any female,

(5)   Exposes wounds to gather alms,

(6)   Procures charitable contributions under fraudulent pretence,

(7)   Runs away and leaves his family as a charge on the parish,

(8)   Is in possession of implements with felonious intent,

(9)   Is found in a building for an unlawful purpose,

(10) Is twice convicted as an idle and disorderly person.

A rogue and a vagabond is liable to a £25 and or three months imprisonment.
* The Housing Bill 1988 as initiated proposes the repeal of this offence.

Incorrigible rogue S. 5
A person shall be deemed to be an incorrigible rogue where such person :
(1) Escapes from legal confinement,
(2) Commits an offence under section 4 above, having been previously convicted as a rogue and a vagabond,
(3) When apprehended as a rogue and a vagabond, he violently resists any constable.
An incorrigible rogue shall be imprisoned until the next court session.

The Vagrancy (Ireland) Act 1847
This Act at section 3 provides as follows : That every person wandering abroad and begging, or placing himself in any public place, ..to beg, or encouraging any child or children to do so, shall be liable to one months imprisonment.

DRUNKENNESS

Drunkenness is not of itself a criminal offence, but being drunk in certain circumstances can constitute an offence, as where it violates public peace and order.

Habitual drunkards
There are, certain provisions which enable a criminal habitual drunkard to be dealt with on indictment. The Habitual Drunkards Act 1879, at section 3 declares that a "Habitual Drunkard" means a person who, not being amenable to any jurisdiction in lunacy, is notwithstanding, by reason of habitual intemperate drinking of intoxication liquor, at times dangerous to himself or herself or to others, or incapable of managing himself or herself, and his or her affairs.
A person who commits any of certain offences, as is mentioned in the first schedule to the Inebriates Act 1898, and who within the previous twelve months has been convicted summarily at least three times, and who is a habitual drunkard,

152

is liable on conviction on indictment to be detained for three years. Amongst the offence contained in the schedule to the 1898 Act are :

Being found drunk in a highway or other public place, whether a building or not, or on a licensed premises.

Being guilty while drunk of riotous or disorderly behaviour in a highway or other public place, whether a building or not.

Being drunk while in charge, on any highway or other public place, of any carriage, horse, cattle, or steam-engine.

The Dublin Police Act 1842 provides as follows :

Disorderly conduct in houses of public resort
VII. Every person who shall have or keep any house,shop,room or place of public resort (within the Dublin Police District) wherein provisions, liquors, or refreshments of any kind shall be sold or consumed (whether the same shall be kept or retailed therein or procured elsewhere) and who shall wilfully or knowingly permit drunken or other disorderly conduct therein, or knowingly suffer any unlawful games or any gaming whatsoever therein, or knowingly permit or suffer persons of notoriously bad character to meet and remain therein is guilty of an offence for which the penalty is a £5 fine.

Drunkards guilty of riotous or Indecent behaviour
XV. And be it enacted that every person who shall be found drunk in any street or public Thoroughfare within the Police District, and who while drunk shall be guilty of any riotous or indecent behaviour, and also any person who shall be guilty of any violent or indecent behaviour in any Police station house, shall be liable to a penalty of 40/- for every such offence, or may be committed for 7 days. The Towns Improvement Act (Ireland)1854, makes similar provision.

CRIMINAL LIBEL

A criminal libel is a malicious defamation expressed either in printing or writing. or by signs or pictures, tending either to blacken the memory of one who is dead or the reputation of one who is alive and thereby exposing him to public hatred, contempt, ridicule. Because of its tendency to provoke a breach of the peace such a libel is criminal.

The Defamation Act 1961 makes provision for criminal proceedings for libel.

Newspapers

By Section 8 of the Act, no criminal prosecution shall be commenced without the order of the High Court sitting in camera on notice to the person accused, where he is a newspaper person.

By section 9 of the Act, a Justice of the District Court, upon the hearing of a charge against any person responsible for the publication of a newspaper, may receive evidence as to the publication being for the public benefit, as to the matters charged in the libel being true, as to the report being fair and accurate and published without malice and as to any matter which; might be given in evidence by way of defence and the Justice, if of the opinion that there is a strong or probable presumption that the jury would acquit the person charged, may dismiss the case.

Penalties

By section 10 of the Act, If a Justice of the District Court is of the opinion that, the libel was of a trivial character may with the consent of the accused deal with the case summarily and impose a fine not exceeding £50.

By section 11 of the Act, every person who maliciously publishes any defamatory libel, shall on conviction on indictment be liable to a £200 fine and or one year imprisonment.

By section 12 of the Act, every person who maliciously publishes any defamatory libel, knowing the same to be false, shall on conviction on indictment be liable to a £500 fine and or two years imprisonment.

Also see reference to section 13 for blasphemous or obscene libel below.

To make a writing a libel it must be published, i.e. communicated to some person. In a criminal prosecution communication to a single person, even the person libeled is a sufficient publication even if it be contained in a private letter.

Any person who is concerned in the writing or publishing of a libel is liable to conviction, unless his part in the transaction is innocent or is a lawful act.

Chapter 21

BIGAMY

Bigamy means being married twice; but in law is used as synonymous with polygamy. It was originally an ecclesiastical offence. But in 1603 was made a felony. The present law is contained in the Offences against the Person Act 1861, which at section 57 provides that; Whosoever, being married, shall marry any other person during the life of the former husband or wife, whether the second marriage shall have taken place in Ireland or elsewhere, shall be guilty of a felony and liable on conviction to seven years imprisonment.

"elsewhere" means any other part of the world.

If the other party is aware of the bigamous nature of the marriage he or she is a principal in the second degree. A clergyman who knowingly assists in a bigamous marriage is liable as an aider and abettor.

In order to prove bigamy the prosecution must show;
    (a) Celebration of the first marriage of the accused,
    (b) Proof of the validity of the first marriage,
    (c) The subsistence of the first marriage,
    (d) Proof of the second ceremony of marriage.

Celebration of the first marriage
There must be evidence of the ceremony itself, i.e. by production of a certified copy of the marriage register, also evidence of the identity of the parties must be given.

Proof of the validity of first marriage
The second marriage is not bigamous unless the first marriage was valid; and the validity of the first marriage must be proved by the prosecution. The law will not presume it in the case of bigamy, as in civil cases.

The subsistence of the first marriage
The prosecution must prove that the spouse of the accused was alive at the date of the second ceremony of marriage. Where the evidence shows only that the first spouse was alive at some time before the second ceremony, the jury must decide

whether or not the spouse was alive at the date of that ceremony.

Proof of the second ceremony of marriage
R V Brawn (1843)
Lord Denman stated: "It is the appearing to contract a second marriage and the going through the ceremony which constituted the crime of bigamy, otherwise it would never exist in the ordinary cases"
The second ceremony must be proved as was the first. It is no defence that the second marriage was itself void independently of its bigamous character.

Defence
The statutory exceptions given by the Act are as follows;
1. If it is the case that the second marriage has been contracted outside of Ireland by someone who is not a citizen of Ireland, thus an American, who is already married in Ireland can marry again abroad with impunity despite the still existing prior marriage.
2. In the case of a person marrying a second time whose husband or wife shall have been continually absent for seven years, and shall not have been known by such person to be living within that time.
   R V Taylor (1950)
   This defence is always available even though several bigamous ceremonies have been gone through, the phrase "a second time" is not limited to a second ceremony; it may refer to a third ceremony which forms the basis of the indictment.
3. I In the case of a person who has been divorced abroad, such divorce recognized by the Irish Courts. Because of the provisions of Article 41.3.3, it is not possible for a marriage to be dissolved by the courts in the State, however there are circumstances where a divorce obtained abroad may be recognised.
4. In the case of a person whose former marriage has been declared void. There are a number of grounds upon which a marriage may be declared to be void, however their consideration is beyond the scope of this work.

Mistake
Mistake has been dealt with earlier, but can be mentioned here.

It follows from the doctrine of mens rea, that the defendant would not be guilty of bigamy where, he mistakenly thought that:

(i) his first wife was dead. Where person believed that his spouse was dead, however such belief must be reasonable.

R V Tolson (1889)

T. heard that her husband, who had deserted her, had been lost at sea. Five years after she had last saw him, and reasonably believing him to be dead, she remarried. On appeal her conviction for Bigamy was quashed, it was held that, despite the absence from the section of any word such as "knowingly" or "intentionally", a common law rule applied, The rule was that an honest and reasonable belief in the existence of circumstances which, if true, would make the accused's an innocent act, was a good defence.

(ii) his first marriage had been dissolved or annulled. It was formerly believed that a mistaken belief that a first marriage was dissolved was not a good defence.

R V Gould (1968)

The Court of Appeal held that the statute should not be construed literally but as subject to the presumption that a crime is not committed if the mind of the person was innocent.

(iii) his first marriage was void.

R V King (1964)

An honest and reasonable belief by the defendant, that his first marriage was invalid is a good defence. The mistake must be one of fact and not of law.

Chapter 22

OFFENCES CONCERNING RELIGION

Blasphemy and obscenity

The Constitution of Ireland Article 40.6.1.i. provides:

The State guarantees liberty for the exercise, subject to public order and morality, the right of the citizens to express freely their convictions and opinions. The publication or utterance of blasphemous, seditious, or indecent matter is an offence which shall be punishable in accordance with law.

Statutory provision is made for this in the Defamation Act 1961 section 13. Every person who composes, prints or publishes any blasphemous or obscene libel shall, on conviction thereof on indictment, be liable to a £500 fine and or seven years imprisonment.

Blasphemy is the denial God and Religion, and Religion is not necessarily Christian. There is no statutory provision for the offence of uttering a blasphemy.

Obscenity means something that is filthy, lewd, or disgusting. It is in general applied to the area of sex.

The Post Office Act 1908 prohibits the sending of indecent prints through the post see section 63 of that Act below. Also not the Dublin Police Act 1842, section 14(12) above, which is similar to a provision contained in the Town Improvement Act (Ireland) 1854.

Obscene or indecent performance

It is an offence at common law to show an obscene or indecent performance. In general all open lewdness, grossly scandalous, and whatever openly outrages decency or is offensive and disgusting, or is injurious to public morals by tending to corrupt the mind and destroy the love of decency, morality and good order, is a misdemeanour indictable at common law.

Indecent publications

The Censorship of Publications Act 1929 at section 14(1) provides that: It shall not be lawful to print or publish or cause to procure to be printed or published in relation to any judicial proceedings -

(a) any indecent matter the publication of which would be calculated to injure public morals, or

(b) any indecent medical, surgical or physiological details the publication of which be calculated to injure public morals.

Obstructing a clergyman

The Offences Against the Person Act, 1861, at section 36 provides that Whosoever shall, by threats or force, obstruct or prevent, or endeavour to obstruct or prevent any clergyman, or other minister, in or from celebrating Divine service, or otherwise officiating in any church, chapel, meeting-house, or other place of Divine worship, or in or from the performance of his duty in the lawful burial of the dead in any churchyard or other burial place, or shall strike or offer any violence to, or shall, upon any civil process, or under the pretence of executing any civil process, arrest any clergyman or other minister who is engaged in, or, to the knowledge of the offender, is about to engage in, any of the rites or duties in this section aforesaid, or who to the knowledge of the offender shall be going to perform the same, or returning from the performance thereof, shall be guilty of a misdemeanour for which the penalty is two years imprisonment.

Disturbing religious worship

The Ecclesiastical Courts Jurisdiction Act, 1860 at section 2 provides that; Any person who shall be guilty of riotous, violent or indecent behaviour in any place of religious worship, whether during the celebration of divine service or at any other time, or in any churchyard or burial ground, or who shall molest, disturb, vex or trouble, or, by any other unlawful means, disquiet or misuse any preacher duly authorized to preach therein, or any clergyman in holy orders ministering or celebrating any sacrament or any divine service, rite or office, in any cathedral, church or chapel, or in any churchyard or burial ground, shall be guilty of of an offence for which the penalty is a £5 fine and or 2 months imprisonment .

This offence can be committed by a clergyman who acts in a violent or indecent way in his own church. An offender may be apprehended immediately after commission of the offence. This offence is known as "brawling".

Violent behaviour at a burial

The Burial Laws Amendment Act 1880 at section 7 makes it an offence to wilfully obstruct a burial or any service thereat, or to there bring into contempt the Christian religion at any graveyard under the colour of any religious service.

Chapter 23

OFFENCES OF A PUBLIC NATURE

POSTAL AND TELECOMMUNICATIONS OFFENCES

The Post Office Act, 1908 makes provision for offences in relation to the Post Office. Section's 50, 52, and 55 of the Act which relate to larceny, embezzlement and receiving have been reproduced in sections 12, 18 and 33(2) of the Larceny Act 1916 and reference should be made to them in chapter 11. The Postal and Telecommunications Service Act 1983, divided theDepartment of Posts and Telegraphs into two, setting up a postal company and a telecommunications company, An Post and Bord Telecom Eireann.

Postal offences

Opening or delaying postal packets
Section 84 of the 1983 Act provides that; a person who-
(a) opens or attempts to open a postal packet addresses to another person or delays or detains any such postal packet or does anything to prevent its due delivery or authorises, suffers or permits another person (who is not the person to whom the postal packet is addressed) to do so, or
(b) discloses the existence or contents of any such postal packet, or
(c) uses for any purpose any information obtained from any such postal packet, or
(d) tampers with any such postal packet,
without the agreement of the person to whom the postal packet is addressed shall be guilty of an offence, for which the penalty on summary conviction is an £800 fine and or twelve months imprisonment; and on conviction on indictment is a £50,000 fine and or five years imprisonment. This section does not apply to a person who is acting under lawful authority.

Unlawfully taking away or opening the mail
Section 51 provides that; If any person unlawfully takes away or opens a mail bag sent by any vessel employed by or under An Post for the transmission of postal packets under contract, or unlawfully takes a postal packet in course of transmission by post out of a mail bag sent, he shall be guilty of a felony.

Fraudulent retention

Section 53 provides that; If any person fraudulently retains, or wilfully secretes or keeps, or detains or, when required by an officer of An Post, neglects or refuses to deliver up--

(a) any postal packet which is in course of transmission by post and which ought to have been delivered to any other person, or

(b) any postal packet in course of transmission by post or any mail bag, which shall have been found by him or by any other person,

he shall be guilty of a misdemeanour.

Inviolability of mail

Section 53A provides that; Any person who unlawfully and maliciously damages or interferes with a mail box shall be guilty of an offence, for which the penalty on summary conviction is an £800 fine and or twelve months imprisonment; and on conviction on indictment is a £50,000 fine and or five years imprisonment.

Offences by postal employees

Section 57 provides that; Any carelessness, negligence, or misconduct of persons while employed to convey or deliver postal packets, shall be an offence for which the penalty is on summary conviction is a £20 fine.

Section 58 provides that; Any officer who fraudulently issues any money order, shall commit a felony for which the penalty is seven years imprisonment.

Forgery and stealing of money orders

Section 59(2) If any person, with intent to defraud, obliterates, adds to, or alters ...a money order . or knowingly offers, alters or disposes of any money order with such fraudulent obliteration, addition, or alteration, he shall be guilty of a felony and the penalty is the same as in the case of cheques.

Public offences

Section 61 provides that;. Placing injurious substances or committing a nuisance in or against post office boxes, is an offence for which the penalty is a £10 fine and or twelve months imprisonment.

Section 62 provides that;. Affixing placards, notices, etc., on post office letter box, telegraph post or other property of An Post or in any way disfiguring same is an offence for which the penalty is a £2 fine.

Section 63 provides that;. Sending by post explosive, inflammable, or deleterious substances, or indecent prints, words, etc. is a misdemeanour for which the penalty on summary conviction is a £10 fine and or twelve months imprisonment.

Section 64 provides that; Imitation of post office stamps, forms and marks, is an offence for which the penalty on summary conviction is a £2 fine.

Section 66 provides that; The displaying without lawful authority the words "Post Office" or "Postal Telegraph Office", or "Letter Box",etc., is an offence for which the penalty on summary conviction is a £2 fine plus 25p each day that the offence continues.

Obstruction

Section 67 provides that;. Obstructing an officer of An Post in the execution of his duty, or obstructing the course of business of An Post is an offence for which the penalty is a £2 fine. Any officer of An Post may require person offending under this section to leave a Post Office, and if he refuses he is liable to a further fine(£5) and may be removed by any officer of An Post, and all members of the Garda Siochana are required on demand to remove or assist in removing such person.

Procurement of an offence

Section 69 provides that; Endeavouring to procure the commission of any felony or misdemeanour under this Act is a misdemeanour for which the penalty is two years imprisonment.

Definitions

Section 89 provides as follows :

"mail" includes every conveyance by which postal packets are carried, whether it be a carriage, coach, cart, horse, or any other conveyance, and also a person employed in conveying or delivering postal packets, and also any vessel:

"mail bag"includes a bag, box, parcel, or any other envelope or covering in which postal packets in course of transmissions by post are conveyed, whether it does or does not contain any such packets:

"Postal packet" means a letter, post card, reply post card,

162

newspaper, book packet, pattern or sample packet, or parcel, and every packet or article transmissible by post, and includes a telegram;

"officer of An Post" includes the Postmaster-General , and any person employed in any business of An Post, whether employed by the Postmaster General, or by any person under him or on behalf of An Post.

Telecommunications offences

Offensive telecommunication messages
The Post Office (Amendment) Act 1951 at section 13(1)   as amended provides that if any person :

(a) sends by means of the telecommunications system operated by Bord   Telecom Eireann, any message or other matter which is grossly offensive or of an indecent, obscene or menacing character, whether addressed to an operator or any other person, or

(b) sends by those means, for the purpose of causing annoyance, inconvenience, or needless anxiety to another, a message which he knows to be false, or persistently makes use of those means for that purpose,

shall be guilty of an offence. This has been amended by the 1983 Act,as it stood originally it was confined to telephone messages, but now it is much broader in scope.

Interception of telecommunications messages
Section 98 of the 1983 Act provides that a person who-

(a) intercepts or attempts to intercept, or

(b) authorises, suffers or permits another person to intercept, o r

(c) does anything that will enable him or another person to intercept,

telecommunications messages being transmitted by the company or who discloses the existence, substance or purport of any such message which has been intercepted or uses for any purpose any information obtained from any such message shall be guilty of an offence. This section does not apply to persons acting under lawful authority.

Fraudulent use of telecommunications system.
Section 99 of the 1983 Act provides that;

(1) A person who wilfully causes the company to suffer loss in respect of any rental, fee or charge properly payable for

the use of the telecommunications system or any part of the system or who by any false statement or misrepresentation or otherwise with intent to defraud avoids or attempts to avoid payment of any such rental, fee or charge shall be guilty of an offence.

(2) A person who connects or causes to be connected any apparatus or device to, or places or causes to be placed any apparatus or device in association with or conjunction with, the telecommunications system operated by Bord Telecom Eireann or any part of the system the effect of which might result in the provision by Bord Telecom Eireann of a service to any person without payment of the appropriate rental, fee or charge shall be guilty of an offence.

Penalties

The penalties in respect of the above offences are; on summary conviction a an £800 fine and or twelve months imprisonment; and on conviction on indictment a £50,000 fine and or five years imprisonment.

GAMING

The law in contained in the Gaming and Lotteries act 1956 as amended.

Unlawful gaming S.4

No person shall promote or assist in promoting or provide facilities for any kind of gaming-

(a) in which by reason of the nature of the game, the chances of all the players, including the banker, are not equal, or

(b) in which any portion of the stakes is retained by the promoter or is retained by the banker otherwise than as winnings on the result of the play, or

(c) by means of any slot-machine.

See D P P V Flanagan (1979) in respect of (c).

Use of buildings for unlawful gaming S.5

No person shall open, keep or use any buildings, room or place, enclosed or unenclosed, or permit it to be opened, kept or used for unlawful gaming or take part in the care and management of or in any way assist in conducting the business of any building, room or place so opened, kept or used.

Cheating   S. 11
Every person who by any fraud or cheat in promoting or operating or assisting in promoting or operating or in providing facilities for any game or in acting as banker for those who play or in playing at, or in wagering on the event of, any game, sport pastime or exercise wins from any other person or causes or procures any person to win from another anything capable of being stolen shall be deemed guilty of obtaining such thing from such other person by a false pretence, with intent to defraud, within the meaning of section 10 of the Criminal Justice Act, 1951 (No. 2 of 1951), and on conviction shall be punished accordingly. See also chapter 11.

Proof   S. 43
It shall not be necessary in support of a prosecution in relation to unlawful gaming to prove that any person found playing at any game was playing for any money, wager or stake.

Penalty   S.44
A person who contravenes any provision of this Act for which a penalty is not specifically provided shall be guilty of an offence and shall on summary conviction thereof be liable to a £100 fine and or three months imprisonment.

CORRUPTION

The law in this area is contained in the following :
>   The Public Bodies Corrupt Practices Act 1889,
>   The Prevention of Corruption Act 1906, and
>   The Prevention of Corruption Act 1916.
The three Acts should be read as one.

Corruption in public bodies
Section 1 of the 1889 Act provides that;
(1) Every person who shall by himself or by or in conjunction with any other person corruptly solicit, or receive or agree to receive, for himself or any other person, any gift, loan, fee, reward, or advantage whatsoever as an inducement to, or reward for, or otherwise on account of any member, officer, or servant of a public body doing or forbearing to do anything in respect of any matter or

transaction whether actual or proposed in which the said public body is concerned, shall be guilty of a misdemeanour.

(2) Every person who shall by himself or by or in conjunction with any other person corruptly give, promise or offer any gift, loan, fee, reward, or advantage whatsoever to any person, whether for the benefit of that person or of another person, as an inducement to, or reward for, or otherwise on account of any member, officer, or servant of a public body doing or forbearing to do anything in respect of any matter or transaction whether actual or proposed in which the said public body is concerned,

shall be guilty of a misdemeanour. The penalty on conviction is £500 fine and or two years imprisonment, together with the return of any gift etc..

"Corruptly" means a deliberate offering of cash or something similar with the intention that it should operate on the mind of the person to whom it is offered to persuade him to enter into the contract.

"public body" means any council of a county, or council of a city or town, also any board of Commissioners which has power to act under any Act relating to Local Government or the public health, or otherwise to administer money raised by rates in pursuance of any public general Act.

"advantage" includes any office or dignity and any forbearance to demand any money or money's worth or valuable thing, and includes any aid, consent, vote or influence or pretended aid, vote consent or influence and also includes any promise or procurement of or agreement or endeavour to procure, or the holding out of any expectation of any gift, loan fee, reward or advantage as defined.

Corruption of and by agents
Section 1 of the 1906 Act provides that; If any agent corruptly accepts or obtains or agrees to accept or attempt to obtain, or any person corruptly gives or agrees to give or corruptly offer any gift or consideration to any agent as a bribe in connection with his principal's business he shall be guilty of a misdemeanour. The penalty on indictment is £500 fine and or two years imprisonment and on summary conviction is £50 and or four months imprisonment.

"agent" in this Act and in the Act of 1916 includes any person employed by or acting for another.

State contracts

Section 1 of the 1916 Act provides that; A person convicted on indictment of a misdemeanour under the Act of 1889 or the Act of 1906 may be liable to a greater penalty of seven years imprisonment in certain cases where State contracts are involved.

A prosecution shall not be instituted under either of the above Acts without the consent of the Director of Public Prosecutions. In addition if it is proved that any money gift or other consideration has been paid or given to or received by any person in the employment of any Government department or public body, by or from a person, or his agent holding or seeking to obtain a contract from any Government department or public body, the money gift or other consideration shall be deemed to have been paid or given and received corruptly as such inducement or reward as is mentioned in the Acts, unless the contrary is proved.

CORRUPT PRACTICES AT ELECTIONS

Bribery, Undue Influence

The Prevention of Electoral Abuses Act 1923 provides that any person guilty of bribery or undue influence as defined in the Act shall be guilty of an offence and liable to a £1,000 fine and or twelve months imprisonment.

Personation

The Prevention of Electoral Abuses Act 1982 provides a new definition of personation in the 1923 Act; a person who -

(a) at an election applies for a ballot paper in the name of some other person, whether that name be the name of a living person or of a dead person or of a fictitious person, or

(b) having obtained a ballot paper once at an election applies at the same election for a ballot paper in his own name

shall be guilty of the offence of personation. The penalty on summary conviction, for a first offence shall be a £500 fine and or two months imprisonment, for a second or subsequent offence a £500 fine and or twelve months imprisonment and on conviction on indictment shall be three years imprisonment.

Chapter 24

OFFENCES AGAINST GOVERNMENT

TREASON

The Constitution of Ireland at Article 39 defines treason as levying war against the State, or assisting any State or persons or inciting or conspiring with any person to levy war against the State, or attempting by force of arms or other violent means to overthrow the organs of Government established by the Constitution, or taking part in or being concerned in or inciting or conspiring with any person to make or take part or be concerned in any such attempt. It can therefore be seen that an attempt at treason is itself treason.

The Treason Act 1939 was passed to give effect to this provision of the Constitution.
Section 1
(1) Every person who commits treason within the State shall be liable to suffer death.
(2) Every person who, being an Irish citizen or ordinarily resident within the State, commits treason outside the State shall be liable to suffer death.
(3) Treason is to be tried by the Central Criminal Court.
(4) No person shall be convicted of treason on the uncorroborated evidence of one witness.
The penalty for treason has been restated by section 1(1)(a) of the Criminal Justice Act 1964.

Treason Felony
Section 2, creates the offence of Treason Felony
(1) Every person who encourages, harbours, or comforts any person whom he knows or has reasonable grounds for believing to be engaged in committing treason shall be guilty of a felony.
(2) No person shall be convicted of treason felony on the uncorroborated evidence of one witness.
The penalty for treason felony is a £500 fine and or twenty years imprisonment.

Misprision of Treason

Section 3, creates the offence of misprision of treason

Every person who knowing that any act the commission of which would be treason is intended or proposed to be or is being, or has been committed, does not disclose the same to a District Justice or officer of the Garda Siochana or some other lawful person shall be guilty of the felony of misprision of treason. The penalty for misprision of treason is five years imprisonment.

OFFICIAL SECRETS

The law relating to official secrets is contained in the Official Secrets Act 1963, which repealed the earlier acts of 1911 and 1920.

Unlawful Communication of Official Information

By Section 4 of the Act a person shall not communicate any official information to any other person unless he is duly authorized to do so or does in the course of and in accordance with his duties as the holder of a public office or when it is his duty in the interest of the State to communicate it. This section also provides that a person shall not obtain official information where he is aware or has reasonable grounds for believing that the communication of such information would be a contravention.

By Section 5 of the act a person shall not disclose any confidential information relating to a contract with the State.

By section 6 of the act a person shall not retain any official document or anything which contains official information. Also by this section a person shall comply with a direction to return such documentation.

Possession of official dies

By section 7 of the Act a person shall not use or have in possession, any official die, seal or stamp, or any counterfeit of same, or manufacture or sell such.

Forging official documents

By section 8 of the Act a person shall not forge or alter any official document or have in his possession any forged or altered official document.

Communication of Information to the Prejudice of the Safety or Preservation of the State.

By section 9 of the Act ; A person shall not :

(a) obtain, record, communicate to any other person, or

(b) have in his possession any document or other record of information on :

   (1) the Defence Forces

   (2) operatives of the Defence Forces or Garda Siochana,

   (3) defences or fortifications,

   (4) munitions of war,

   (5) any other matter whatsoever prejudicial to the safety or preservation of the State.

When a person is charged with this offence the fact that he has been in communication with a foreign or a member of an unlawful organization shall be evidence that the act with which he is charged has been done in a manner prejudicial to the State.

Harbouring

By section 2 of the Act a person shall not knowingly harbour any person whom he knows or has reasonable grounds for supposing to have contravened or to be about to contravene section 9.

If in the course of proceedings for an offence under section 9 or in relation to the unlawful communication of official information, application is made by the prosecution that part of the hearing shall be in camera, the court shall make such order, but the verdict and sentence shall be announced in public.

Penalties

By section 17 of the Act it is an offence if a person fails to give information in relation to a suspected offence under section 9 to an authorized member of the Garda Siochana not below the rank of Inspector,the penalty being £100 and or six months imprisonment.

The penalty for any offence under the Act shall without prejudice be a £100 fine and or six months imprisonment.The penalty on indictment for an offence under Section 9 or for any offence prejudicial to the safety or preservation of the State shall be two years imprisonment or seven years penal servitude.

Proceedings for any offence under Official Secrets Act 1963 shall not be instituted except by or with the consent of the Attorney General.

CUSTOMS OFFENCES

The law in this area is principally governed by the Customs Consolidation Act 1876, it is particularly concerned with smuggling.

Smuggling.
Smuggling consists in bringing on shore, or in carrying from the shore, dutiable goods, wares, or merchandise for which duty has not been paid, or goods the importation of which is prohibited. Smuggling across the land frontier of the State is an offence.

Prohibited goods
The Customs(Amendment) Act 1942 at section 2(a) provides that the expression "prohibited goods" includes and always included goods the export of which is prohibited as well as goods the import of which is prohibited.

The land frontier
The Adaptation of Enactments Act 1922, section 13 provides that the Minister of Finance may make regulations to apply to the importation and exportation of any goods into and from the State by land, any of the provisions of the Customs Act. He may prohibit the importation and exportation of all goods or of any classes of goods except by such routes within the State and during such hours as may be prescribed. such regulations are contained in the Customs (Land Frontier) Regulations 1968

Forfeiture
Section 177 of the Act, provides that any goods brought into the State without clearance, shall be forfeited together with any goods which shall be found packed with or used in concealing them. Thus a motor vehicle used to transport goods across the land frontier, shall be forfeited.

Powers of search

Section 182 of the Act makes provision for the searching of any ships or boats within the limits of any port.

Section 184 as amended by the Customs and Inland Revenue Act 1881, section 12 provides;

Any officer of customs or other person duly employed for the prevention of smuggling may search any person on board any ship or boat within the limits of any port, or any person who shall have landed from any ship or boat, provided such officer or other person has good reason to suppose that such person is carrying or has in his possession uncustomed or prohibited goods.

Any person who

(1) breaks or destroys goods to prevent their seizure by any customs officer;

(2) breaks or destroys any goods seized by a customs officer; or

(3) rescues any person arrested for any customs offence; or

(4) prevents the arrest of any such person; or

(5) assaults or obstructs any customs officer or other person duly employed in the prevention of smuggling, acting in the execution of his duty; or

(6) attempts or endeavours to commit or aids, abets or assists in committing any of the above offences.

commits an offence, for which the penalty is a £100 fine.

Penalty

Section 186 of the Act provides that: Every person who shall illegally import, remove or shall knowingly harbour, keep or conceal upon his premises or person any dutiable or prohibited goods which shall have been illegally unshipped or removed without payment of duty; or shall be in any way knowingly concerned in carrying, removing, depositing, concealing, or in any manner dealing with any such goods with intent to, or shall evade the duties of customs,is liable to the penalty of treble the value or the goods, or £100, and may be detained or proceeded against by summons. The Finance Act 1963 section 34(4)(c)(i) provides that in case treble the estimated value of goods exceeds £100, the offence shall be triable on indictment.

Melling V O'Mathghamhna (1962)

It was held by the Supreme Court that smuggling offences are criminal offences and are minor which can be tried summarily.

Prohibited book or periodical publication
The Censorship of Publications Act 1946 section 18 provides:
(1) No person shall, except under and in accordance with a permit, import any prohibited book or any prohibited periodical publication
(2) Where a person is charged, under section 186 with the importation of a prohibited book or a prohibited periodical publication it shall be a good defence for him to prove that the book or prohibited periodical publication was imported otherwise than for sale or distribution or that it was not a prohibited book or prohibited periodical publication at the time he ordered it.

Assembling for smuggling
Section 188 of the Act provides that; All persons to the number of three or more who shall assemble for the purpose of landing, carrying, concealing, or having so assembled shall land, run, carry, or conceal any prohibited, restricted, or uncustomed goods shall commit an offence for which the penalty is a £500 fine.
Section 189 of the Act provides that; Every person procuring or hiring persons to assemble for the purpose of being concerned in the landing or carrying, or concealing smuggled goods shall be guilty of a misdemeanour for which the penalty is twelve months imprisonment, however if offensive weapons are involved the penalty is three years imprisonment.

Shooting at ships
Section 193 of the Act provides that; any person maliciously shooting at boats belonging to navy or revenue service, or maliciously shoots at anyone employed in the prevention of smuggling shall be guilty of a felony for which the penalty is five years imprisonment.

Chapter 25

OFFENCES AGAINST PUBLIC ORDER

Unlawful Assembly

Unlawful Assembly is committed where three or more persons gather together for the purpose of committing or preparing to commit a crime involving the use of violence, or in order to carry out a lawful or unlawful purpose in such a way as to lead to alarm being caused to bystanders of ordinary courage, that there will be a breach of the peace as a direct result of their conduct.

An assembly which was originally lawful may become unlawful, if a proposal is made at the meeting to do an act of violence to the disturbance of the public and the proposal is acted upon. The offence will have been committed even though the parties involved have departed without having done anything to carry out their purpose.

The moment when persons in a crowd begin to act for some shared common purpose and thus causing alarm the assembly becomes unlawful, alarm is likely to be caused by, the tone of any speeches, or the carrying of any offensive weapons, or the late hour of the meeting.

An unlawful assembly need not take place in public. Private citizens may on their own initative disperse an unlawful assembly forcibly. Unlawful assembly is an indictable misdemeanour at common law punishable by imprisonment.

ROUT

Rout is a misdemeanour at common law it stands midway between unlawful assembly and a riot, it is committed when an unlawful assembly makes some move towards the execution of its common purpose.

RIOT

A rout becomes a riot when an unlawful assembly executes its common purpose. It does not matter whether the purpose is lawful or not or whether the Riot Act (see below) has been read or not. It is a misdemeanour at common law, the elements of which are :

(1) three or more persons,
(2) such persons must have a common purpose,
(3) they must have begun to execute such purpose,
(4) they must have an intent to help one another by force if necessary against any person who may oppose them,
(5) force or violence must be displayed in such a manner as to alarm at least one person of reasonable firmness and courage.

The degree of force used to suppress a riot must be reasonable and proportionate to the circumstances of the case, as the rioters are guilty only of a misdemeanour.

RIOTOUS ASSEMBLY

Riotous Assembly is a statutory offence created by the Riot Act 1787, By this Act if an unlawful assembly of twelve or more persons do not disperse within an hour after a Justice of the Peace has read or has attempted to read, a proclamation calling on them to disperse, they become felons.

In such circumstances the rioters become liable to any amount of force, including military or armed police. However such force that is to be used must be proportionate to that of the rioters, a riotous assembly may be fired upon but only where this is necessary as a last resort to preserve life. Any persons hindering the making of such proclamation are deemed felons. See: *Lynch V Fitzgerald and Others* .

175

Chapter 26

FIREARMS AND EXPLOSIVES OFFENCES

FIREARMS OFFENCES

Given the use of firearms in the commission of offence, one way of discouraging serious offences against the person is by regulating the use of firearms, and the law on this subject is contained in the following :
> The Firearms Act 1925
> The Firearms Act 1964
> The Firearms (Proofing) Act 1968
> The Firearms Act 1971
> The Firearms (Dangerous Weapons) Order 1972
> The Firearms Regulations 1976

A number of amendments and insertions to the Firearms Acts have been made by the Criminal Law (Jurisdiction) Act 1976. These statutes have been further added to by the Criminal Justice Act 1984 which also increased the penalties for offences under the earlier Acts.

Definitions
By the 1925 Act Section 1 (as amended) :

"firearm" means a lethal weapon of any description from which any shot bullet, or other missile can be discharged and save where the context otherwise requires, includes a component part of a firearm.

"ammunition" means ammunition for a firearm but also includes grenades, bombs and other similar missiles whether the same are or are not capable of being used with a firearm and also includes any ingredient or component part of any such ammunition or missile.

By the 1964 Act section 2 :

"firearms" shall include an airgun (which expression includes an air rifle and an air pistol) and any other weapon incorporating a barrel form which metal or other slugs can be discharged and a prohibited weapon.

By the 1964 Act section 25(as amended): In section 28 of the Larceny Act 1916, "offensive weapon" shall include a firearm that is not loaded and an imitation forearm. "imitation firearm" means anything which is not a firearm but has the appearance of being a firearm.

Flack V Baldry (1988)

The defendant was convicted of possessing a stun gun. On appeal to the House of Lords it was held that it was capable of being a weapon designed to discharge a noxious thing.

Unlawful possession of firearms

By the 1925 Act Section 2 : it shall not be lawful for any person to have in his possession, use or carry any firearm or ammunition unless authorized by a firearm certificate.

Where a person is guilty of this offence, he shall be liable :

(a) in a case where an offence relates to a sporting firearm or to any firearm in respect of which a firearm certificate was held on summary conviction, in the case of a first offence, to a £50 fine and, in the case of any subsequent offence to a £50 fine and or three months imprisonment.

(b) in any other case, on summary conviction to a £200 fine and or one years imprisonment, or, on conviction on indictment to a £50 fine and or five years imprisonment.

A number of persons may lawfully be in possession of firearms, otherwise a firearm certificate granted by the Garda Superintendent of the district shall be required.

Possession of firearms in suspicious circumstances

By the 1964 Act Section 27A (as inserted) A person who has a firearm or ammunition in his possession or under his control in such circumstances as to give rise to a reasonable inference that such possession or control is not for a lawful purpose, shall be guilty of an offence and be liable to ten years imprisonment.

R V Whelan (1972)

It was held that the finding of a revolver and ammunition in a room in which three brothers were sleeping is not sufficient to found an inference that all three were in possession, nor was there anything to indicate which, if any had possession.

The D. P. P. V Kelso and Others (1984)

Three armed R.U.C. men were charged with an offence under the Firearms Act 1964 Section 27(a). The question was whether the possession of a firearm in all the circumstances obtaining, was for a lawful purpose? The defendants stated that they carried firearms to protect their lives should the necessity arise. The court held that it had been established as a probability that each of the accused reasonably and honestly believed that his life might be in danger and that it's protection required him to carry his gun.

Possession of firearms while taking a vehicle
By the 1964 Act section 26 (as amended): A person who contravenes section 112 of the Road Traffic Act 1961 (see chapter 11) and who at the time has with him a firearm or an imitation firearm shall be guilty of an offence and be liable to fourteen years imprisonment.

Carrying firearms with criminal intent
By the 1964 Act section 27B (as inserted): A person who has with him a firearm or an imitation firearm with intent to commit an indictable offence, or to resist or prevent the arrest of himself or another, shall be guilty of an offence and be liable to fourteen years imprisonment. In a proceeding for an offence under this section proof that the accused had a firearm or imitation firearm with him and intended to commit an indictable offence or to resist or prevent arrest is evidence that he intended to have it with him while doing so.

Possession of firearms with intent
By the 1925 Act Section 15 (as amended) : Any person who has in his possession or under his control any firearms:
(a) with intent to endanger life or cause serious injury to property, or
(b) with intent to enable any other person by means of such firearm to endanger life or cause serious injury to property,
shall, whether any injury to person or property has, or has not been caused thereby, be guilty of felony and liable to life imprisonment. By the 1971 Act section 4 references to life and property includes references to life and property outside the area of application of the laws enacted by the Oireachtas.

Use of firearms to resist arrest or aid escape
By the 1964 Act Section 27 (as amended): A person shall not use or produce a firearm or an imitation firearm
(a) for the purpose of or while resisting the arrest of such person or of another person by a member of the Garda Siochana, or
(b) for the purpose of aiding of in the course of the escape or rescue of such person or another person from custody.

A person who contravenes this shall be guilty of an offence and be liable to life imprisonment.

Aggravated burglary
By the Larceny Act 1916, section 23B (as inserted): Aggravated Burglary for which the penalty is life imprisonment is committed where the person has with him any firearm or imitation firearm, any weapon of offence or any explosive. See also chapter

Manufacture, sell or repair
By the 1925 Act section 10 (as amended) : It shall not be lawful for any person to manufacture, sell, repair, test, or prove, or expose for sale, or have in his possession for sale.... any firearm or ammunition unless such person is registered in the register of firearm dealers.

The offences under the Firearms Acts 1925 - 1971 are scheduled offences for the purposes of Part V of the Offences Against the State Act 1939, and as such where a person is charged with such an offence, he is brought before the Special Criminal Court.

Withholding information regarding firearms
The Criminal Justice Act 1984, at section 15 provides that;
(1) Where a member of the Garda Siochana -
  (a) finds a person in possession of any firearm or ammunition,
  (b) has reasonable grounds for believing that the person is in possession of the firearms or ammunition in contravention of the criminal law, and
  (c) informs that person of his belief,
  he may require that person to give him any information which is in his possession, or which he can obtain by taking reasonable steps, as to how he came by the firearm or ammunition and as to any previous dealings with it, whether by himself or by any other person.
(2) If that person fails or refuses, without reasonable excuse, to give the information or gives information that he knows to be false or misleading,
he shall be guilty of an offence and shall be liable summarily £800 and or twelve months and on indictment £10,000 and or

five years imprisonment.

Any information given by a person shall not be admissible in evidence against that person, other than for an offence under sub-section 2

OFFENCES INVOLVING EXPLOSIVES

The law is principally contained in the Explosive Substances Act 1883, which has been amended by the Criminal Law (Jurisdiction) Act 1976. There are additional offences contained in the Offences against the Person Act 1861 and the Malicious Damage Act 1861.

Explosive Substances Act 1883

Explosive substance S.9
This expression shall be deemed to include any materials for making any explosive substance; also any apparatus, machine, implement, or materials used, or intended to be used, or adapted for causing, or aiding in causing, any explosion in or with any explosive substance; also any part of any such apparatus, machine, or implement.

Causing explosion to endanger life or property S.2
A person who in the State or (being an Irish citizen) outside the State unlawfully and maliciously causes by any explosive substance an explosion of a nature likely to endanger life, or cause serious injury to property, shall, whether any injury to person or property is actually caused lor not, be guilty of an offence and, on conviction on indictment, shall be liable to imprisonment for life.

Intent to cause explosions S.3
A person who in the State or (being an Irish citizen) outside the State unlawfully and maliciously-
(a) does any act with intent to cause, or conspire to cause, by an explosive substance an explosion of a nature likely to endanger life, or cause serious injury to property, whether in the State or elsewhere, or
(b) makes or has in his possession or under his control an explosive substance with intent by means thereof to endanger life, or cause serious injury to property, whether in the State or elsewhere, or to enable any other person so

to do,

shall whether any explosion does or does not take place, and whether any injury to person or property is actually caused or not, be guilty of an offence and, on conviction on indictment liable to twenty years imprisonment.

Possession under suspicious circumstances S.4

Any person who makes or knowingly has in his possession or under his control any explosive substance, under such circumstances as to give rise to a reasonable suspicion that he is not making it or does not have it in his possession or under his control for a lawful object shall, unless he can show that he made it or had it in his possession or control for a lawful object, shall be guilty of felony and on conviction liable to fourteen years imprisonment.

Offences against the Person Act 1861

Causing bodily injury by gunpowder S. 28

Whosoever shall unlawfully and maliciously, by explosion of gunpowder or other explosive substance, burn, maim, disfigure, or do grievous bodily harm to any person, shall be guilty of felony and on conviction liable to life.

Causing gunpowder to explode S.29

Whosoever shall unlawfully and maliciously, cause any gunpowder or other explosive substance to explode, or send or deliver to or cause to be taken or received by any person any explosive substance or any other dangerous or noxious thing, or put or lay at any place, or cast or throw at or upon or otherwise apply to any person, any corrosive fluid or any destructive or explosive substance, with intent in any of the cases aforesaid to burn, maim, disfigure, or do grievous bodily harm to any person, shall, whether any bodily injury is effected or not, be guilty of felony and on conviction liable to life.

Placing gunpowder near a building with intent S.30

Whosoever shall unlawfully and maliciously place or throw in, into,upon, against,or near any building, ship, or vessel any gunpowder or other explosive substance, with intent to do any bodily injury to any person, shall, whether or not any explosion

181

take place, and whether or not any bodily injury be effected be guilty of felony and on conviction liable to fourteen years imprisonment.

Malicious Damage Act 1861

Endangering life or property by explosives S.9
Whosoever shall unlawfully and maliciously, by explosion of gunpowder or other explosive substance, destroy, throw down, or damage the whole of any part of any dwelling-house, any person being therein, or of any building, whereby the life of any person shall be endangered, shall be guilty of felony and on conviction liable to life.

Putting explosives near building with intent S.10
Whosoever shall unlawfully and maliciously place or throw in, into, upon, under, against, or near, any building any gunpowder, or other explosive substance, with intent to destroy or damage any building, or any engine, machinery, working-tools, fixtures, goods, or chattels, shall whether or not any explosion takes place, and whether or not any damage be caused, be guilty of felony and on conviction liable to fourteen years imprisonment.

Attempting to damage ships with explosives S. 45
Whosoever shall unlawfully and maliciously place or throw in, into, upon, under, against, or near, any ship or vessel, any gunpowder, or other explosive substance, with intent to destroy or damage any ship or vessel, or any machinery, working-tools, fixtures, goods, or chattels, shall whether or not any explosion takes place, and whether or not any injury be effected, be guilty of felony and on conviction liable to fourteen years imprisonment.

Manufacturing explosive substances for purpose of committing offences S.54
Whosoever shall make or manufacture, or knowingly have in his possession, any gunpowder or other explosive substance, or any dangerous or noxious thing, or any machine, engine, instrument, or thing, with intent thereby or by means thereof to commit, or for the purpose of enabling any other person to commit, any of the felonies in this Act mentioned, shall be guilty of a misdemeanour and on conviction liable to two years imprisonment.

Chapter 27

THE OFFENCES AGAINST THE STATE ACT

The Offences Against the State Act 1939 as amended makes provisions in relation to actions and conduct calculated to undermine public order and the authority of the state.
The Offences Against the State created by the Act are principally contained in Part II as follows;

Usurpation of functions of government S.6
Every person who usurps or unlawfully exercises any function of government, whether by setting up, maintaining, or taking part in any way in any body of persons purporting to be a Government or a legislation but not authorized in that behalf by or under the Constitution, shall be guilty of a felony.

Obstruction of government S.7
Every person who prevents or obstructs, or attempts or is concerned in any attempt to prevent or obstruct, by force of arms or other violent means or by any form of intimidation the carrying on of the government of the state shall be guilty of a felony.
The People (D.P.P.) V Kehoe (1983)
The accused was convicted in the Special Criminal Court of this offence. There was evidence that he had used a pole, to aim blows at a Garda, who was guarding the British embassy. It was held by the Court of Criminal Appeal, that the conduct of the accused, as established by the evidence, constituted the commission of the offence.

Obstruction of the President S.8
Every person who prevents or obstructs, by force of arms or other violent means, the exercise by the President of his functions shall be guilty of a felony.

Interferences with military or other employees S.9
Every person who shall with intent to undermine public order or the authority of the state commit any act of violence against or of interference with a member of a lawfully established military or police force shall be guilty of a misdemeanour.

Printing of certain documents S.10

It is a summary offence to print, publish, or distribute, incriminating, treasonable,or seditious documents.

Section 2 of the Act, defines such documents as follows :

"incriminating document" means a document, issued by or emanating from an unlawful organisation or appearing to be so issued or so to emanate or purporting or appearing to aid or abet any such organisation or calculated to promote the formation of an unlawful organisation.

"treasonable document" includes a document which relates directly or indirectly to the commission of treason.

"seditious document" includes-

(a) a document consisting of or containing matter calculated or tending to undermine the public order or the authority of the state, and

(b) a document which alleges, implies, or suggests or is calculated to suggest that the government functioning under the Constitution is not the lawful government of the State or that there is in existence in the State any body or organisation not functioning under the Constitution which is entitled to be recognized as being the government of the country, and

(c) a document which alleges, implies, or suggests or is calculated to suggest that the military forces maintained under the Constitution are not the lawful military forces of the State, or that there is in existence in the State a body or organisation not established and maintained by virtue of the Constitution which is entitled to be recognized as a military force, and

(d) a document in which words, abbreviations, or symbols referable to a military body are used in referring to an unlawful organisation.

By section 11 of the Act the Minister for Justice may prohibit the importation of any foreign periodicals which he considers contains any seditious matter, the importation of which shall not be lawful.

Possession of documents S.12

It shall be a summary offence to be in possession of incriminating,
treasonable, or seditious documents. Where a person is charged with this offence,it shall be a good defence for such a person to prove:

184

(a) That he had custody of the document as an officer of the State,

(b) That he did not know that the document was in his possession,

(c) That he did not know the nature of the document.

Documents printed for reward S.13

It shall be a summary offence, for a person who prints documents for reward not to retain for six months the name and address of his client in order that it may be available to the Garda Siochana. A person who prints documents for reward is required to print his own name and address on such documents.

Unauthorised military exercises S.15

It shall not be lawful for any assembly of persons to practise or to train or drill in the use of arms or the performance of military exercises. To do so is a misdemeanour.

Secret societies in army or police S.16

Every person who shall administer any oath to bind persons with regard to the commission of any crime or any person who takes such an oath shall be guilty of a misdemeanour.

Administering unlawful oaths S.17

Every person who shall administer, or cause to be administered or take part in, be present at, or consent to the administering or taking in any form or manner of any oath, declaration, or engagement purporting or intended to bind the person taking the same to do any one of a number of unlawful acts, shall be guilty of a misdemeanour.

UNLAWFUL ORGANISATIONS

Part III of the Act deals with unlawful organisations

Unlawful organisations S.18

The government may by means of a suppression order declare any organisation to be an unlawful organisation. Membership of an unlawful organisations is an indictable offence,by the Criminal Law Act 1976, section 2 the penalty is up to seven years imprisonment. It is also a summary offence with a penalty of three months imprisonment. It is a good defence for a person charged with such membership that:

(a) That he did not know that such organisations was unlawful,

(b) He had ceased to be a member thereof.

The possession of an incriminating document shall be evidence until the contrary is proved of membership of an unlawful organisation.

By the Offences against the State (Amendment) Act 1972 any statement or any conduct leading to a reasonable inference that an accused person was a member of an unlawful organisation shall be evidence of such. Also by that Act the evidence of a member of the Garda Siochana not below the rank of Chief Superintendent that he believes an accused to have been a member of an unlawful organisation shall be evidence of such, this provision shall only be in force as long as Part V of the 1939 Act is in force.

Unlawful public meetings   S.27

It shall not be lawful to hold a public meeting on behalf of an unlawful organisation. In addition any meeting may be rendered unlawful by a member of the Garda Siochana not below the rank of Chief Superintendent by giving notice of such.

Prohibition of meetings near Oireachtas   S.28

It shall not be lawful for any public meeting to be held or any procession to pass within one half of a mile of a sitting of either house of the Oireachtas. Where:

(a) An officer of the Garda Siochana not below the rank of Chief Superintendent has by notice prohibited such, or

(b) A member of the Garda Siochana has called on persons taking part to disperse.

Section 30
ARREST AND   DETENTION OF SUSPECTED   PERSONS

(1) A member of the Garda Siochana may without warrant stop, search, interrogate and arrest any person, whom he suspects of having committed or being about to commit or being or having been concerned in the commission of an offence under this Act or an offence which is a scheduled offence or whom he suspects of being in possession of information relating to any such offence.

(2) Any member of the Garda Siochana may for the purpose of exercising the powers in sub-section 1, stop and search

any vehicle or any ship, boat, or other vessel which he suspects contains a person whom he may arrest without warrant.

(3) Whenever a person is arrested under this section, he may be detained in custody for a period of twenty-four hours and may if an officer of the Garda Siochana not below the rank of Chief Superintendent so directs, be detained for a further period of twenty-four hours.

(4) A detained person may be charged before the District Court, the Special Criminal Court or be released at the end of the detention period.

(5) By virtue of the Criminal Law Act 1976 section 7, any person detained under section 30 or under section 2 of the following in respect of him;
   (a) demand of him his name and address;
   (b) search him or cause him to be searched;
   (c) photograph him or cause him to be photographed;
   (d) take, or cause to be taken, his fingerprints and palm prints;
   (e) make or cause to be made any test in respect of firearms or explosives;
   (f) seize and retain for testing anything that he has in his possession

(6) Every person who obstructs the Garda Siochana in respect of the powers in the sub-section 5 shall by the Criminal Law Act 1976 section 7 (2) be liable:
   (a) on summary conviction to a £1,000 fine and or twelve months imprisonment

Trimbole V Governor of Mountjoy (1985)

Trimbole an Australian citizen, was arrested under section 30. On the same day the Government applied the Extradition Act 1965, part II to Australia and on his release by the High Court, he was arrested under that Act. It was held by Egan J. in the High Court that since no genuine suspicion grounding the arrest under section 30 existed, the arrest was a misuse of that section amounting to a conscious and deliberate violation of right guaranteed by the Constitution. It was subsequently held by the Supreme Court, that the Courts have a positive duty, to protect persons against invasion of their constitutional rights and to ensure as far as possible that persons acting on behalf of the executive who consciously and deliberately violate the constitutional rights of citizens do not for themselves or their superiors obtain the planned results of that invasion.

POWERS OF INTERNMENT

The Offences Against the State (Amendment) Act, 1940 provides for powers of internment, whenever the Government proclaims that Part II of the Act is to be in force. Whenever a Minister of State is of opinion that any particular person is engaged in activities which in his opinion are prejudicial to the preservation of public peace and order, or security of the State, such Minister may by warrant under his hand and seal, order the arrest and detention of such person.

Any member of the Garda Siochana may arrest without other warrant such person.

It shall be lawful for any member of the Garda Siochana to do all or any of the following things in respect of any person who is arrested and detained;

(a) to demand of such person his name and address;
(b) to search such person or cause him to be searched;
(c) to photograph such person or cause him to photographed;
(d) to take or cause to be taken his finger-prints.

A Minister of State may by writing, order the release of any particular person who is detained under the Act. By virtue of Article 34.3.3 of the Constitution of Ireland, because the Act was referred by the President to the Supreme Court, it is immune from challenge on constitutional grounds.

re O'Laighleis (1960)

The applicant was detained by warrant of the Minister of Justice under the Act. He obtained in the High Court a conditional order of habeas corpus contending that his detention was was unlawful as it contravened the European Convention of Human Rights, to which the State was a party. It was held by the Supreme Court that the Convention was not part of the domestic law of the State, and that the applicant was detained in accordance with law.

THE EMERGENCY POWERS ACT 1976

Under the provisions of the Constitution of Ireland Article 28.3.3, nothing in the Constitution shall be invoked to invalidate any law which is expressed to be for the purpose of securing the public safety and the preservation of the State in times of war or armed rebellion, where each of the House of the

188

Oireachtas have resolved that a national emergency exists. Such a resolution was adopted on the first day of September 1976 in relation to the Emergency Powers Act 1976.

Detention

Section 2 of the Act provides :

(1) A member of the Garda Siochana may without warrant stop, search, question and arrest any person, if he suspects with reasonable cause that that person has committed an offence under the Offences against the State Act 1939, or an offence which is a scheduled offence under part V of the Act, or if he suspects with reasonable cause that the person is carrying anything, or is in possession of information relating to such an offence.

(2) Any vehicle or vessel which he suspects may also be stopped.

(3) Whenever a person is arrested, he may be kept on custody for 48 hours and may, if a member of the Garda Siochana not below the rank of chief superintendent so directs, be kept in custody for another five days.

(4) A detained person may be charged before the District Court, the Special Criminal Court or be released at the end of the detention period.

During the period when this section is in force, the powers conferred by Section 30 of Offences against the State Act 1939 shall not be exercisable. However this should be seen in light of section 7 of the Criminal Law Act 1976. At the time of writing this Act is not in force, the Government may by order, bring it into force for a period of twelve months, subject to such an order being laid before both Houses of the Oireachtas. The major difference between Section 2 of this Act and Section 30 of the Offences against the State Act 1939 are the detention period a maximum of seven days rather than two days and the use of the words "suspects with reasonable cause" rather than "suspects".

The State (Hoey) V Garvey (1978)

It was held by the High Court that section 2 did not authorize the arrest and detention of a person on a second occasion, if the second arrest was grounded on the same suspicion as had justified the first arrest, even though the police had acquired further information between the dates of the two arrests.

Chapter 28

OFFENCES OF AN INTERNATIONAL NATURE

Piracy

Piracy *jure gentium* (piracy at common law) involves an act of armed violence committed upon the high seas within the jurisdiction of the admiralty, and not being an act of war.

The common law offence was supplemented by the Piracy Act 1837, section 2 of the Act provides Whosoever, with intent to commit or at the time of or immediately before or immediately after committing the crime of piracy in respect of any ship or vessel, shall assault, with intent to murder, any person being on board of or belonging to such ship or vessel, or shall stab, cut, or wound any such person, or unlawfully do any act by which the life of such person may be endangered, shall be guilty of a felony, the penalty for which would now be life imprisonment.

Piracy is an offence under international law and can be tried by the courts of any country even though it was not committed within its territorial waters.

WAR CRIMES

Geneva Convention Act 1962

This Act gives effect to the Geneva Convention of the 12th August 1949. Those protected by the convention, include the sick, wounded and shipwrecked members of armed forces, prisoners of war and civilians. Prisoners of war may not be compelled to serve in the forces of a hostile power, nor may they be deprived of of the right of a fair and regular trial.

The wilful killing, torture or inhuman treatment, including biological experimentation, wilfully causing great suffering or serious injury to body or health of persons is prohibited.

The extensive destruction of and appropriation of property, not justified by military necessity and carried out unlawfully and wantonly is prohibited.

Grave breaches

Section 3 of the Act provides that any person, whatever his

nationality, who, whether in or outside the State, commits, or aids, abets or procures the commission by any other person of any grave breach of the convention shall be guilty of an offence. The penalty where the offence involved a wilful killing would now be life imprisonment, in any other case the penalty is fourteen years. Proceedings for an offence under this section can only be instituted, with the consent of the Attorney General.

Minor breaches

Section 4 of the Act provides that, any persons, whether in the State or outside the State if a citizen of Ireland, who commits, or aids, or abets or procures the commission by any other person of, any minor breach of the Convention shall be guilty of an offence. The penalty on summary conviction is £60 and or six months imprisonment and on indictment is £300 and or two years imprisonment.

AIRCRAFT CRIMES

Air Navigation and Transport Act 1973

This Act writes into Irish law, the provisions of the Tokyo Convention on offences and certain other acts committed on board aircraft, of the 14th September 1963 and the Hague Convention for the Suppression of Unlawful Seizure of Aircraft, of the 16th. December 1970.

Tokyo Convention

Section 2 of the Act provides that, any act or omission which, if taking place in the State, would constitute an offence under the law of the State, shall, if it takes place on board an Irish controlled aircraft while in flight elsewhere that in or over the State, constitute that offence. The offence is treated as having taken place in the State. So if, for example a person steals a wallet on board an Irish aircraft while it is in flight over Germany, he may be arrested in Dublin and tried under the Larceny Act 1916.

The Hague Convention

Unlawful seizure of aircraft

Section 11 of the Act provides that; A person who on board an aircraft in flight anywhere -

(a) unlawfully, by force or threat thereof, or by any other form of intimidation, seizes or exercises control of or otherwise interference with the control of that aircraft, or

(b) attempt to perform any such act or aides or abets a person who performs or attempts to perform any such act of counsels or procures the performance of any such act.

shall be guilty of an offence. By section 16 of the Act the penalty is imprisonment for life.

GENOCIDE

The General Assembly of the United Nations in 1946 declared genocide to be a crime. A Genocide Convention was drawn up, which Ireland later adhered to. The Genocide Act 1973 gives effect to the Genocide Convention.

Definition

Genocide means any of the following acts committed with intent to destroy, in whole or in part, a national, ethnical, racial or religious group, as such:

(a) Killing members of the group;

(b) Causing serious bodily mental harm to members of the group;

(c) Deliberately inflicting on the group conditions of life calculated to bring about its physical destruction in whole or in part;

(d) Imposing measures intended to prevent births within the group;

(e) Forcibly transferring children of the group to another group.

Acts punishable

The following acts shall be punishable:

     (a) Genocide;

     (b) Conspiracy to commit genocide;

     (c) Direct and public incitement to commit genocide;

     (d) Attempt to commit genocide;

     (e) Complicity in genocide.

Penalties

A person guilty of an offence of genocide shall on conviction on

192

indictment-
(a) in case the offence consists of the killing of any person, be sentenced to imprisonment for life, and
(b) in any other case, be liable to imprisonment for a term not exceeding fourteen years.

Proceedings for an offence of genocide shall not be instituted except by or with the consent of the Attorney general.

A person charged with an offence of genocide or any attempt, conspiracy or incitement to commit genocide shall be tried by the Central Criminal Court. Genocide is an extraditable offence in any form and it shall not be regarded as a political offence or an offence connected with a political offence for the purposes of the Extradition Act 1965.

DIPLOMATS

Hindering diplomats

As stated in chapter 4 the Diplomatic Relations and Immunities Act 1967, gives force of law to the Vienna Conventions. The Act at section 46(1) provides that; a person who wilfully hinders, restricts or prevents the enjoyment or exercise of inviolability or an exemption, facility, immunity, privilege or right conferred by the Act shall be guilty of an offence, for which the penalty on summary conviction is a £100 fine and or six months imprisonment. A prosecution for this offence may not be instituted without a certificate from the Minister for Foreign Affairs.

Chapter 29

OFFENCES AGAINST THE ADMINISTRATION OF JUSTICE

PERJURY

Perjury is a misdemeanour at common law, it consists in knowingly giving false evidence on oath in a material matter in a judicial proceeding.

Judicial proceeding

The evidence must be given in a judicial proceeding. This includes the various courts, any commission established by such courts to hear evidence and all statutory tribunals at which evidence must be given on oath, and proceedings before those who are authorized by law to take evidence. Affidavits depositions, answers to interrogatories, and examinations are included.

Oath

The making of the oath must be proved, together with the lawful authority of such oath.

Material

The evidence given must be to something material to the issue. If the statement is not material, then even though it is false, it is not perjury. A statement is material if it is likely to influence a court in making its decision.

False evidence

False evidence given by a person who is not competent is not perjury. False evidence need not necessarily be untrue, as a person is only bound to give evidence as to what he knows and believes. Thus a truthful statement which is believed to be false could be perjury. The false statement must be deliberate, negligence will not suffice to constitute the mens rea of perjury.

In order to convict of perjury it is necessary to prove all of the above, corroboration is also necessary.

European Court of Justice
The Court of Justice of the European Communities(Perjury) Act, 1975 at section 1 provides; A person who before the Court of Justice of the European Communities swears anything which he knows to be false or does not believe to be true shall, whatever his nationality, be guilty of perjury.

Subornation of Perjury
The counseling, procuring, or inciting of another to commit perjury, where it is actually committed is also a misdemeanour at common law.

The Perjury Act 1729
This provides that the penalty on indictment is seven years penal servitude or two years imprisonment, on summary conviction with the consent of the D.P.P. it is a £100 fine and or twelve months imprisonment.

CONTEMPT OF COURT

Contempt of court is of two kinds; civil and criminal. Criminal contempt is a misdemeanour at common law, it is an offence against the due administration of justice.

At common law
The courts have given consideration as to what is meant by contempt, or more importantly what amounts to contempt.
Keegan V DeBurca (1973)
The defendant refused to answer a relevant question asked by a judge. The Judge thereupon sentenced her to be imprisoned "until she purge her said contempt". The Supreme Court gave consideration to what is meant by contempt of court
O'Dalaigh C.J. stated: "The distinction between civil and criminal contempt is not new in law. Criminal contempt consists in behaviour calculated to prejudice the due course of justice, such as contempt in facie curiae, words written or spoken or acts calculated to prejudice the due course of justice or disobedience to a writ of habeas corpus by the person to whom it is directed - to give but some examples of this class of

contempt. Civil contempt usually arises where there is a disobedience to an order of the court by a party to the proceedings and in which the court has generally no interest to interfere unless moved by the party for whose benefit the order was made. Criminal contempt is a common law misdemeanour and, as such, is punishable by both imprisonment and fine at discretion, that is to say without statutory limit, its object is punitive . . ." Accordingly punishment by imprisonment should be imposed by sentencing the defendant to imprisonment for a period of definite duration.

There is no one type of contempt of court and it is established that there is no limitation as to the contempts, that the courts may hold there to be.

M.M. and H.M. (1933)

This case related to criminal contempt by obstruction.

State (Quinn) V. Ryan (1965)

The carrying away of an arrested person across the border while his legal advisers backs were turned thus denying access to the Courts was a contempt of court by the police.

Re: Kevin O'Kelly

The refusal of a journalist to give evidence of an interview he had had with an accused person, on the grounds of journalistic ethics was held to be a contempt.

The State (D.P.P.) V. Walsh

A newspaper report that the Special Criminal Court was a "sentencing tribunal" was held a contempt.

Attorney- General V. O'Ryan and Boyd (1946)

The High Court has full jurisdiction under Art.34, Section 3(1) of the Constitution of Ireland to deal with contempt of court where the Circuit Court is scandalized and will, in its discretion, exercise that jurisdiction in a proper case. Such jurisdiction will be exercised in the case of an editor of a newspaper who is liable to be punished for contempt of court in respect of matter published in his newspaper.

In the matter of Kelly and Deighan (1984)

A witness stated that he had been approached by K. and D., they had attempted to suborn him and also suggested that he not attend to give evidence. It was held by the High Court that; the evidence established that a contempt in the face of the Court had been committed which, in the interests of the proper administration of justice required to be tried summarily and immediately at the instance of the trial judge without reference to the D.P.P.. It was held by the Supreme Court that having regard to the sequence of evidence in this case, the necessity for the judge to hear and determine the contempt issue did not exist.

Statutory provision

The common law on contempt has been supplemented by statute: The Offences Against the State (Amendment) Act 1972, at section 4(1) provides :

(a) Any public statement made orally, in writing or otherwise, or any meeting, procession or demonstration in public, that constitute an interference with the course of justice shall be unlawful.

(b) A statement, meeting, procession or demonstration shall be deemed to constitute an interference with the course of justice if it is intended, or is of such a character as to be likely, directly or indirectly to influence any court, person or authority concerned with the institution, conduct or defence of any civil or criminal proceedings (including a party or witness) as to whether or how the proceedings should be instituted, conducted, continued or defended, or as to what should be their outcome.

The penalty for the above on summary conviction is a £200 fine and or twelve months imprisonment: on conviction on indictment is a £1,000 fine and or five years imprisonment.

Sub-section 3 states that nothing in this section shall affect the law as to contempt of court.

The Enforcement of Court Orders Act 1926, at section 24 provides :

every person who resists, obstructs, or impedes an undersheriff, court messenger, or other person in the lawful execution of an execution order or resists, obstructs, or impedes any member of the Garda Siochana in the lawful execution of an execution order shall be guilty of a misdemeanour. The penalty on conviction on indictment is a £100 fine and or twelve months imprisonment; on summary conviction is a £50 fine and or six months imprisonment.

See also the Offences Against the State Act 1939 Section 7, chapter 27 above.

EMBRACERY

Embracery is a misdemeanour which is indictable at common law, punishable by fine and imprisonment, it consists in attempting by bribes or any corrupt means whatsoever, other than evidence and argument in open court, to influence or instruct jurors, or to incline them to favour one party to a judicial proceeding

INTERFERENCE WITH WITNESSES

At common law interference with witnesses by threats or persuasion to induce them not to give evidence, is a misdemeanour, punishable on indictment or on information.
The offence seems to be committed whether the prisoner dissuades him from giving evidence at all or dissuades him from giving certain evidence. There is no distinction between the offence of endeavouring to persuade a witness to alter evidence already given, and the offence of attempting to dissuade a witness from giving evidence of a certain character. The offence is also summarily punishable as a contempt of court To prevent a witness duly summoned from attending court is punishable as a contempt or, in the event of combination, is indictable as a conspiracy to pervert the course of justice, see conspiracy in chapter 5 above.

BARRATRY

It is an indictable misdemeanour at common law to be a common barrator, i.e., habitually to move, excite or maintain suits and quarrels either at law or otherwise: The offence is now rarely heard of.

MAINTENANCE

Maintenance is said to consist in the unlawful taking in hand or upholding of or assisting in civil suits or quarrels of others, to the disturbance of common right, and from other than charitable motives. It would seem to be immaterial whether the maintenance is of the plaintiff or of the defendant. A man may lawfully maintain a suit respecting any property in which he has an equitable interest. It is not maintenance to assist another in a criminal prosecution. Maintenance is an indictable misdemeanour at common law, and is punishable by fine and or imprisonment

CHAMPERTY

Champerty is a species of maintenance, being a bargain with a plaintiff or defendant to divide the land or other matter sued for between them if they prevail at law; whereupon the champerter is to carry on the party's suit at his own expense. Champerty is an indictable misdemeanour at common law.

BRIBERY

The receiving or offering of any undue reward by or to any person whatsoever, whose ordinary profession or business relates to the administration of public justice in order to his behaviour in office and incline him to act contrary to the known rules of honesty and integrity is a common law misdemeanour, an attempt at bribery is also a misdemeanour.

PERSONATING A JURYMAN

To personate a juryman, even though there is no intention to pervert the course of justice is a misdemeanour at common law.

PUBLIC MISCHIEF

The wasteful employment of the police has been held to be a public mischief.

D.P.P. (Vizzard) V Carew (1981)

The accused was charged as follows : " For that you ...did by means of certain false statements, to wit, report the larceny of £2,000 in cash, cause officers of an Garda Siochana, maintained at public expense for the public benefit, to devote their time and services to the investigation of false allegations, thereby temporarily depriving the public of the services of these police officers and rendering certain persons liable to suspicion, accusation and arrest, and in doing so did unlawfully effect a public mischief contrary to common law." The District Justice stated a case for the opinion of the High Court as to whether this offence is known to the common law of Ireland. It was held by the court that the offence of effecting a public mischief is known to the common law of Ireland and that the facts set out in the charge prepared against the accused, if established, would constitute the offence.

The English cases of *R V Manley (1933)* and *R V Newland (1954)* may be referred to here.

ESCAPE OF PRISONERS

At common law

It is a misdemeanour at common law for a person who is lawfully confined in connection with a criminal offence, whether before or after trial ;

(a) To break out of the prison or other building in which he is confined.

(b) To escape from confinement without any breaking.

The prisoner escaping is deemed to have regained his liberty as soon as he gets out of sight of the person from whom he escapes, and not before.

It is a distinct offence for an officer of the law or a private person to either voluntarily or negligently permit the escape of a prisoner in his custody, to do so is a misdemeanour.

A negligent escape has been defined to be when the party arrested or imprisoned escapes against the will of him in whose custody he is, and is not immediately pursued and taken again before he had been lost sight of.

Penalty

The offence, is punishable in the same degree as that of which the prisoner is guilty, and for which he is in custody, whether treason, felony, or misdemeanour.

In the case of a prisoner in custody for a felony whose escape is voluntarily permitted by the person who has him in custody such person cannot be punished for until the prisoner has been convicted of the felony. He would of course be guilty of misdemeanour.

Statutory provision
The Criminal Law Act 1976, at section 6(1)
(1) Any person who-
  (a) aids any person in escaping or attempting to escape from lawful custody or, with intent to facilitate the escape of any person from lawful custody or enable a person after escape to remain unlawfully at large, or with intent to cause injury to persons or property in a place where a person is in lawful custody, conveys any article or thing into or out of such place or to a person in such a place or places any article or thing inside or outside such a place, or
  (b) makes, or takes part in, any arrangement for the purpose of enabling a person to escape from lawful custody, facilitating such an escape, enabling a person after escape to remain unlawfully at large, or causing injury to persons or property in a place where a person is in lawful custody,
  shall be guilty of an offence, for which the penalty on indictment is ten years imprisonment.
(2) Any person who, contrary to any rules or regulations in force in relation to a prison, conveys or attempt to convey any article or thing into or out of the prison or to a person in the prison, or places any article or thing in any place inside or outside the prison with intent that it shall come into the possession of a person in the prison,
shall be guilty of an offence, for which the penalty on summary conviction shall be a £500 fine and or twelve months imprisonment, and on indictment to five years imprisonment.

Chapter 30

THE COURTS OF CRIMINAL JURISDICTION

The Constitution of Ireland in Article 34.1 provides that justice shall be administered in courts established by law by judges appointed in the manner provided, and save in such special and limited cases as may be prescribed by law, shall be administered in public.

The Courts (Establishment and Constitution) Act 1961 and the Courts (Supplemental Provisions) Act 1961 gave legislative effect to the provisions of the Constitution.

The Courts (S.P.) Act 1961 provides in section 45 (1) :

Justice may be administered otherwise than in public in the following cases :

(a) applications of an urgent nature for relief by way of habeas corpus, bail, prohibition or injunction ;

(b) matrimonial causes and matters ;

(c) lunacy and minor matters ;

(d) proceedings involving the disclosure of a secret manufacturing process

The Criminal Procedure Act 1967 provides in section 16 (2) :

Where the court is satisfied, because of the nature or circumstances of the case or otherwise in the interests of justice, that it is desirable, the court may exclude the public or any particular person or persons except bona fide representatives of the press from the court during the hearing. The reference here is to the District Court, any members of the press who may be present are not free to report the proceedings.

The Criminal Justice Act 1951 provides in section 20 (3) :

In any criminal proceedings for an offence which is, in the opinion of the court of an indecent or obscene nature, the court may, subject to a parent or other relative or friend of a young person involved in the case being present, exclude from the court during the hearing all persons except officers of the court, persons directly concerned in the proceedings, bona fide representatives of the press and such other persons as the court may, in its discretion, permit to remain.

The Courts that now stand established by law are as follows;

THE DISTRICT COURT

The District Court is a court of first instance, it is presided over by a Justice who sits without a jury. The District Court by its nature is restricted by the Constitution which provides in Article 38.2 that Minor Offences (see Chapter 2) may be tried by courts of summary jurisdiction, and by article 38.5 which provides that save in the case of the trial of certain offences no person shall be tried on any criminal charge without a jury.

The Criminal Justice Act 1951 at section 2.2 provides that; The District Court may try summarily a person charged with a scheduled offence if -

(i) the court is of opinion that the facts proved or alleged constitute a minor offence fit to be so tried, and

(ii) the accused, on being informed by the court of his right to be tried with a jury, does not object to being tried summarily.

The offences triable summarily in this way are public mischief, obstruction of the administration of justice or the enforcement of the law, or perjury, which may not be tried in this way without the consent of the Director of Public Prosecutions. The other offences which may be tried summarily in this way include; riot or unlawful assembly, assault occasioning actual bodily harm, indecent assault, offences under the Larceny Acts 1861 and 1961 involving property worth not more than £50, assault resisting arrest, concealing the birth of a child, gross indecency where the accused is over sixteen years of age and the other person involved is under sixteen years or is an idiot, an imbecile or a feeble-minded person, and attempted carnal knowledge under sections; 1(2), 2(2), or 4 of the Criminal Law Amendment Act 1935.

The Criminal Procedure Act 1967 at section 13 provides that: Where an accused pleads guilty in the District Court to an indictable offence, other than an offence under the Treason Act 1939, murder, attempt to murder, conspiracy to murder, piracy or a grave breach of the Geneva Conventions Act 1962, or an offence by an accessory before or after the fact. The District Court, if it is satisfied that the accused understands the nature of the offence and if the Director of Public Prosecutions consents may deal with the offence summarily. In this case where a District Court deals with an offence summarily, the accused is liable to a fine and or twelve months imprisonment.

CHILDRENS COURT
Where an offence has been committed by a child under the age of sixteen years, A Justice of the District Court sits as a Childrens Court and deals in such manner as shall seem just with all offences except those of a very grave nature.

The District Court in addition to its own jurisdiction as outlined above, is responsible for the conducting of the preliminary examination of indictable offences (see Chapter 31).

THE CIRCUIT CRIMINAL COURT
The Central Criminal Court i.e. the Circuit Court exercising its criminal jurisdiction is a court of first instance. It is presided over by a Judge who may sit with or without a jury. The Courts (S.P.) Act 1961 at section 25 outlines the jurisdiction of the Circuit Court in relation to indictable offence. It has subject to a number of exceptions the same jurisdictions as the Central Criminal Court (see below). This jurisdiction is exercisable by the Judge of the circuit in which the offence charged has been committed or in which the accused person has been arrested or resides.

A Judge of the Circuit Court may, on the application of the D.P.P. or of an accused, transfer a criminal trial from one part of his circuit to another part of his circuit. A Judge of the Circuit Court is obliged on the application of the D.P.P. or of an accused, to transfer a criminal trial to the Central Criminal Court.

An appeal lies from the Circuit Court from a decision of the District Court. A criminal appeal consists of a rehearing of the case and fresh evidence may be introduced. In the case of an appeal, the Circuit Court sits without a jury, it may confirm, vary or reverse the order of the District Court. On appeal the decision of the Circuit Court is final, conclusive and may not itself be appealed.

THE CENTRAL CRIMINAL COURT
The Constitution of Ireland at article 34.3.1 provides that; The courts of first instance shall include a High Court invested with

full original jurisdiction in and power to determine all matters and questions whether of law or fact, civil or criminal.

The Courts (S.P.) Act 1961 at section 11(1) provides that; the High Court when exercising its criminal jurisdiction shall be known as the Central Criminal Court. The jurisdiction of the High Court is exercisable by a Judge or Judges of the High Court nominated by the President of the High Court, the High Court may sit with or without a jury. The Central Criminal Court has exclusive jurisdiction in relation to offences under the Treason Act 1939, major offences under the Offences Against the State Act 1939, murder, attempt to murder, piracy and offences under the Genocide Act 1973.

The Courts (S.P.) Act 1961 provides :

Section 52 (1) Section 2 of the Summary Jurisdiction Act 1857 is extended to enable any party in proceedings in the District Court if dissatisfied with its determination as been erroneous on a point of law to appeal to the High Court.

Section 52 (1) A Justice of the District Court shall, if requested by any person before him, unless he considers the request frivolous, refer any question of law to the High Court for determination.

If a case is stated under section 51, appeal lies from the High Court to the Supreme Court. However if a case is stated under section 52, appeal only lies to the Supreme Court with the permission of the High Court.

In respect of inferior tribunals such as the District Court, the Circuit Court, and the Special Criminal Court, the High Court may grant a judicial review of the exercise of their functions.

THE COURT OF CRIMINAL APPEAL

The Courts (E. & C.) Act 1961 at section 3, established the Court of Criminal Appeal. It consists of not less than three Judges, one of whom shall be the Chief Justice or an ordinary Judge of the Supreme Court nominated by him, and the other two, Judges of the High Court nominated by the Chief Justice.

The Court of Criminal Appeal has jurisdiction to hear appeals from the Central Criminal Court, the Special Criminal Court and the Circuit Criminal Court. A person convicted on indictment may appeal to the Court of Criminal Appeal, but only where the trial judge gives a certificate for leave to appeal, or where the Court of Criminal Appeal itself grants leave to appeal. The Court of Criminal Appeal may affirm a conviction, reverse it in whole or in part, and reduce or increase the sentence. In exceptional circumstances fresh evidence may be introduced. The Court of Criminal Appeal may also order a new trial.

THE SUPREME COURT

The Constitution of Ireland at Article 34.4 makes provision for the Supreme Court:

1. The Court of final appeal shall be called the Supreme Court.
2. The president of the Supreme Court shall be called the Chief Justice.
3. The Supreme Court shall, with such exceptions and subject to such regulations as may be prescribed by law, have appellate jurisdiction from all decisions of the High Court, and shall also have appellate jurisdiction from such decisions of other courts as may be prescribed by law.
4. No law shall be enacted excepting from the appellate jurisdiction of the Supreme Court cases which involve questions as to the validity of any law having regard to the provisions of this Constitution.

Where an application is made for a judicial review in respect of the District Court, an appeal lies to the Supreme Court in respect of a decision of the High Court.

The Court of Justice Act 1947 at section 16 provides that; a Judge of the Circuit Court may, on the application of any party to any matter before him, refer any question of law arising in such matter to the Supreme Court by way of case stated.

An appeal lies from the grant or refusal of the High Court for an order of habeas corpus to the Supreme Court.

An appeal lies from the Central Criminal Court to the Supreme Court in respect of interlocutory orders.

The Criminal Procedure Act 1967 at section 34 (1) provides that: Where on a question of law, a verdict in favour of an accused person is found by direction of the trial judge, the D. P. P. may without prejudice to the verdict in favour of the accused, refer the question of law to the Supreme Court for determination.

The Court of Justice Act 1924 at section 29 makes provision that; an accused may appeal from a decision of the Court of Criminal Appeal to the Supreme Court, if the D.P.P. or the Court of Criminal Appeal itself certifies that the decision involves a point of law of exceptional public importance and that it is desirable in the public interest that the opinion of the Supreme Court be taken thereon.

In addition to the ordinary courts there are other courts.

THE SPECIAL CRIMINAL COURT

The Constitution of Ireland at Article 38.3 makes provision for Special Courts :

3.1 Special Courts may be established by law for the trial of offences in cases where it may be determined in accordance with such law that the ordinary courts are inadequate to secure the effective administration of justice, and the preservation of public peace and order.

3.2 The constitution, powers, jurisdiction and procedure of such special courts shall be prescribed by law.

Statutory effect to these provisions is made by Part V of the Offences Against the State Act 1939.

Section 35 of that Act provides that whenever the Government is satisfied that the ordinary courts are inadequate to secure the effective administration of justice and the preservation of public peace and order and that it is necessary that Part V of the Act should come into force, the Government may make a proclamation to that effect. Such a proclamation was made on the 26th Day of May 1972.

Section 38 of the Act establishes Special Criminal Courts, at the present time there is only one such court, which sits in Dublin.

Section 39. of the Act outlines the constitution of such courts. The court consists of an uneven number of persons not being less than three; it sits without a jury and delivers only one decision. At present the court is composed of a judge of the High Court, of the Circuit Court and a justice of the District Court.

Section 43. of the Act gives the Special Criminal Court jurisdiction to try convict, or acquit any person brought before it.

The offences declared to be scheduled offences for the purposes of Part V of the Act are offences under the following Acts :

    Malicious Damage Act 1861
    Explosive Substances Act 1883
    Firearms Acts 1925 to 1971
    Offences Against the State Act 1939
    Conspiracy and Protection of Property Act 1875 (S.7)

Section 45. of the Act provides that; Whenever it is intended to charge a person with a scheduled offence, the Director of Public Prosecution may direct that the person be brought before the Special Criminal Court instead of the District Court and such person shall be charged and eventually tried there.

Section 46. of the act provides that; Whenever it is intended to charge a person with an offence which is not a scheduled offence, if the Director of Public Prosecutions certifies that in his opinion that the ordinary courts are not adequate to secure the effective administration of justice and the preservation of public peace and order. The District Court shall transfer the person charged to the Special Criminal Court to be charged and tried.

MILITARY TRIBUNALS

The Constitution of Ireland Article 38.4.1 makes provision for Military Tribunals; Military tribunals may be established for the trial of offences against military law alleged to have been committed by persons while subject to military law, and also to deal with a state of war or armed rebellion.

By virtue of section 39(3) above, a Special Criminal Court may be composed entirely of officers of the Defence Forces not below the rank of commandant.

Court-martials

The Defence Act 1954 Part V provides for the convening of military courts called courts-martials. This part of the Act also deals with the categories of persons subject to military law and the application of military law. The membership of courts-martial is confined to officers of the Defence Forces.

Section 192(3) of the Act provides that a court-martial may not try a person for treason, murder, manslaughter, or rape unless such person is on active service.

COURTS-MARTIAL APPEAL COURT

The Courts-Martial Appeals Act 1983 at section 9 established this court, to which a person convicted by a court martial may appeal. The Court shall consist of not less than three judges, i.e. the Chief Justice and two ordinary judges of the Supreme Court nominated by him. An appeal shall not lie to the Supreme Court unless the court itself or the Attorney General certify that the decision involves a point of law of exceptional public importance and that such appeal is desirable in the public interest.

LIMITATIONS ON JURISDICTION

Limitation by Territory

The criminal jurisdiction of the courts in Ireland, extends to all offences committed within the State and within the territorial seas.

The jurisdiction extend as well to all offences committed aboard Irish ships, on the high seas and such ships within the territorial waters of other states.

The People(A. G.) V Thomas (1954)

The accused was convicted of the manslaughter of his friend. The accused and his friend were on board an Irish ship on its way from Liverpool to Dublin. They came into hand grips, as a result of which his friend was thrown into the sea. The body was never recovered. It was held by the Supreme Court, that there was ample evidence before the jury on which they might conclude that the death had been proved, so as to leave no grounds for reasonable doubt. Also, the evidence pointed only to a death by drowning on the high sea and that the act that caused the death occurred on board an Irish ship. The two elements necessary to give jurisdiction were both present and the accused was properly triable in the Central Criminal Court.

The Criminal Law (Jurisdiction) Act 1976 extends the jurisdiction of the courts to the whole island of Ireland in respect of certain specified offences, the offences specified in the schedule to the Act include all the major criminal offences.

The Aliens Act 1935, at section 4 provides that; an alien is amenable to and triable under the law of Ireland in like manner and to the like extent in all respects as a citizen of Ireland.

Exceptions to the general rule

In general offences committed by Irish citizens, or by persons who are ordinarily resident within the State outside the State are not triable within the State. However there are a number of exceptions to this, most of which have been referred to earlier, but are here summarized:

Piracy

The jurisdiction of the former Court of Admiralty to piracy jure genitum (Against the Law of Nations) committed on the high Seas by persons of any nationality or by ships of any country, would be retained by the present courts.

Murder or Manslaughter

The Offences Against the Person Act 1861, Section 9 provides that where any murder or manslaughter is committed outside the State, and whether the person killed was an Irish citizen or not, any offence committed by an Irish citizen whether murder or manslaughter, or of being accessory to murder or manslaughter, may be dealt with inquired of, tried, determined and punished in the State.

Bigamy

The Offences Against the Person Act 1861, Section 56 provides that whosoever shall marry any other person during the lifetime of a spouse in Ireland or "elsewhere" may be tried in Ireland.

Explosive Substances Act 1883

Section's 2 and 3 of this Act as amended provides "A person who in the State or (being an Irish citizen) outside the State unlawfully and maliciously.." causes an explosion or, does any act with intent to cause an explosion, or has in his possession an explosive substance is guilty of an offence.

Merchant Shipping Act 1894

Section 687 of the Act provides for the trial of offences against persons or property in any place either ashore or afloat by any master, seaman or apprentice.

Treason Act 1939

The Act at section 1(2) provides that; every person who, being an Irish citizen or ordinarily resident within the State who commits treason outside the State shall be liable to suffer death.

Maritime Jurisdiction Act 1959

This Act as amended defines the exclusive jurisdiction of the State this being, all sea areas which are twelve nautical miles from the baseline. Under the Act the Government may by order extend the fishery limits and make special provision for citizens and ships of other states.

Geneva Convention Act 1962

The Act at section 3(2) provides that; the Irish courts have jurisdiction to try any person, whatever his nationality who, whether in or outside the State, commits, or aids, abets or procures the commission of grave breaches of the Geneva conventions.

Broadcasting (Offences) Act 1968

By section 2 of the Act, it is an offence for any person to broadcast from any ship or aircraft registered in the State which is in or over waters adjacent to the State within the territorial waters of the State, or from any ship or aircraft registered in the State which is outside such waters.

Air Navigation and Transport Act 1973

The Act at section 2(1) provides that; Any act or omission which, if taking place in the State, would constitute an offence under the law of the State, shall, if it takes place on board an Irish controlled aircraft while in flight elsewhere than in or over the State, constitute that offence.

Court of Justice of the European Communities (Perjury) Act 1975

The Act at section 1 provides that; A person who before the court of Justice of the European Communities swears anything which he knows to be false or does not believe to be true shall, whatsoever his nationality, be guilty of perjury.

Misuse of Drugs Act 1977

The Act at section 20 provides that; It is an offence for any person to aid, abet, counsel or induce the commission outside the State of an offence punishable under a corresponding law.

LIMITATION BY TIME

At common law there is no time limit for the commencement of proceedings for indictable offences; nullum tempus occurrit regi, (the time does not run against the Crown). There are a number of statutory exceptions to the general rule, for example prosecution must be commenced within twelve months for offences under Sections 2 and 4 of the Criminal Law Amendment Act 1935.

In relation to summary offences, there is a six months time limit laid down in the Petty Sessions (Ireland) Act 1851 section 10(4). Some statutes contain specific provisions in relation to particular offences. This does not apply to an indictable offence which may be dealt with summarily by a District Justice as a minor offence.

Chapter 31

CRIMINAL PROCEDURE

PRELIMINARY   EXAMINATION

Where an accused person is brought before the District Court charged with an indictable offence, then unless the case is being tried summarily or the accused pleads guilty, or waives his right to a preliminary examination, the District Justice is obliged to conduct a preliminary examination of the charge. The procedure on preliminary examinations as laid down in part II of the Criminal Procedure Act 1967.

Book of evidence
Section 6 of the Act provides that certain documents shall be served on the accused by the prosecutor, before the preliminary examination.
This "Book of Evidence" contains the following;
(a) a statement of the charges,
(b) a copy of any sworn information in writing upon which the proceedings were initiated,
(c) a list of the witnesses whom it is proposed to call at the trial,
(d) a statement of the evidence that is to be given by each of them,
(e) a list of exhibits, if any, which may be inspected by the accused.
A copy of the Book of Evidence shall also be inspected by the accused.
  After the Book of Evidence has been served, further evidence may become available and the prosecutor may cause to be served on the accused and furnished to the Court a copy of such further evidence.

Examination
Section 7 of the Act deals with the preliminary examination itself.
The District Justice shall consider the documents and exhibits, any deposition or statement taken and any submission that may be made to him.
The prosecutor and the accused shall be entitled to give

evidence on sworn deposition and also to require the attendance of any person, whether included in the supplied list of witnesses or not, and to examine him by way of sworn deposition.

However by section 18 of the Criminal Law(Jurisdiction) Act 1976, there is no entitlement to require the attendance before the justice of a person or to examine him by way of sworn deposition if it appears to the justice that the person is outside the State and that it is not reasonably practicable to secure his attendance before the justice for examination.

Such a witness may be cross-examined and re-examined on his evidence. His deposition shall be taken down in writing, read over to him and signed by him and by the District Justice.

Decision

Section 8 of the Act deals with the Decision on preliminary examination.

If the District Justice is of the opinion that there is a sufficient case to put the accused on trial for the offence with which he has been charged, he shall send him forward for trial.

If the District Justice is of the opinion that there is a sufficient case to put the accused on trial for some indictable offence other than that charged, he shall cause him to be charged with that offence and unless he deals with the case himself, send him forward for trial.

If the District Justice is of the opinion that a summary offence only is disclosed, and the Director of Public Prosecutions consents, he shall cause the accused to be charged with the summary offence and deal with the case accordingly.

In any other case the District Justice shall order the accused to be discharged as to the offence under examination.

Waiver

Section 12 of the Act deals with waiver by the accused of the preliminary examination. The accused may waive the preliminary examination and elect to be sent forward for trial with a plea of not guilty, unless the prosecutor requires the attendance of a witness to give evidence on deposition. An accused under the age of seventeen years may only exercise a waiver with the consent of a parent or guardian.

THE INDICTMENT

When an accused person is sent forward to the Circuit Court or the Central Criminal Court for trial the prosecution must prepare an indictment. An indictment is a written accusation of crime made by "The People at the suit of the Director of Public Prosecutions" against one or more persons and preferred to a jury.

Form of Indictment

The Criminal Justice (Administration) Act 1924 determines the form of an indictment, the First Schedule to that Act contains the Indictment Rules and the Appendix to such schedule, contains forms of indictment covering many of the more serious or more common crimes.

Every indictment shall contain, a statement of the specific offence or offences with which the accused person is charged, together with particulars giving reasonable information as to such charge. At any time before or during a trial a Court may amend an indictment, order a separate trial for one or more offences, or it may order the postponement of a trial. Where two or more persons are charged with the same offence, they may be tried together, however if an accused would be prejudiced, separate trials may be ordered.

Count

Where more than one offence is charged in an indictment then a description of each offence charged, shall be set out in a separate paragraph called a count, each count shall be numbered consecutively.

Each count shall commence with a statement of the offence charged, called the Statement of Offence, it shall describe the offence shortly in ordinary language, and if the offence is one created by statute, shall contain a reference to the relevant section of such statute.

Particulars of the offence

After the statement of the offence, particulars of the offence shall be set out in ordinary language, in which the use of technical terms shall not be necessary.

Description of property shall be in ordinary language and such as to indicate with reasonable clearness the property referred to.

It shall be sufficient to describe any document by any name or designation by which it is usually known. The description of any accused or any person in an indictment, shall be such as is reasonably sufficient to identify him without necessarily being correct and "a person unknown" is sufficient.

Example of Indictment
The forms set out in the Appendix to the rules shall be used in cases to which they are applicable, and in other cases forms to the like effect shall be used.
The commencement of the indictment is normally as follows:

The People of Ireland at the suit of the Director of Public Prosecutions
V.
A. B.
The Central Criminal Court.
Charge preferred to the Jury.
Statement of offence
Arson,
contrary to section 2 of the Malicious Damage Act, 1861.
Particulars of offence.
A. B., on the first day of October 1988, at Letterkenny in the County of Donegal, maliciously set fire to a dwelling-house, C.D., being therein.
Charges for any offences, whether felonies or misdemeanours, may be joined in the same indictment.

ARRAIGNMENT

After an accused person has been sent forward for trial the next step will normally be the arraignment, this consists of calling the prisoner to the bar by naming him, reading the indictment to him and asking him whether he pleads guilty or not guilty. A prisoner who has signed a plea of guilty in the District Court may, when arraigned plead not guilty.

Where a question arises as to the competence of an accused person to plead, the issue must be determined by a jury empanelled for the purpose. The onus of proving insanity is on the accused person and the standard of proof required is on the balance of probabilities. The test is whether the accused is of sufficient intellect to comprehend the course of the proceedings, so as to make a proper defence.

If the accused person does not plead guilty or not guilty, he may:

<u>Stand Mute</u>; If he is found to be "mute of malice", a plea of not guilty will be entered on his behalf. If he is found to be "mute by visitation of God" i.e. deaf and dumb an attempt will be made to make him understand by some means. Otherwise the question must be considered whether the accused is unfit to plead.

<u>Plea Autrefois Acquit or Autrefois Convict</u>; These pleas are based on the principle that a person cannot be tried for a crime that he has previously been convicted or acquitted. To succeed in either of these pleas the accused must show that the previous acquittal or conviction was for the offence charged in the present indictment and that it was for the offence of which he could have been convicted on the previous indictment and that in the case of an acquittal it was a valid one after a trial on its merits.

Minister for Supplies V Connor (1945)

It was held by the High Court, that an order made by the District Court to "strike out" a summons constitutes a dismissal of the summons and may not be raised on a plea of *autrefois acquit.*

The State (A. G.) V Deale (1973)

It was held by the High Court, that the plea of *autrefois convict* is a matter to be tried by a jury.

Where the accused person pleads guilty, the judge will hear the facts of the case from the prosecution, hear evidence of character and any plea in mitigation, before he passes sentence. The Criminal Justice (Administration) Act 1924 Section 12 provides that at the trial of a prisoner on indictment, a nolle prosequi ("unwilling to prosecute") may be entered after the indictment is preferred to a jury and before a verdict is found.

THE TRIAL

The Criminal Justice Act 1984

This Act introduced a number of changes with regard to trial on indictment :

<u>Notice of alibi</u> S. 20

An accused shall not without leave of the court adduce evidence in support of an alibi unless, he gives notice of particulars of the alibi.

<u>Proof by written statement</u> S. 21

Where a witness does not appear in court, a written statement shall be admissible as evidence to the like extent as oral evidence by such witness.

Proof by formal admission S.22

Any fact of which oral evidence may be given may be admitted and such a formal admission shall be conclusive evidence

Additional changes are referred to below.

Prosecution case

Counsel for the prosecution normally opens the case, he will outline the matters he intends to prove, will state the facts on which he intends to rely, and the evidence it is proposed to call.

Having opened the case, counsel for the prosecution calls the witness for the prosecution, they are subject to examination-in-chief by him, followed by cross-examination by the defence and re-examination by him. The defence is entitled to know the case to be answered and matter should not be introduced unless it is contained in the book of evidence.

No case to answer

When council for the prosecution has concluded his case, the defence may ask the judge, or the judge may determine his own imitative, to direct the jury as a matter of law to find the accused not guilty on the ground that on the evidence the accused has no case to answer. The judge may accept the submission and direct the jury to return a verdict of not guilty.

The judge may on his own initiative, and at any time during the course of the trial, before the summing up, exercise his power to withdraw a case from the jury.

Defence case

Where the judge has not withdrawn the case from the jury, the next stage is the case for the defence. The defence may decide to call no evidence or may only call witnesses as to the good character of the accused.

The procedure will depend on whether or not the accused person is represented by counsel and on whether evidence other than that of the accused himself and witnesses as to character is adduced.

(a) Where evidence is to be adduced other than that of the defendant himself and witnesses only as to character:

   (i) The defendant, or his counsel, may if he so wishes, open his defence.

   (ii) The defence witnesses (including the defendant, if he wishes to give evidence) will then be examined.

(iii) The prosecuting counsel will sum up the evidence on behalf of the prosecution.

(iv) The defendant, or, where he is represented, counsel, will sum up the evidence for the defence.

(b) Where no evidence is adduced except that of the defendant himself and witnesses as to character, and defendant is not represented by counsel:

    (i) The defendant, if he wishes, will give his evidence and witnesses as to character will give their evidence.

    (ii) The defendant will address the jury.

(c) Where no evidence is adduced save that of the defendant himself and witnesses as to character, and defendant is represented by counsel:

    (i) The defendant gives his evidence, and witnesses as to character will give their evidence.

    (ii) Counsel for the prosecution may sum up his case.

    (iii) Counsel for the defence will sum up his case.

Closing speeches

The Criminal Justice Act 1984, at section 24 provides as follows :

(a) the prosecution shall have the right to a closing speech in all cases except where the accused is not represented and does not call any witness(other than a witness to character only), and the defence shall have the right to a closing speech in all cases, and

(b) the closing speech for the defence shall be made after that for the prosecution.

Summing up

Following the closing speeches, the judge must sum up the case to the jury. His summing up should include: direction on points of law, a review of the evidence, and direction as to burden and standard of proof, see consideration of proof in chapter 1.

Verdict

After the summing up by the judge, the jury retire and consider their verdict. After retirement the verdict of the jury is announced by their foreman in open court.

The Criminal Justice Act 1984, at section 25(1) declares :

The verdict of a jury in a criminal proceeding need not be unanimous in a case where there are not fewer that eleven jurors if ten of them agree on the verdict. However such majority verdicts is not accepted unless it appears to the court that the jury have not less than two hours for deliberation.

Sentence
The imposition of a sentence is a matter for the judge and not for the jury. The accused may be asked by the judge if he wishes to say anything before he is sentenced. Pleas in mitigation of sentence will then be heard. The "antecedents" of the accused, that is any previous convictions and his character, will be given.

The State(O) V O'Brien (1973)
It was held by the Supreme Court that, the selection of punishment and the determination of the length of a sentence are integral parts of the administration of justice in criminal trials, which are exercisable by the courts in accordance with the provisions of the Constitution.

Absence of jury
All evidence is to be given in the presence of a jury, however they are not concerned with purely legal argument, and are asked by the judge to retire during the course of such an argument.

THE JURY

The law with regard to juries is laid down in the Juries Act 1976. Every citizen aged 18 years and upwards and under the age of 70 years, who is entered in a register of Dail Eireann electors in a particular jury district is qualified and liable to serve as a juror for the trial of all issues are for the time being triable with a jury drawn from that district unless for the time being ineligible or disqualified.

Ineligible
Those declared to be ineligible include the President of Ireland, persons concerned with the administration of justice, members of the Defence Forces, deaf or illiterate persons and mental patients.

Disqualified
A person is qualified for jury service and may likewise not serve if he wishes, if he has been convicted of an offence in any part of Ireland and has at any time been sentenced to imprisonment.

Excusable

Certain persons, who are entitled to serve on a jury if they wish, may be excused. Those excusable as of a right include persons who have recently served as jurors, members of the Oireachtas, members of the religious, registered medical practitioners, nurse, chemists, students, and those aged from 65 to 70 years. Such persons may inform the County Registrar that they wish to be excused. Others in the public service on production of a certificate from their head of department. Others may be excused at the discretion of the County Registrar or the Court.

Offences

Failing to attend for jury service is an offence for which the penalty on summary conviction is a £50 fine, the Act also creates a number of other offences.

Challenges

The Act provides that the prosecution and each accused person may, challenge seven jurors without showing cause and any person challenged will not be include in the jury. The Act further provides that the prosecution and each accused may challenge any number of jurors for cause shown. The cause of the challenge must be shown immediately upon it being made and it is then a matter for the judge to allow or disallow it as he thinks proper.

BAIL

Bail is a recognizance or bond entered into by an authorized person, who undertakes to ensure that an accused person will appear for trial.

The law is contained in the Criminal Procedure Act 1967 Part III, which has been supplemented by the Criminal Justice Act 1984.

Admission to bail

A District Justice or a peace commissioner shall admit to bail a person charged before him with an offence, if it appears to him to be a case in which bail ought to be allowed and he is satisfied as to the sufficiency of the persons proposed to be accepted to bailsmen.

In the case of treason, murder and certain other offences, a person shall not be admitted to bail except by order of the High Court.

A District Justice or a peace commissioner on issuing a warrant for the arrest of any person may, by endorsement on the warrant, direct that the person named be on arrest released on his entering into such a recognizance, with or without sureties as may be specified.

An accused person may be released on his own personal bail, but in serious cases independent bailsmen may be required. A court cannot reject persons as sureties on account of their moral character or political opinion, the chief consideration is that he will have sufficient property in the event of the estreatment of his recognizance.

Criteria
The People (A.G)   v.   O'Callaghan (1966)
The Supreme Court reviewed the law as to the granting of bail.   The test in deciding whether to allow bail is the probability of the accused evading justice. The Supreme Court approved the following which may be taken into consideration with regard to such a probability:
1.   The seriousness of the offence charged,
2.   The strength of the evidence,
3.   The likely sentence to be imposed on conviction,
4.   The fact that the accused was caught in the Act,
5.   The accused's failure to answer bail on a previous occasion,
6.   The possibility of the disposal of illegally obtained property,
7.   The possibility of interference with witnesses or jurors.

Where a person charged with an offence has been admitted to bail, a District Justice or a peace commissioner may, on the application of the surety or a member of the Garda Siochana and upon information being made in writing and on oath that the accused is about to abscond for the purpose of evading justice, issue a warrant for the arrest of the accused.

The Court of Criminal Appeal may admit a convicted person to bail pending the determination of his appeal, if it thinks fit.

Consecutive sentences
The Criminal Justice Act 1984 at section 11 provides that ;
Any sentence of imprisonment passed on a person for an offence committed, while he was on bail shall be consecutive on

any sentence passed on him for a previous offence.

Failure to surrender to bail

The Criminal Justice Act 1984 at section 13 provides that : If a person has been released on bail and fails to appear before a court in accordance with his recognizance, he shall be guilty of a an offence and shall be liable on summary conviction to a £1,000 fine and or twelve months imprisonment. The offence shall be treated as an offence committed while on bail.

Bail a right

As an accused person is presumed innocent, the granting of bail is a right to which he is entitled. The wrongful refusal or a delay in admitting a person to bail is itself a common law offence.

LEGAL AID IN CRIMINAL CASES

The Criminal Justice (Legal Aid) Act 1962 makes provision for the grant by the state of free legal aid to poor persons in certain criminal cases. The act has been supplemented by the Criminal Procedure (Amendment) Act 1973 and the Criminal Justice (Legal Aid) regulations 1965.

Five different kinds of legal aid certificates are contemplated by the act.

Legal Aid (District Court) Certificates
Legal Aid (Trial on Indictment) Certificate
Legal Aid (Appeal) Certificate
Legal Aid (Case Stated) Certificate
Legal Aid (Supreme Court) Certificate

If it appears to the Court, that the means of a person charged before it with an offence are insufficient to enable him to obtain legal aid, and by reason of the gravity of the change or of exceptional circumstances it is essential in the interests of justice that he should have legal aid in the preparation and conduct of his defence. The court shall on application being made to it, grant the appropriate legal aid certificate.

Where a person has been granted a certificate for free legal aid, he shall be entitled to free legal aid in the preparation and conduct of his case and to have solicitor and counsel(where appropriate) assigned to him.

INDEX

225

Supplement 1991

Criminal Law

in

Ireland

Sean E. Quinn
Barrister-at-Law

Magh Itha Teoranta
1991

Published in 1991 by
Magh Itha Teoranta
15 Rathclaren, Bray, Co. Wicklow, Ireland

Printed in Ireland
by
The Leinster Leader Limited, Naas, Co. Kildare.

Contents

Prohibition of Incitement to Hatred Act, 1989

The Prohibition of Incitement to Hatred Act, 1989 was passed to prohibit incitement to hatred on account of race, religion, nationality or sexual orientation. It enables Ireland to ratify the United Nations Covenant on Civil and Political Rights, which was adopted on 16th December 1966.

The Bill as initiated was amended to include hatred against a group of persons on account of their membership of the travelling community or sexual orientation.

Actions likely to stir up hatred

By section 2 of the Act, it shall be an offence for a person -
(a) to publish or distribute written material,
(b) to use words, behave or display written material -
    (i) in any place other than inside a private residence, or
    (ii) inside a private residence so that the words, behaviour or
        material are heard or seen by persons outside the residence, or
(c) to distribute, show or play a recording of visual images or sounds,
if the written material, words, behaviour, visual images or sounds, as the case may be, are threatening, abusive or insulting and are intended or, having regard to all the circumstances, are likely to stir up hatred.

Hatred

Hatred means hatred against a group of persons in the State or elsewhere on account of their race, colour, nationality, religion, ethnic or national origins, membership of the travelling community or sexual orientation.

Group of persons

It should be noted that hatred must be directed against a "group" of persons, rather than individual persons.

Private residence

By section 2(3), private residence does not include any part not used as a dwelling, or any part in which a public meeting is being held; "public meeting" means a meeting at which the public are entitled to be present, on payment or otherwise and as a right or by virtue of an express or implied permission.

State or elsewhere

In relation to this offence and an offence under section 4 below and given the definition of hatred, all offence created by the Act are of an extra jurisdictional effect.

Defence

By sub-section 2, if the accused person is not shown to have intended to stir up hatred, it shall be a defence for him to prove that he was not aware of the content of the material or recording concerned and did not suspect, and had no reason to suspect, that the material or recording was threatening, abusive or insulting.

In relation to b(i), it shall be a defence for the accused person -

(i) to prove that he was inside a private residence at the relevant time and had no reason to believe that the words, behaviour or material concerned would be heard or seen by a person outside the residence, or

(ii) if he is not shown to have intended to stir up hatred, to prove that he did not intend the words, behaviour or material concerned to be, and was not aware that they might be, threatening, abusive or insulting.

Broadcasts likely to stir up hatred

By section 3 of the Act, If an item involving threatening, abusive or insulting visual images or sounds is broadcast, each of the persons mentioned below is guilty of an offence if he intends thereby to stir up hatred or, having regard to all the circumstances, hatred is likely to be stirred up thereby.

The persons referred to are:

(a) the person providing the broadcasting service concerned,

(b) any person by whom the item concerned is produced or directed,

(c) any person whose words or behaviour in the item concerned are threatening, abusive or insulting.

Defence

In proceedings against a person referred to in paragraph (a) or (b) for an offence, if the person is not shown to have intended to stir up hatred, it is a defence for him to prove-

(a) that he did not know and had no reason to suspect that the item concerned would involve the material to which the offence relates, or

(b) in a case other than (a) relates, that, having regard to the circumstances in which the item was broadcast, it was not reasonably practicable for him to secure the removal of the material aforesaid.

In proceedings against a person referred to in (b), it is a defence for the person to prove that he did not know and had no reason to suspect -

(a) that the item would be broadcast, or

(b) that the circumstances in which the item would be broadcast would be such that hatred would be likely to stirred up.

In proceedings against a person referred to in (c), it is a defence for the person to prove that he did not know and had no reason to suspect -

(a) that an item involving the use of the material to which the offence relates would be broadcast, or

(b) that the circumstances in which such an item would be broadcast would be such that hatred would be likely to be stirred up.

It shall be a defence for him to prove that he did not know, and had no reason to suspect, that the material to which the offence relates was threatening, abusive or insulting.

Powers of Garda Síochána

If a member of the Garda Síochána not below the rank of superintendent has reasonable grounds for suspecting -
(i) that an offence under section 3 has been committed by a person in respect of an item included in a broadcast, or
(ii) that an item is to be so included and that an offence under the section is likely to be committed by a person in respect of the item, he may make an order in writing authorising any member of the Garda Síochána, to require any person named in the order to produce, if such thing exists-
(A) a script, or (B) a recording, and if produced, to require the person to afford him an opportunity of causing a copy thereof to be made.

Any person who without reasonable excuse fails or refuses to comply with a requirement made shall be guilty of an offence.

Preparation and possession of material

By section 4 of the Act, it shall be an offence for a person-
(a) to prepare or be in possession of any written material with a view to it being distributed, displayed, broadcast or otherwise published, in the State or elsewhere, whether by himself or another, or
(b) to make or be in possession of a recording of sounds or visual images with a view to its being distributed, shown, played, broadcast or otherwise published, in the State or elsewhere, whether by himself or another,
if the material or recording is threatening, abusive or insulting and is intended or, having regard to all the circumstances, including such distribution, display, broadcasting, showing, playing or other publication thereof as the person has, or it may reasonably be inferred that he has, in view, is likely to stir up hatred.

This section of the Act was included to deal with the situation where racist material was being prepared in the State for distribution outside the State.

Defence

If the accused is not shown to have intended to stir up hatred, it shall be a defence for him to prove that he was not aware of the content of the material or recording concerned and did not suspect, and had no reason to suspect, that the material or recording was threatening,

230

abusive or insulting. Where it is proved that the accused person was in possession of material or a recording such as is referred to above and it is reasonable to assume that the material or recording was not intended for the personal use of the person, he shall be presumed, until the contrary is proved, to have been in possession of the material or recording in contravention of the above offence.

Penalties
By section 6 of the Act, a person guilty of an offence under section 2, 3 or 4 shall be liable -

(a) on summary conviction, to a fine not exceeding £1,000 or to imprisonment for a term not exceeding 6 months or to both, or

(b) on conviction on indictment, to a fine not exceeding £10,000 or to imprisonment for a term not exceeding two years or to both.

Consent of Director of Public Prosecutions
By section 8 of the Act, where a person is charged with an offence under section 2, 3, or 4 no further proceedings in the matter (other than any remand in custody or on bail) shall be taken except by or with the consent of the Director of Public Prosecutions.

Search and seizure
By section 9 of the Act: If a justice of the District Court or a Peace Commissioner is satisfied on the sworn information of a member of the Garda Síochána not below the rank of sergeant that there are reasonable grounds for suspecting that an offence under sections 3 or 4 has been or is being committed on any premises, he may issue a warrant.

Powers of arrest
By section 10 of the Act, if a member of the Garda Síochána reasonably suspects that a person has committed an offence :

(i) under section 2(1)(b), he may arrest him without warrant.

(ii) referred to above, he may require him to give him his name and address and, if the person fails or refuses to do so or gives a name or address that the member reasonably suspects to be false or misleading, the member may arrest him without warrant.

Forfeiture
By section 11 of the Act, the court by or before which a person is convicted of an offence under section 2, 3 or 4 may order any written material or recording shown to the satisfaction of the court to relate to the offence to be forfeited and either destroyed or otherwise disposed of in such manner as the court may determine.

The Larceny Act, 1990 (No. 9)

Possession of articles

The Larceny Act, 1990 amended the Larceny Act 1916. The principal act at section 28 dealt with possession of housebreaking implements, a new section 28 deals with possession of articles. The section as it now stands creates two offences. Unlike the older offence the new offences are not confined to "night", in addition they are both felonies whereas the older offence was a misdemeanour.

Possession of articles with intent

(1) A person who is, when not at his place of abode, in possession of any article with the intention that it be used in the course of or in connection with-

(a) larceny or burglary, or

(b) an offence under section 29, 30, 31 or 32 of this Act, or

(c) an offence under section 112 (which deals with taking a vehicle without lawful authority) of the Road Traffic Act, 1961,

shall be guilty of felony and be liable on conviction on indictment to imprisonment for a term not exceeding 5 years or to a fine or to both.

For this offence a person must not be at his place of abode, and must have an intention to use any article that he is in possession of, in the commission of any of the seven specified offences.

Place of abode

R v Bundy (1972)

It was held that "place of abode" means a fixed place, so that a car out on the road is not a place of abode.

Any article

This is very broad especially when compared with the older offence, which was confined to implements of housebreaking. Amongst the items covered could be bankcards, coathangers, keys and screwdrivers. It would be for the jury to decide whether the article could be used in the commission of the specified offences.

Intention

It must be shown that there was an intention on the part of the accused, to use the article in the commission of one of the specified offence. The offence under section 1(b) above, in addition to larceny, burglary and taking a vehicle without lawful authority are the blackmail offences of :

Section 29, demanding with menaces,

Section 30, demanding with menaces with intent to steal,
Section 31, threatening to publish with intent to exhort, and
Section 32, obtaining by false pretence in the Larceny Act 1916.

Section 9 of the Larceny Act 1990 provides that the penalty for these offences shall be a term of imprisonment not exceeding ten years or a fine or both.

Possession of articles made or adopted for use

(2) A person who is, without lawful authority or reasonable excuse, in possession of any article made or adapted for use in the course of or in connection with-

(a) larceny or burglary, or

(b) an offence under section 29, 30, 31 or 32 of this Act, or

(c) an offence under section 112 (which deals with taking a vehicle without lawful authority) of the Road Traffic Act, 1961,

shall be guilty of felony and be liable on conviction on indictment to imprisonment for a term not exceeding 5 years or to a fine or to both.

Any article made or adapted for use

The reference in subsection (1) to "any article" is added to in subsection (2) by the addition of "made or adapted for use" . A made article is produced for some or a variety of purposes, an adapted article is an article which has undergone some alteration.

R v Simpson (1983) 1 WLR 1494

A court is entitled to take judicial notice of the fact that something is made for a particular use and the fact that it can be used for a particular purpose does not take it out of that category.

The Firearms and Offensive Weapons Act, 1990 at section 10 provides that a "weapon of offence" means any article made or adopted for use for causing injury to or incapacitating a person, or intended by the person having it with him for such use. This is similar to section 23B(1)(b) of the Larceny Act 1916 in relation to aggravated burglary.

Lawful authority or reasonable excuse

For this offence there is no requirement as to intention as above, and a person may be at his place of abode. It would be open to a person to show that he was in possession of the articles with lawful authority or reasonable excuse. Many a person particularly tradesmen would have in their possession articles that could be used in the commission of the specified offences

Forfeiture

(3) Where a person is convicted of an offence under this section, the court may order that any article for the possession of which he was so

convicted shall be forfeited and either destroyed or disposed of in such manner as the court may determine.

(4) An order under subsection (3) of this section shall not take effect until the ordinary time for instituting an appeal against the conviction or order concerned has expired or, where such an appeal is instituted, until it or any further appeal is finally decided or abandoned or the ordinary time for instituting any further appeal has expired.".

The use of "may" is an indication that a court may use its discretion when it comes to forfeiture.

The Larceny Act, 1990 - Handling stolen property

Section 33 of the Larceny Act 1916 as amended by the Larceny Act 1990, at sub-section (1) provides that : A person who handles stolen property knowing or believing it to be stolen property shall be guilty of felony and shall be liable on conviction on indictment to imprisonment for a term not exceeding 14 years or to a fine or both.

Griffiths v Freeman (1970) 1 AER 1117
Nicklin (1977) 2 AER 444

It has been decided by the English courts in relation to section 22 of the Theft Act, 1968 which is similar to this section that only one offence was created. Since the offence may be committed in many different ways, a contrary decision would have had a complicating effect, giving wide scope to possible objections on the grounds of duplicity.

The ingredients of this offence are :
1. The property must be "handled".
2. The property must be stolen.
3. A person must have known or believed it to have been stolen.

Handling
Handling may arise in many different ways. Section 33(2)(a) clarifies what is meant by "handling". It provides that : For the purposes of this Act-

(a) a person handles stolen property if (otherwise than in the course of the stealing), knowing or believing it to be stolen property, he dishonestly-

(i)   receives the property, or
(ii)   undertakes or
                assists
                      in its
                            retention,
                            removal
                            disposal or

234

                        realisation
        by or
        for the benefit of
                another person, or
(iii)   arranges to do any of the things specified in
                sub-paragraph (i) or (ii) of this paragraph;
    The terms used in the sub-section require some explanation.
retention : to keep possession of.
removal : to move from one place to another.
disposal : to get rid of (could include destruction).
realisation : to turn into money or some other property.
    It seems clear that an accused can be convicted of the offence of
handling, without having had physical contact with the stolen property.
All forms of handling other than receiving or arranging to receive are
subject to the qualification that an accused was acting "by or for the
benefit of another person". If this were not the case almost all thieves
would be handlers as well. However the thief may be guilty of handling
if he himself retains etc. for the benefit of another person. This other
person would normally be the thief.
R v Bloxham (1982) 1 AER 582, (1983) 1 AC 109

Receiving

    In order to establish receiving, it must be proved, that an accused
took possession of the stolen property or joined with others to share
possession or control of it. If the "thief" (person other than the
receiver) retains exclusive control there is no receiving. It is not
necessary that the receiver should receive any advantage, or profit in
any way from the possession of the goods.

Undertakes

a person handles stolen property if, he dishonestly :
undertakes in its retention by another person, or
undertakes in its retention for the benefit of another person, or
undertakes in its removal by another person, or
undertakes in its removal for the benefit of another person, or
undertakes in its disposal by another person, or
undertakes in its disposal for the benefit of another person, or
undertakes in its realisation by another person, or
undertakes in its realisation for the benefit of another person,

Assists

a person handles stolen property if, he dishonestly :
assists in its retention by another person, or
assists in its retention for the benefit of another person, or

assists in its removal by another person, or
assists in its removal for the benefit of another person, or
assists in its disposal by another person, or
assists in its disposal for the benefit of another person, or
assists in its realisation by another person, or
assists in its realisation for the benefit of another person,

Arranges
a person handles stolen property if, he dishonestly :
arranges to receive the property, or
arranges to undertake or assist its retention, removal disposal or realisation by or for the benefit of another person.
Where an accused had made preparations to receive and has not yet reached the stage of an attempt to do so, any preparation may constitute a sufficient arrangement.

The property must be stolen
The handling required for the offence must be "otherwise than in the course of the stealing" If an accused received the property in the course of stealing, it followed that he was a principal in the larceny and this necessarily meant that he could not be convicted of receiving.
It is not necessary, to prove from whom or by whom the goods were stolen. The circumstances in which the accused received the goods may of themselves prove that they were stolen.
The People (A.G.) V Mulcahy and Carney
It was held by the Court of Criminal Appeal, that it is a necessary ingredient of the crime of receiving stolen goods that some person other than the receiver should be shown to have stolen them.
A person cannot be guilty of receiving, if he has stolen the goods himself;
O'Leary V Cunningham (1980)
It was held by the Supreme Court that, as the evidence established that the accused was guilty of robbery of money on the occasion mentioned in the charges, the accused could not be convicted of having received that money on the same occasion, knowing it to have been stolen.
See also *Walters v Lunt (1951) 2 AER 645* page 18

Stolen property
Section 7 of the Larceny Act 1990, provides at sub-section 2 ....
references to stolen property shall include, in addition to the property originally stolen and parts of it (whether in its original state or not)-
(a) any property which directly or indirectly represents, or has at any time represented, the stolen property in the hands of the thief as

being the proceeds of any disposal or realisation of the whole or part of the stolen property or of property so representing the stolen property; and

(b) any other property which directly or indirectly represents, or has at any time represented, the stolen property in the hands of a handler of the stolen property or any part of it as being the proceeds of any disposal or realisation of the whole or part of the stolen property handled by him or of property so representing it.

(4) For the purposes specified in subsection (1) of this section, property shall be regarded as stolen property whether it has been stolen, embezzled, fraudulently converted or obtained by false pretences or by the commission of any offence under section 29, (demanding with menaces), 30, (demanding with menaces with intent to steal), or 31, (threatening to publish with intent to exhort), of the Principal Act (Larceny Act 1916); and "steal," "theft" and "thief" shall be construed accordingly.

(5) In section 46(1) of the Principal Act, the definition of property" is hereby amended by the insertion, after "The expression 'property'", of "subject to section 7 of the Larceny Act, 1990,".

Section 46(1) of the Principal Act provides : The expression 'property' includes any description of real and personal property, money, debts, and legacies, and all deeds and instruments relating to evidencing the title or right to any property, or giving a right to recover or receive any money or goods, and also includes not only such property as has been originally in the possession or under the control of any person, but also any property into or for which the same has been converted or exchanged, and anything acquired by such conversion or exchange, whether immediately or otherwise.

Ceasing to be stolen

(3) For the purposes specified in subsection (1) of this section, no property shall be regarded as having continued to be stolen property after it has been restored to the person from whom it was stolen or to other lawful possession or custody, or after that person and any other person claiming through him to have otherwise ceased, as regards that property, to have any right to restitution in respect of the theft.

Known or believed to have been stolen

The Act provides that a person handles stolen property if, knowing or believing it to be stolen property, he dishonestly does any of the things specified in section 33(2)(a) above. This is the *mens rea* of the offence. Section 33(2), (b) and (c) clarifies in some detail what is meant by "knowing or believing the property to be stolen" . They provide that :

(a) where a person-

(i)   receives stolen property, or

(ii)   undertakes or assists in its

retention,

removal,

disposal or

realisation

by or for the benefit of another person, or

(iii)   arranges to do any of the things specified in

sub-paragraph (i) or (ii) of this paragraph,

in such circumstances that it is reasonable to conclude that he knew or believed the property to be stolen property, he shall be taken to have so known or believed unless the court or the jury, as the case may be, is satisfied having regard to all the evidence and that there is a reasonable doubt as to whether he so knew or believed; and

(c) believing property to be stolen property includes thinking that such property was probably stolen property.

Dishonestly

Dishonestly is not defined in the Act. However "Dishonesty" has been considered in English cases.

Feely (1973) 1 AER 341,(1973) 2 WLR 201.

It was held by the Court of Appeal that dishonesty was a question of fact for the jury to decide on the standards of the ordinary decent person.

Ghosh (1982) 2 AER 689, (1982) 3 WLR 110

A two stage test was set for dishonesty :

1. The jury must decide if the behaviour was dishonest by the standards of the ordinary decent person. If he was not, he is not guilty.

2. If the defendant was dishonest by those ordinary decent standards he is only guilty if he realised that people would so regard his behaviour.

The test is subjective but does not allow the defendant to claim he is honest when he knows that by the ordinary standards of society people would regard him as dishonest.

Conviction of principal offender

Section 33(3) provides that: A person to whom this section applies may be indicted and convicted whether the principal offender has or has not been previously convicted or is or is not amendable to justice.

Joint Indictment

Section 44(5) of the Act as now amended provides that : On the trial of two or more persons indicted for jointly handling any stolen property, the court or jury,as the case may be, may find any of the accused guilty if satisfied that he handled all or any part of such property whether he did so jointly with the other accused or with any of them.

Jurisdiction

Section 7(1) of the Larceny Act 1990 provides that : The provisions of the Principal Act and of this Act relating to handling property which has been stolen shall apply whether the property was stolen in the State or elsewhere, and whether the stealing occurred before or after the commencement of this Act, provided that the stealing amounted to an offence where and at the time when the property was stolen; and references to stolen property shall for the purposes of those provisions be construed accordingly.

Alternative verdicts

Section 8(1) of the Larceny Act 1990 provides that : If, on the trial of a person for an offence, consisting of or including the stealing, embezzlement or fraudulent conversion of any property, or the obtaining of any property by false pretences, or for an offence under section 29, (demanding with menaces), 30, (demanding with menaces with intent to steal), or 31, (threatening to publish with intent to exhort), of the Principal Act (Larceny Act 1916), it is proved that the person handled the property the subject of the charge in such circumstances as to constitute an offence under section 33, he may be convicted of that offence, but shall not be sentenced to a term of imprisonment exceeding 10 years.

Section 8(2) of the Act provides that : If, on the trial of a person for an offence, under section 33 ..., of handling property alleged to have been stolen or alleged to have been embezzled, fraudulently converted or obtained by false pretences or by the commission of an offence under section 29, (demanding with menaces), 30, (demanding with menaces with intent to steal), or 31, (threatening to publish with intent to exhort), of the Principal Act (Larceny Act 1916), it is proved that the person stole, embezzled or fraudulently converted the property or obtained it by false pretences or by the commission of an offence under section 29, (demanding with menaces), 30, (demanding with menaces with intent to steal), or 31, (threatening to publish with intent to exhort), of the Principal Act (Larceny Act 1916), as the case may be, he may be convicted of the offence which he is proved to have committed as aforesaid.

Firearms

Part II of the Firearms and Offensive Weapons Act, 1990 amends and extends the Firearms Acts.

Construction

The Firearms Acts, 1925 to 1971, and Part II may be cited together as the Firearms Acts, 1925 to 1990.

Firearms

By section 4 of the Act : In the Firearms Acts, 1925 to 1990 "firearm" means -

(a) a lethal firearm or other lethal weapon of any description from which any shot, bullet or other missile can be discharged;

(b) an air gun (which expression includes an air rifle and an air pistol) or any other weapon incorporating a barrel from which metal or other slugs can be discharged;

(c) a crossbow;

(d) any type of stun gun or other weapon for causing any shock or other disablement to a person by means of electricity or any other kind of energy emission;

(e) a prohibited weapon as defined in section 1(1) of the Firearms Act, 1925; ·

(f) any article which would be a firearm under any of the foregoing paragraphs but for the fact that, owing to the lack of a necessary component part or parts, or to any other defect or condition, it is incapable of discharging a shot, bullet or other missile or of causing a shock or other disablement (as they case may be);

By section 6 of the Act, A superintendent of the Garda Síochána may grant an authorisation to hold a defective firearm without a firearm certificate.

(g) save where the context otherwise requires, any component part of any article referred to in any of the foregoing paragraphs and, for the purposes of this definition, the following articles shall be deemed to be such component parts as aforesaid :

(i) telescope sights with a light beam, or telescope sights with an electronic light amplification device or an infra-red device, designed to be fitted to a firearm specified in paragraph (a), (b), (c), (d), or (e), and

(ii) a silencer designed to be fitted to a firearm specified in paragraph

240

(a), (b) or (e).

The definition of "firearm" in section 1(1) of the Firearms Act,1925, and in section 1 of the Firearms (Proofing) Act, 1968 and section 2 of the Firearms Act, 1964, and section 2 of the Firearms Act, 1971 are repealed.

This new definition of "firearms" includes crossbows and stun guns.

Sell, etc. to a prescribed country

By section 5 of the Act, the Firearms Act, 1925 is amended by the addition of section 10(3A) : A person shall not sell, transfer or otherwise dispose of a firearm or ammunition for a firearm to a person, or to a body, in a country that stands prescribed for the time being for the purposes of this section unless the superintendent of the Garda Síochána of the district in which the firearm or ammunition is kept, being satisfied that the transaction is authorised by the competent authorities of that country, also authorises it.

Possession, sale, etc., of silencers

By section 7 of the Act : A person shall be guilty of an offence if he has in his possession or sells or transfers to another person a silencer unless the possession, sale, or transfer is authorised in writing by the superintendent of the district in which the first-mentioned person resides.

The penalty on summary conviction is a £1,000 fine and or one years imprisonment, or on conviction on indictment is a fine and or five years imprisonment.

Reckless discharge of firearm

By section 8 of the Act : A person who discharges a firearm being reckless as to whether any person will be injured or not, shall be guilty of an offence, whether any such injury is caused or not.

The penalty on summary conviction is a £1,000 fine and or twelve months imprisonment, or on conviction on indictment is a fine and or five years imprisonment.

Offensive weapons

Part III of the Firearms and Offensive Weapons Act, 1990 introduces controls on the availability and possession of Offensive weapons and other articles. This came into operation on the 1st May 1991.

By section 9 of the Act, there are a number of offences of possession of knives and other articles.

Possession of knives etc.
(1) Where a person has with him in any public place any knife or other article which has a blade or which is sharply pointed, he shall be guilty of an offence.

The penalty on summary conviction is a £1,000 fine and or twelve months imprisonment.

It shall be a defence for a person charged with an offence to prove that he had good reason or lawful authority for having the article with him in a public place. It shall be a defence to prove that he had the article with him for use at work or for a recreational purpose.

"public place"
"public place" includes any highway and any other premises or place to which at the material time the public have or are permitted to have access, whether on payment or otherwise, and includes any club premises and any train, vessel or vehicle used for the carriage of persons for reward.

Possession of flick-knifes etc.
(4) Where a person, without lawful authority or reasonable excuse (the onus of proving shall lie on him), has with him in any public place -
(a) any flick-knife, he shall be guilty of an offence.

The penalty on summary conviction is a £1,000 fine and or twelve months imprisonment, or on conviction on indictment is a fine and or five years imprisonment.

"flick-knife"
"flick-knife" means a knife -
(a) which has a blade which opens when hand pressure is applied to a button, spring, lever or other device in or attached to the handle, or
(b) which has a blade which is released from the handle or sheath by the force of gravity or the application of centrifugal force and when released is locked in an open position by means of a button, spring, lever or other device.

242

Possession of any other article made or adopted

(4) Where a person, without lawful authority or reasonable excuse (the onus of proving shall lie on him), has with him in any public place -

(b) any other article whatsoever made or adapted for use for causing injury to or incapacitating a person,

he shall be guilty of an offence.

The penalty on summary conviction is a £1,000 fine and or twelve months imprisonment, or on conviction on indictment is a fine and or five years imprisonment.

Any article with intent

(5) Where a person has with him in any public place any article intended by him unlawfully to cause injury to, incapacitate or intimidate any person either in a particular eventuality or otherwise, he shall be guilty of an offence. The penalty is the same as in the case of flick-knives above.

Evidence of intent

In a prosecution for this offence, it shall not be necessary for the prosecution to allege or prove that the intent to cause injury, incapacitate or intimidate was intent to cause injury to, incapacitate or intimidate a particular person; and if, having regard to all the circumstances (including the type of the article alleged to have been intended to cause injury, incapacitate or intimidate, the time of the day or night, and the place), the court (or the jury as the case may be) thinks it reasonable to do so, it may regard possession of the article as sufficient evidence of intent in the absence of any adequate explanation by the accused.

Trespassing with a knife, weapon of offence etc.

By section 10 of the Act : Where a person is on any premises, he shall be guilty of an offence if he has with him _

(a) any knife or other article which has a blade or which is sharply pointed, or

(b) any weapon of offence

The penalty on summary conviction is a £1,000 fine and or twelve months imprisonment, or on conviction on indictment is a fine and or five years imprisonment.

"premises"

"premises" means any building, any part of a building and any land ancillary to a building.

"weapon of offence"

"weapon of offence" means any article -

made or
adapted for use for causing injury to or incapacitating a person, or
intended by the person having it with him for such use.

A court is entitled to take judicial notice of a made article, see *R V
Simpson (1983) 1 WLR 1494* page 234.

An article may be adapted that is altered in some way, e.g. a broken
bottle.

Where an article is neither made or adapted, an intention on the part
of a person having the article with him to cause injury to another or to
incapacitate another will be sufficient.

Production of article capable of inflicting serious injury

By section 11 of the Act : Where a person, while committing or
appearing to be about to commit an offence, or in the course of a
dispute or fight, produces in a manner likely unlawfully to intimidate
another person any article capable of inflicting serious injury, he shall
be guilty of an offence.

The penalty on summary conviction is a £1,000 fine and or twelve
months imprisonment, or on conviction on indictment is a fine and or
five years imprisonment.

Power to prohibit manufacture, etc.

By section 12 of the Act: Any person who -

(a) manufactures, sells or hires, or offers or exposes for sale or
hire, or by way of business repairs or modifies, or

(b) has in his possession for the purpose of sale or hire or for the
purpose of repair or modification by way of business, or

(c) puts on display, or lends or gives to any other person,
a weapon to which this section applies shall be guilty of an offence.

The Minister for Justice may by order direct that this section shall
apply to any description of weapon specified in the order except any
firearm subject to the Firearms Acts, 1925 to 1990.

The penalty on summary conviction is a £1,000 fine and or twelve
months imprisonment, or on conviction on indictment is a fine and or
five years imprisonment.

Forfeiture

By section 13 of the Act : Where a person is convicted of an offence
under Part III of the Act, the court may order any article in respect of
which the offence was committed to be forfeited and either destroyed
or otherwise disposed of.

Power of arrest without warrant

By section 14 of the Act : A member of the Garda Síochána may arrest without warrant any person who is, or whom the member, with reasonable cause suspects to be, in the act of committing an offence under section 9, 10 or 11.

Search warrants

By section 15 of the Act: If a justice of the District Court or a Peace Commissioner is satisfied on the sworn information of a member of the Garda Síochána that there are reasonable grounds for suspecting that an offence under section 12 has been or is being committed on any premises, he may issue a warrant.

Power of search

By section 16 of the Act : Where a number of people are congregated in any public place and a breach of the peace is occurring, or a member of the Garda Síochána has reasonable grounds for believing that a breach of the peace has occurred, or may occur, in that place when the people were or are congregated there.

If a member of the Garda Síochána suspect with reasonable cause that a person has with him any article in contravention of section 9, he may search him in order to ascertain whether this is the case.

If a member of the Garda Síochána suspect with reasonable cause that some one or more of the people present has or have with him or them an article or articles in contravention of section 9, then, even if the member has no reason to suspect that any particular one of the people present has with him any such article, the member may search any of those people if he considers that a search is necessary in order to ascertain whether any of them has with him any such article or articles.

The Criminal Justice Act, 1990 (No. 16)

The Criminal Justice Act, 1990 abolishes the death penalty and substitutes imprisonment for life and provides that minimum periods of imprisonment shall be served by persons convicted of treason or of certain categories of murder.

Abolition of death penalty

By section 1 of the Act ; No person shall suffer death for any offence. "any" would cover every offence.

Sentence

By section 2 of the Act : A person convicted of treason or murder shall be sentenced to imprisonment for life.

Special provisions

By subsection 1 of section 3, the Act applies to :

(i) murder of a member of the Garda Siochana acting in the course of his duty, or

(ii) murder of a prison officer acting in the course of his duty, or

(iii) murder done in the course or futherance of an offence under section 6, 7, 8 or 9 of the Offences Against the State Act 1939, or in the course or furtherance of the activities of an unlawful organisation within the meaning of section 18 (other than paragraph (f)) of that Act, and

(iv) murder, committed within the State for a political motive, of the head of a foreign state or of a member of the government of, or a diplomatic officer of, a foreign state; and

an attempt to commit any such murder.

The Offences Against the State Act, 1939 at the above provide :

Section 6: usurpation of the functions of government,

Section 7: obstruction of government,

Section 8 : obstruction of the President,

Section 9 : interference with certain public servants,

Section 18(f) : relates to organisations which advocate the non-payment of monies to the public purse.

Distinct offence

2 (a) ..murder to which this section applies, and an attempt to commit such a murder, shall be a distinct offence from murder an from an attempt to commit murder and a person shall not be convicted of murder to which this section applies or of an attempt to commit such a murder unless it is proved that he knew of the existence of each ingredient of the offence specified in the relevant paragraph of

subsection (1) or was reckless as to whether or not that ingredient existed.

Murder to which section 3 applies is a new offence replacing the offence of capital murder. See *The People (DPP) v Murray [1977] IR 360,* see page 43.

Minimum period of imprisonment

By section 4 of the Act : Where a person (other than a child or young person) is convicted of treason or murder or attempt to murder to which section 3 applies, the court -

(a) in the case of treason or murder, shall in passing sentence specify as a minimum period of imprisonment to be served by that person a period of not less than forty years,

(b) in the case of an attempt to commit murder, shall pass a sentence of imprisonment of not less than twenty years as the minimum period of imprisonment to be served by that person.

Restriction on power to commute

By section 5(1) of the Act : The power conferred by section 23 of the Criminal Justice Act, 1951, to commute or remit a punishment shall not, in respect of a person convicted under section 3, be exercisable before the minimum period specified above, less any reduction under (2) below.

Presidential pardon

The Constitution of Ireland at Article 13 provides:

6. The right of pardon and the power to commute or remit punishment imposed by any court exercising criminal jurisdiction are hereby vested in the President, but such power of commutation or remission may, except in capital cases, also be conferred by law on other authorities.

9. The powers and functions conferred on the President, ... shall be exercisable and performable by him only on the advise of the Government, ...

A Presidential pardon is unaffected by the provisions of the Act.

Remission by good conduct

By section 5(2) of the Act : The rule of practice whereby prisoners generally may earn remission of sentence by industry and good conduct shall apply in the case of a person convicted under section 3.

It is the practice to grant one-quarter remission of sentences of penal servitude for good conduct

Temporary release

By section 5(3) of the Act : Any power conferred by rules made under section 2 of the Criminal Justice, Act 1960, to release temporarily a person serving a sentence of imprisonment shall not, in the case of a person convicted under section 3, be exercisable during the period for which the commutation or remission of his punishment is prohibited by section 5(1) unless for grave reasons of a humanitarian nature, and any release so granted shall be only of such limited duration as is justified by those reasons.

Procedure

By section 6 of the Act :

(1) Where a person is accused of murder to which section 3 applies or of any attempt to commit such a murder, he shall be charged in the indictment with murder to which that section applies or, as the case may be, with an attempt to commit such a murder.

(2) A person indicted for murder to which section 3 applies may-
(a) if the evidence does not warrant a conviction for such murder but warrants a conviction for murder be found guilty of murder,
(b) if the evidence does not warrant a conviction murder but warrants a conviction for manslaughter be found guilty of manslaughter.

(3) A person indicted for an attempt to commit a murder to which section 3 applies may, if the evidence does not warrant a conviction for such an attempt but warrants a conviction for an attempt to commit murder, be found guilty of an attempt to commit murder.

It follows from the provisions of this section that where a person is charged with murder, he may not afterwards be convicted of murder to which section 3 applies.

Consequential amendments

By section 7 of the Act there are a number of consequential amendments to the effect that the sentence of "death" is replaced by "imprisonment for life".

The Acts affected are :

> The Piracy Act, 1837;
> The Treason Act, 1939;
> The Defence Act, 1954;

The Criminal Justice Act, 1964

The Criminal Justice Act, 1964 has been amended to such an extent that only section 4 which deals with malice remains. That section provides :

(1) Where a person kills another unlawfully the killing shall not be

murder unless the accused person intended to kill, or cause serious injury to, some person, whether the person actually killed or not.

(2) The accused person shall be presumed to have intended the natural and probable consequences of his conduct; but this presumption may be rebutted.

Intention
The accused person must have
> intended to kill, or
> cause serious injury to,

some person, whether the person actually killed or not.

Section 3, 2(a) provides that : a person shall not be convicted of murder to which this section applies or of an attempt to commit such a murder unless it is proved that :

1. he knew of the existence of each ingredient of the offence specified in the relevant paragraph of subsection (1) or
2. was reckless as to whether or not that ingredient existed.

In respect of section 3 1(i) this could require proof of :

(a) That the accused intended to kill or cause serious injury to the victim,

(b) That the victim was a member of the Garda Síochána,

(c) That the victim was acting in the course of his duty,

(d) That the accused knew the victim to be a member of the Garda Síochána,

(e) That the accused knew that the victim was acting as a member of the Garda Síochána in the course of his duty.

Presumption
The accused person shall be presumed to have intended the natural and probable consequences of his conduct; but this presumption may be rebutted.

The Criminal Law (Rape) (Amendment) Act, 1990 (No. 32)

The Criminal Law (Rape) (Amendment) Act, 1990 amends the law relating to rape and to sexual assault offences. The law is changed in particular by amendment to the Criminal Law (Rape) Act, 1981, which is referred to as the Principal Act.

A sexual assault offence

A sexual assault offence means a rape offence and any of the following, namely, aggravated sexual assault, attempted aggravated sexual assault, sexual assault, attempted sexual assault, aiding, abetting, counselling and procuring aggravated sexual assault, attempted aggravated sexual assault, sexual assault or attempted sexual assault, incitement to aggravated sexual assault or sexual assault and conspiracy to commit any of the foregoing. The term "sexual assault offence" is substituted for "rape offence" throughout the 1981 Act, thus broadening the application of the 1981 Act from rape to all sexual assault offences.

There are accordingly three types of sexual assault offences :

> Rape offences,
> Aggravated sexual assault and
> Sexual assault

In addition to the actual sexual offence, there are ancillary offences in relation to :

attempt : this is to make an effort to accomplish something. page 30
aiding : this is to help another in doing something
abetting : this is to encourage or assist in something.
counselling : this is to advise or suggest something.
procuring : this is to obtain or acquire, and
incitement : this is to urge on or stir up. page 34

A rape offence

A rape offence means any of the following, namely rape, attempted rape, burglary with intent to commit rape, aiding, abetting, counselling and procuring rape, attempted rape or burglary with intent to commit rape, and incitement to rape and, rape under section 4, attempted rape under section 4, aiding, abetting, counselling and procuring rape under section 4, attempted rape under section 4, and incitement to rape under section 4.

There are three types of rape offence :

> Rape,
> Burglary with intent to commit rape, and
> Rape under section 4 of the Act

250

Complainant

A complainant means a person in relation to whom a sexual assault offence is alleged to have been committed. Throughout the 1981 Act the term "person" is substituted for the term "woman".

Meaning of rape

Section 2 of the 1981 Act is amended by the repeal of the word "unlawful". Thus a man commits rape if he has sexual intercourse with a woman who at the time of the intercourse does not consent to it.

Sexual intercourse

Sexual intercourse must be taken to mean "carnal knowledge" and regard should be taken of section 63 of the Offences against the Person Act, 1861.

Kaitamaki v The Queen (1984)

This New Zealand case was referred to the Judicial Committee of the Privy Council. The evidence of the accused was that after he had penetrated the woman he became aware that she was not consenting; he did not however desist from intercourse. The trial judge directed the jury that if, having realised the woman was not willing, the defendant continued with the act of intercourse, it then became rape. On appeal to the Privy Council, the defence sought to establish the proposition that rape is penetration without consent: once penetration is complete the act of rape is concluded. Intercourse if it continues, is not rape, it was argued, because for the purposes of (section 63) it is complete upon penetration.

The appeal was dismissed, their Lordships agreed with the Court of Appeal of New Zealand. The Court, had expressed the opinion that the purpose of the section was to remove any doubts as to the minimum conduct needed to prove the fact of sexual intercourse. "Complete" is used in the sense of having come into existence, but not in the sense of being at an end. Sexual intercourse is a continuing act which only ends with withdrawal. Accordingly a man is guilty of rape if he continued intercourse after he realised that the woman was no longer consenting.

Sexual assault

By section 2 of the Act : The offence of indecent assault upon any male person and the offence of indecent assault upon any female person shall be known as sexual assault. The penalty on conviction on indictment is imprisonment for five years.

Sexual assault may be defined as an assault accompanied by circumstances of indecency. Assault as used here may mean an assault or a battery. Indecency could refer to a touching or threatened touching by, or of the sexual parts of the body.

251

Aggravated sexual assault

By section 3 of the Act : Aggravated sexual assault is a felony and means a sexual assault that involves serious violence or the threat of serious violence or is such as to cause injury, humiliation or degradation of a grave nature to the person assaulted. The penalty on conviction on indictment is imprisonment for life. This offence may be committed by either a man or a woman and against either a man or woman.

Aggravated sexual assault involves either :
(a) serious violence, or
(b) the threat of serious violence, or
(c) is such as to cause injury of a grave nature to the person assaulted,
(d) is such as to cause humiliation of a grave nature to the person assaulted, or
(e) is such as to cause degradation of a grave nature to the person assaulted.

"injury" may be either damage or harm,
"humiliation" would cause a person to feel disgraced, and
"degradation" would bring disgrace on a person or reduce them to a lower status.

Rape under section 4

By the Act rape under section 4 is a felony and means a sexual assault that includes -
(a) penetration (however slight) of the anus or mouth by the penis, or
(b) penetration (however slight) of the vagina by any object held or manipulated by another person.

The penalty on conviction on indictment is imprisonment for life. This offence may be committed by either a man or a woman. While (b) may only be committed against a woman, (a) may be committed against either a man or woman.
(a) is confined to a penetration by the penis only.
(b) is confined to a penetration of the vagina only. An "object" is something solid that can be seen or touched, examples might be a banana, bottle, knife or stick.

Buggery as it relates to mankind and which is an offence under section 61 of the Offences Against the Person Act, 1861 and which consists of a penetration of the anus by the penis, is now included as a type of "rape under section 4".

Abolition of marital exemption

By section 5 of the Act : Any rule of law by virtue of which a husband cannot be guilty of rape of his wife is hereby abolished.

252

However proceedings shall not be instituted against a husband except by or with the consent of the Director of Public Prosecutions.

Capacity to commit

By section 6 of the Act: Any rule of law by virtue of which a male person is treated by reason of his age as being physically incapable of committing an offence of a sexual nature is hereby abolished. This abolishes the irrebutable presumption of law in respect of boys under the age of fourteen years.

Corroboration of evidence

By section 7 of the Act : Where a person is charged with an offence of a sexual nature and where there would be a requirement that that the jury be given a warning about the danger of convicting on uncorroborated evidence, it shall be for the judge to decide in his discretion whether the jury should be given a warning.

Alternative verdicts

By section 8 of the Act :

(1) A person indicted for rape may, if the evidence does not warrant a conviction for rape but warrants a conviction for rape under section 4 or aggravated sexual assault or sexual assault, be found guilty of rape under section 4 or of aggravated sexual assault or of sexual assault, as may be appropriate.

(2) A person indicted for rape may, if the evidence does not warrant a conviction for rape but warrants a conviction for an offence under section 1 (Defilement of girl under fifteen years of age) or 2 (Defilement of a girl under seventeen years) of the Criminal Law amendment Act, 1935 or under section 3 of the Criminal Law Amendment Act 1885 (Procurement), be found guilty of an offence under the said section 1, 2 or 3, as may be appropriate.

(3) A person indicted for rape under section 4 may, if the evidence does not warrant a conviction for rape under section 4 but warrants a conviction for aggravated sexual assault or for sexual assault, be found guilty of aggravated sexual assault or of sexual assault, as may be appropriate.

(4) A person indicted for aggravated sexual assault may, if the evidence does not warrant a conviction for aggravated sexual assault but warrants a conviction for sexual assault, be found guilty of sexual assault.

(5) A person indicted for an offence made felony by section 1 of the Criminal Law Amendment Act, 1935, may, if the evidence does not warrant a conviction for the felony or an attempt to commit the felony but warrants a conviction for an offence under section 2 of the Criminal

Law amendment Act, 1935 or section 3 of the Criminal Law Amendment Act 1885, or rape under section 4 or aggravated sexual assault or sexual assault, be found guilty of an offence under the said section 2 or 3 or of rape under section 4, or of aggravated sexual assault or of sexual assault, as may be appropriate.

Consent

By section 9 of the Act: It is hereby declared that in relation to an offence that consists of or includes the doing of an act to a person without the consent of that person any failure or omission by that person to offer resistance to the act does not of itself constitute consent to the act.

Trial by Central Criminal Court

By section 10 of the Act : A person indicted for a rape offence or the offence of aggravated sexual assault shall be tried by the Central Criminal Court.

The offence of sexual assault continues to be tried in the Circuit Criminal Court.

Exclusion of the public

By section 6 of the 1981 Act as now amended : In any proceedings for a rape offence or the offence of aggravated sexual assault, the judge shall exclude from the court during the hearing all persons except officers of the court, persons directly concerned in the proceedings, *bona fide* representatives of the press and such other persons as the judge, may in his discretion permit to remain. This is without prejudice to the right of a parent, relative or friend of the complainant. The verdict or decision and the sentence (if any) shall be announced in public.

This provision does not apply to proceedings for the offence of sexual assault.

Anonymity of accused

By section 8 of the 1981 Act as now amended : After a person is charged with a sexual assault offence no matter likely to lead members of the public to identify him, as the person against whom the charge is made shall be published ... or be broadcast except after he has been convicted of the offence. This may be dispensed with, but not where it might enable members of the public to identify a person as a complainant.

The previous provision was confined to the offence of rape only, the provision now is much wider.

254

The Criminal Justice (Forensic Evidence) Act, 1990 amends and extends the law to authorise the taking of bodily samples for forensic testing from persons suspected of certain criminal offences.

Power to take bodily samples

By section 2 of the Act : Where a person is in custody under the provisions of section 30 of the Offences against the State Act, 1939, or section 4 of the Criminal Justice Act, 1984, a member of the Garda Síochána may take, or cause to be taken, from that person for the purpose of forensic testing all or any of the following samples :

(a) a sample of -

(i) blood, *

(ii) pubic hair, *

(iii) urine, *

(iv) saliva, *

(v) hair other than pubic hair,

(vi) a nail,

(vii) any material found under a nail,

(b) a swab from any part of the body other than a body orifice or a genital region,

(c) a swab from a body orifice or a genital region, *

(d) a dental impression, *

(e) a footprint or similar impression of any part of the person's body other than a part of his hand or mouth.

Where a person is in prison, a member of the Garda Síochána may take, or cause to be taken, from that person for the purpose of forensic testing all or any of the samples specified.

Authorisation

A sample may be taken only if -

(a) a member of the Garda Síochána not below the rank of superintendent authorises it to be taken, (this may be given orally but, it shall be confirmed in writing as soon as is practicable) and

(b) in the case of certain samples * , the appropriate consent has been given in writing.

An authorisation shall not be given unless the member of the Garda Síochána giving it has reasonable grounds -

(a) for suspecting the involvement of the person from whom the sample is to be taken -

(i) in a case where the person is in custody, in the offence in respect of which he is in custody, or

(ii) in a case where the person is in prison, in the commission of an offence under the Offence against the State Act, 1939, or an offence which is for the time being a scheduled offence for the purposes of Part V of that Act or an offence to which section 4 of the Criminal Justice Act, 1984, applies, and

(b) for believing that the sample will tend to confirm or disprove the involvement of the person from whom the sample is to be taken in the said offence.

Consent

Before a member of the Garda Síochána takes, or cause to be taken, a sample, or seeks the consent of the person from whom the sample is required to the taking of such a sample, the member shall inform the person -

(a) of the nature of the offence in which it is suspected that that person has been involved,

(b) that an authorisation has been given and of the grounds on which it has been given, and

(c) that the results of any tests on the samples may be given in evidence in any proceedings.

"seeks the consent"

"seeks the consent" would imply that there is no obligation on a detained person to give such consent. By section 3 below; inferences may be drawn where a consent is refused without good cause. What is meant by "good cause".

Registered medical practitioner

A sample of the kind specified in (a) (i) or (ii), or in (c) may be taken only by a registered medical practitioner and a dental impression may be taken only by a registered dentist or by a registered medical practitioner.

Obstruction

A person who obstruct or attempts to obstruct any member of the Garda Síochána or any other person acting under the powers conferred above shall be guilty of an offence and shall be liable on summary conviction to a fine not exceeding £1,000 or to imprisonment for a term not exceeding 12 months or to both.

Inferences from refusal to consent

By section 3 of the Act : Where a consent is refused without good cause, in any proceeding against a person for the offence -

(a) the court, in determining -

(i) whether to send forward that person for trial, or

256

(ii) whether there is a case to answer, and

(b) the court, in determining whether that person is guilty of the offence charged, may draw such inferences, if any, from the refusal as appear proper; and the refusal may on the basis of such inferences, be treated as, or as being capable of amounting to, corroboration of any evidence in relation to which the material is material, but a person shall not be convicted of an offence solely on an inference drawn from such refusal.

This section shall not have effect in relation to an accused unless he has been told in ordinary language by a member of the Garda Síochána when seeking his consent that the sample was required for the purpose of forensic testing, that his consent was necessary and, if his consent was not given, what the effect of a refusal by him of such consent could be.

This section shall not apply -

(a) to a person who has not attained the age of 14 years, or

(b) in a case where an appropriate consent has been refused by a parent or guardian.

Destruction of records and samples

By section 4 of the Act provision is made for the destruction of records and samples.

Regulations

By section 5 of the Act provision is made for the Minister for Justice to make regulation regarding the taking of samples.

Chapter 1 : Introduction

Codification of criminal law page 3
The present Government has declared itself in favour of the codification of the criminal law. A Select Committee on Crime has now been established.

Juvenile Justice Bill
The Minister for Justice has stated that a Juvenile Justice Bill will be introduced in 1992.

Chapter 2 : Classification of crimes

Minor offence page 12
Robert A. Cartmill v Ireland [1988] 430
Held by Mr. Justice Murphy in the High Court :
(1) In determining whether an offence is of a minor or major nature, the only punishment which must be examined is that which must be referred to as "primary punishment", i.e., punishment in the ordinary sense, be it a custodial sentence or the intentional penal deprivation of property whether by means of fine or other direct method of deprivation.

Other punitive and unpleasant consequences flowing from a conviction, such as the loss of a licence to carry on business or the forfeiture of equipment in connection with that business, however drastic the effect, even on the very livelihood of the convicted person, are too remote in character to be considered in weighing the seriousness of an offence by the punishment it may attract.

(2) The test whether the particular offence is major or minor will normally depend on the effective penalty validly imposed.

(3) It is not necessary in all cases to await the decision of the District Justice before forming an opinion of the seriousness or otherwise of the offence concerned. For example, a mandatory or maximum penalty laid down by the legislature will constitute a reliable guide as to the minor or major nature of that offence.

Chapter 3 Criminal participation and association

Participation in a crime page 14
The People (D. P. P.) v Michael Egan (1989) IR 681
Held by the Court of Criminal Appeal that :
(1) A person could aid and abet the commission of a crime without being present when the crime was committed, and accordingly be liable

to be dealt with as a principal offender.

(2) In order to be convicted of the principal offence, it was not necessary for the prosecution to establish that a person who had aided and abetted the principal offender before the crime was committed had knowledge of the actual crime intended. It is sufficient that a person who gave assistance knew the nature of the intended crime.

(3) The applicant in this case was an accessory before the fact of the crime committed by the principal offender because he knew that a crime was to be committed, that it involved the theft of goods and with this knowledge he assisted the principal offender when he agreed before the crime took place to make his workshop available to hide stolen goods.

Chapter 4 : Defences to criminal responsibility

Insanity page 25
D. P. P. v John Gallagher S.C. 12/2/91

Where a person detained under section 2(2) of the Trial of Lunatics Act, 1883 seeks to secure release from detention, he may apply to the executive for his release on the grounds that he is not suffering from any mental disorder. Where such an application is made, the executive, must inquire into all the relevant circumstances of the case and in so doing must use fair and constitutional procedures and such an inquiry and its result may be the subject of judicial review so as to ensure compliance with such procedures.

Mr. Justice McCarthy in the course of his judgment noted that at the Central Criminal Court, a jury had returned a special verdict as provided for in the Act. He said that the overriding consideration is that this special verdict is a verdict of acquittal. In his view the making of an order did not involve the administration of justice, but rather constituted the carrying out of the role of the executive in caring for society and protecting the common good.

The Trial of Lunatics Act, 1883 at section 2 provides :

(1) Where in any indictment or information any act or omission is charged against any person as an offence, and it is given in evidence on the trial of such person for that offence that he was insane, so as not to be responsible, according to law, for his actions at the time when the act was done or omission made, then, if it appears to the jury before whom such person is tried that he did the act or made the omission charged, but was insane as aforesaid at the time when he did or made the same, the jury shall return a special verdict to the effect that the accused was guilty of the act or omission charged against him, but was insane as aforesaid at the time when he did the act or made the omission.

(2) Where such special verdict is found, the Court shall order the accused to be kept in custody as a criminal lunatic, in such place and in such manner as the Court shall direct till the pleasure of the (Government) shall be known; and it shall be lawful for the (Government) thereupon, and from time to time, to give such order for the safe custody of the said person during (its) pleasure in such place and in such manner as (the Government) may seem fit.

Chapter 5 : The inchoate offences

Conspiracy page 32
Desmond Ellis v O'Dea & Governor of Portlaoise Prison ITLR 14/1/91
Finlay C.J. stated that it is a fundamental principle of the Irish common law that a person joining in a conspiracy or a joint venture outside the State, in furtherance of which an overt criminal act is committed within the State, will be amenable to the jurisdiction of the Irish courts even where he has not committed an overt act within the State.

Chapter 6 : Homicide

Suicide page 48
A Suicide Bill is to be introduced in the Seanad which will propose that suicide no longer be a crime. However a person who aids, abets, counsels or procures the suicide of another or an attempt by another to commit suicide, shall be liable on conviction on indictment to imprisonment for a term of ten years.

Chapter 8 : Sexual offences

Re, Norris v A. G. (1984) page 75
The European Court of Human Rights has found Ireland to be in breach of the European Convention on Human Rights. The Government has indicated its intention to change the criminal law in the area of homosexuality.

Chapter 9 : Offences concerning children and young persons. page 76

The Tobacco (Health, Promotion and Protection) Act, 1988 makes the following provisions :

Restriction on sale of tobacco products S.3
(1) Any person who sells, offers to sell, or makes available in relation to the sale of any other product, any tobacco product to a person under the age of 16 years, whether for his own use or

otherwise, or who sells to any person, acting on behalf of a person under the age of 16 years, any tobacco products, shall be guilty of an offence and shall be liable, on summary conviction, to a fine not exceeding £500.

(3) Whenever a person is prosecuted for an offence under this section, it shall be a defence for him to establish that he had taken all reasonable steps to assure himself that the person to whom the tobacco products were sold, offered for sale or made available had attained the age of 16 years.

Restriction on sale of cigarettes S.4

Any person who sells, offers to sell or makes available in relation to the sale of any other products, cigarettes to a person otherwise than in packets of ten or more cigarettes shall be guilty of an offence and shall be liable on summary conviction to a fine not exceeding £500.

The Intoxicating Liquor Act, 1988 at section 31 provides :

(3) A person who contravenes subsection (1) or (2) of this section shall be guilty of an offence and shall be liable on summary conviction to a fine not exceeding-

(a) £300, in case of a first offence, or

(b), in the case of a second or any subsequent offence,

and the offence shall be deemed for the purposes of Part III (which relates to the endorsement of licences) of the Act of 1927 to be an offence to which that Part of that Act applies.

(4) In any proceedings against a person for a contravention of subsection (1) or (2) of this section, it shall be a defence for such person to prove that the person in respect of whom the charge is brought produced to him an age card relating to such person or that he had other reasonable grounds for believing that such person was over the age of 18 years, or, if the person is charged with permitting another person to sell or deliver intoxicating liquor contrary to the said subsection (1) or (2), to prove that an age card was produced by the person concerned to that other person or that that other person had other reasonable grounds for believing as aforesaid.

Chapter 11 : What constitutes larceny

Director of Public Prosecutions v *Edward Keating [1989] 561*
It was held by Mr. Justice Lynch in the High Court that :

(1) Where the offence of larceny depends upon the fraudulent intention of an accused, which intention is to be ascertained from his conduct at the time of the alleged offence.

(2) Where, on the evidence, the conduct of a person accused of the larceny of goods in a shop is such as to indicate, in the absence of a

261

plausible explanation, that he intended to fraudulently deprive the shipowner thereof, the offence of larceny has been committed even before such person has left the premises.

Simple larceny page 88
Director of Public Prosecutions v Robert Cassidy [1990] ILRM 310
The accused took goods the property of his employer without his authority or consent. At the time of taking the goods, the accused had the intention of permanently depriving his employer thereof. The accused was charged and convicted under section 2. The District Justice stated a case for the High Court, as to whether the accused could be convicted of an offence under section 2 notwithstanding that he might on the same facts be charged with and punished for an offence under section 17(1)(a).

It was held by Mr. Justice Gannon: that section 2 provides for the punishment of larceny where it is not provided for by any other section of the Act or any other statute. Punishment under section 2 is not precluded merely because an accused person may also be penalised under another section.

Husband or wife page 89
The Married Women's Status Act 1957, at section 9 provides :

(1) Subject to subsection (3), every married woman shall have in her own name against all persons whomsoever, including her husband, the same remedies and redress by way of criminal proceedings for the protection and security of her property as if she were unmarried.

(2) Subject to subsection (3), a husband shall have against his wife the same remedies and redress by way of criminal proceedings for the protection and security of his property as if she were not his wife.

(3) No criminal proceedings concerning any property claimed by one spouse (in this section referred to as the claimant) shall, by virtue of subsection (1) or subsection (2), be taken by the claimant against the other spouse while they are living together, nor, while they are living apart, concerning any act done while living together by the other spouse, unless such property was wrongfully taken by the other spouse when leaving or deserting or about to leave or desert the claimant.

Subjects of larceny page 89
The Larceny Act, 1990 at section 9 provides that a person convicted on indictment of an offence under the following sections of the Larceny Act, 1916 : 3, 4, 5, 6, 7, 8, 9, 10, 11, shall be liable to a term of imprisonment not exceeding ten years or a fine or both.

The same Act provides for the repeal of section 12 : Postal packets page 91

Chapter 12 : Receiving stolen goods page 93

See consideration of Handling stolen property

Possession page 96
Minister for Posts and Telegraphs v Campbell (1966) IR 69
   In the High Court Davitt P. stated "A person cannot in the context of a criminal case, be properly said to keep or have possession of an article unless he has control of it either personally or by someone else. He cannot be said to have actual possession of it unless he personally can exercise physical control over it; and he cannot be said to have constructive possession of it unless it is in the actual possession of some other person overwhom he has control so that it would be available to him if and when he wanted it. ... He cannot properly be said to be in control or possession of something of whose existence and presence he has no knowledge."

The People (Attorney General) v Nugent and Byrne (1964) 1 Fre. 294
   The applicants were convicted of receiving stolen monies contrary to section 33(1). Monies stolen in a shop were found in Nugent's car. The car had been under observation by the Gardai, but there was a period of five minutes after its arrival when the car was not under observation. Byrne was a passenger in the car. Both denied all knowledge of the stolen monies.
   Held by the Court of Criminal Appeal that there was no evidence that Byrne was aware, or should have been aware, that there were stolen monies in the car. The only evidence connecting him with the car was his own evidence that he had been merely a passenger in the car.
   Davitt P. stated "... If Nugent was aware that the money was in his car then he was in control of it, and it could properly be said to be in his possession. ... If he was not aware that the money was in his car then it must have been put there by somebody else without his knowledge. ... A person is not necessarily aware at all times of what is in the back of his car."

The People (Attorney General) v Kelly & Robinson (1953) 1 Fre. 147
   The applicant Kelly was convicted under section 26(1) of the Larceny Act, 1916, while Robinson was convicted under section 33(1) of the same Act. Certain articles were stolen from a shop. Robinson was seen in the vicinity with others, and his car was used in committing the offence. The following night a house was raided by the Gardai. Kelly was seen through a window with three others, sorting the stolen goods. By the time the Gardai were admitted the stolen goods were hidden. Two of the four pleaded not guilty, claiming that they had been visiting the house at the time it was raided.

The trial judge stated in explaining the nature of the offence of receiving goods knowing them to have been stolen "... A person may have joint possession of the property with one person or others, though the property may be in the physical custody of another person. If you were satisfied that Hand had in his house this stolen property and that all the people that were there had some control over this property, or that he was holding it for them, they would have what is called constructive possession of it -- if that was the position, they would have received the property knowing it to be stolen. If they knew it was stolen, they of course must know it was stolen property at that particular time.."

It was held by the Court of Criminal Appeal that the trial judge had correctly and adequately instructed the jury on the nature of "constructive possession".

Chapter 13 : Larceny in property page 98

The Larceny Act, 1990 at section 9 provides that a person convicted on indictment of an offence under the following sections of the Larceny Act, 1916 : 13, 15, 16, shall be liable to a term of imprisonment not exceeding ten years or a fine or both.

The same Act provides for the repeal of section 28 : Being found by night page 101

Chapter 14 : Larceny from people page 103

The Larceny Act, 1990 at section 9 provides that a person convicted on indictment of an offence under the following sections of the Larceny Act, 1916 : 13, 14, 29, 30, 32, shall be liable to a term of imprisonment not exceeding ten years or a fine or both.

Chapter 15 : Embezzlement and fraudulent conversion page 108

The Larceny Act, 1990 at section 9 provides that a person convicted on indictment of an offence under the following sections of the Larceny Act, 1916 : 17, 19, 20, 21, 22, shall be liable to a term of imprisonment not exceeding ten years or a fine or both.

The same Act provides for the repeal of section 18 Embezzlement by officers of An Post, page 110.

Chapter 18 : Road Traffic offences

Being in charge while drunk page 131
Section 50, inserted by the Road Traffic(Amendment) Act, 1978 provides as follows :

1 (a) a person shall be guilty of an offence who, when in charge of a mechanically propelled vehicle in a public place with intent to drive or attempt to drive the vehicle (but not driving or attempting to drive it), is under the influence of an intoxicant to such an extent as to be incapable of having proper control of the vehicle.

2. a person shall be guilty of an offence who is in charge of a mechanically propelled vehicle in a public place with intent to drive or attempt to drive the vehicle (but not driving or attempting to drive it) and in whose body there is present a quantity of alcohol such that, within three hours after having been so in charge of the vehicle, the concentration of alcohol in his blood will exceed a concentration of 100 milligrammes of alcohol per 100 millilitres of blood.

3. a person shall be guilty of an offence who is in charge of a mechanically propelled vehicle in a public place with intent to drive or attempt to drive the vehicle (but not driving or attempting to drive it) and in whose body there is present a quantity of alcohol such that, within three hours after having been so in charge of the vehicle, the concentration of alcohol in his urine will exceed a concentration of 135 milligrammes of alcohol per 100 millilitres of urine.

The penalty on summary conviction, in the case of a first offence is a £350 fine and or three months imprisonment or in the case of a second or subsequent offence is £1,000 fine and or six months imprisonment.

Where a person is charged with an offence under Section 50, he may be found guilty of an offence under Section 49 above.

Road Traffic Bill 1991

A Road Traffic Bill is to be introduced by the Government it is to propose the reduction in the proportion of alcohol in respect of the above offences. The reduction in respect of blood is expected to be from 100 milligrammes to 80 milligrammes and in respect of urine is expected to be from 135 milligrammes to 107 milligrammes.

Endorsement page 136

Director of Public Prosecutions v Maria O'Brien [1989] IR 266

It was held by the Supreme Court, that on a construction of section 52 of the Act, a conviction of an offence under that section led to a mandatory endorsement pursuant to the provisions of section 36, of the particulars of the offence on the defendant's driving licence.

Chapter 19 : Misuse of drugs

Possession S.3 page 138

The State (Gleeson) v District Justice Connellan [1988] IR 559

Held by the Supreme Court : Section 3 created only one offence of possession *simpliciter,* the question of the use of the drug was not an ingredient of the offence and arose only in relation to the penalty to be imposed under section 27.

The State (Bloomfield) v Nelyon & D. P. P. (1985) page 141
"The judgment of O'Hanlon J. ... , is not a correct statement of the law." Hederman J. in the above.

Search Warrants page 146
The People (D. P. P.) v Mark Kenny [1990] ILRM 569
It was held by the Supreme Court that an information required to obtain a search warrant under section 26(1) must state facts from which a district justice or peace commissioner could be satisfied there were reasonable grounds for the issue thereof. In the absence of an independent decision by a district justice or a peace commissioner that a search warrant is justified beyond a suspicion by members of the Garda Síochána that controlled drugs are on the premises, there may be a failure to adequately protect the inviolability of the dwelling under Article 40.5 of the Constitution of Ireland.

Chapter 20 : Offences against the public peace

A rogue and a vagabond S. 4 page 151
Delete (2) and (8)

Chapter 23 : Offences of a public nature page 160

The Larceny Act, 1990 at section 10 provides that The Post Office Act, 1908 is amended by -
(a) the substitution, in section 51, of "and be liable on conviction on indictment to imprisonment of a term not exceeding 10 years or to fine or to both" for existing penalty.
(b) the substitution, in section 53, of "and be liable on conviction on indictment to imprisonment of a term not exceeding 2 years or to fine or to both" for existing penalty.
(c) the substitution of the following for section 55:

Secreting or destroying by officer of An Post
If any officer of An Post for any purpose whatsoever secrets or destroys a postal packet in course of transmission by post, he shall be guilty of felony, and shall be liable on conviction on indictment to imprisonment for a term not exceeding 10 years or to a fine or to both.

Chapter 24 : Offences against Government

Treason page 168

As noted above the Criminal Justice Act, 1990 at section 2 provides that a person convicted of Treason shall be sentenced to imprisonment for life. Also take note that the provisions of sections 4 and 5 apply to Treason.

Chapter 27 : The Offences Against the State act

Unlawful organisations page 185
The People v O'Leary 1987/137 CCA 29/7/88

The appellant was convicted in the Special Criminal Court on a count which charged him with being a member of an unlawful organisation contrary to section 21 and on a count which charged him with possessing incriminating documents contrary to section 12. The Gardai found on the appellant's premises, thirty-seven copes of a poster which was held to be incriminating, and this was taken to be evidence of membership of an unlawful organisation.

It was held on appeal that the appellant had failed to displace the *prima facie* evidence furnished by his possession of such documents. The conviction was upheld.

Section 30 page 186
The People (Director of Public Prosecutions) v Byrne [1987] IR 363

The respondent was arrested under section 30. He was detained in Garda custody for a period of 24 hours, during which time a Chief Superintendent authorised his detention for a further period of 24 hours. Counsel for the accused objected to the manner in which the validity of the extension order was proved by the prosecution. The Chief Superintendent who had signed the extension order had died prior to the trial.

It was held by the Supreme Court, that the trial judge had been correct in ruling that, in the absence of direct evidence from the Chief Superintendent as to his state of mind when making the extension order, the prosecution had failed to establish that the continued detention of the respondent after the expiration of the initial 24 hour period was lawful; and the evidence of the Garda officer who was present when the Chief Superintendent issued the authorisation was irrelevant to the validity of the respondent's further period of detention.

The People (D. P. P.) v Sean Howley [1989] 629

The applicant was arrested under section 30, on suspicion of having committed the scheduled offence of cattle maiming. During a further period of detention the appellant made a statement confessing to a murder, which was subsequently admitted as evidence at his trial.

It was held by the Supreme Court that :

(1) The trial judge was correct in concluding that the arrest in respect of the scheduled offence of cattle maiming was not in any sense a "colourable device" to allow the Gardai an opportunity to question the accused in relation to the alleged murder. There is no requirement that an arrest under section 30 must be predominantly motivated by a desire to investigate a scheduled offence.

(2) There are no grounds for holding that the extension of the period of detention was unlawful. Where the Garda officer empowered to make the extension order *bona fide* suspects the accused person of being involved in the offence for which he was originally arrested, the extended period of detention is lawful.

Chapter 30 : The courts of criminal jurisdiction

The Court of Criminal Appeal page 205
The People (D. P. P.) v Luke Egan [1990] ILRM 780

Held by the Supreme Court that the Court of Criminal Appeal has no jurisdiction to substitute its own subjective view of evidence for the verdict of a jury. If there is credible evidence to support the verdict of the jury the Court of Criminal Appeal has no power to interfere with it save only where a verdict may be identified as perverse.

Special Criminal Court page 207
Thomas Cox v Ireland etc. ITLR 21/1/91

Mr. Justice Barr in the High Court held that for legislation to provide that whenever a person, convicted in the Special Criminal Court of a scheduled offence, is employed in the public service, he shall forfeit his employment and that any such convicted person shall be disqualified from any such employment for a further seven years, is to interfere to an unreasonable and unjustified extent with the personal rights, particularly the right to practise a particular profession or vocation, of those within its wombat. Further, any such legislation also amounts to unfair discrimination contrary to Article 40.1 of the Constitution of Ireland, in that it would be so patently capricious as to be a denial of equality before the law. Accordingly section 34 (1) to (IV) of the Offences Against the State Act, 1939 are contrary to the Constitution and are void.

Chapter 31 : Criminal procedure

Preliminary examination page 212
Richard Glavin v Governor .... of Mountjoy Prison etc. ITLR 25/3/91

The Supreme Court stated that the entitlement of an accused person to a proper valid preliminary examination of an indictable offence is so inexorably bound up with the trial of that person on indictment that a failure to hold a proper preliminary examination means that there has been a failure to afford to the accused the due process that is required by Article 38.1 of the Constitution of Ireland. Mr. Justice O'Flaherty stated "...Part II of the Criminal Procedure Act, 1967 as amended afforded a valuable protection for an accused person charged with an indictable crime. It meant that he was afforded a full opportunity of considering the case that was to be mounted against him and might in certain circumstances exercise his entitlement to have witnesses make sworn depositions. Before an accused person could be sent forth for trial the District Justice must decide that there was in fact a sufficient case to put him on trial."

Verdict page 218
Director of Public Prosecutions v *Jackie Kelly [1989] ILRM 370*
It was held by the Court of Criminal Appeal

(1) The minimum period of time which must be afforded to a jury for deliberation to arrive at a majority verdict is two hours - No impairment, however small, of that period may be permitted.

(2) The time spent by a jury back in court listening to the further charge or charges of the trial judge cannot be considered as part of the two hours of deliberation.

Where the facts are clear this leaves no discretionary conclusion for the court of trial.

ERRATA

CRIMINAL LAW IN IRELAND

on page 7 ninth line delete "on a charge"
on page 7 eleventh line "offences" should read "defences"
on page 7 nineteenth line "delegation authority" should read "delegation of authority"
on page 7 twenty-fourth line "licence" should read "licencee"
on page 7 eleventh last line delete "the"
on page 8 first line second "with" should read "without"
on page 9 delete third paragraph
on page 11 fourth last line "or" should read "of"
on page 12 sixteenth delete "are"
on page 12 seventeenth line "of" should read "or
on page 15 twelfth last line "known" should read "knowing that"
on page 26 sixteenth line insert "way" fourth word
on page 31 last line "appear" should read "appears"
on page 40 tenth last line "an" should read "at"
on page 44 sixteenth line delete "where"
on page 45 twelfth line delete first "is"
on page 50 eight last line "was held" should read "was not held"
on page 65 seventh last line "not" should read "note"
on page 82 sixteenth line "not" should read "note"
on page 86 second line first "of" should read "or"
on page 89 paragraph on "Husband or Wife" to be replaced with s. 9, M. W. S. A. 1957
on page 90 thirteenth line insert "or any original document of or belonging to any court of record, or relating to" before "any"
on page 90 thirteenth line "of matte" should read "or matter"
on page 99 eight line "or" should read "of"
on page 101eleventh line "that purpose" should read "such use"
on page 101 sixteenth line "intend" should read "intended" and "fir" should read "for"
on page 101 third last line should read "with intent to commit burglary"
on page 105 last line   add "or"
on page 109 ninth line add "is"
on page 111 fourteenth line "nay" should read "any"
on page 112 "coveted" should read "converted"
on page 112 second last line "on" should read "of"

270

on page 119 ninth last line insert "it" after "threw"

on page 126 fourteenth line insert"for" after "driving,"

on page 128 second last line "provision" should read "proviso"

on page 131 seventh line "interest" should read "intent"

on page 131 twelfth line insert "in a public place with intent to drive or attempt to drive the vehicle" between "vehicle" and "(but"

on page 132 sixth last line "36" should read "38"

on page 152 seventh last line "intoxication" should read "intoxicating"

on page 158 twentieth line "not" should read "note"

on page 160 eleventh line "addresses" should read "addressed"

on page 161 twenty-third line delete "is"

on page 164 sixteenth line delete "an"

on page 164 twentieth line "in" should read "is"

on page 170 fifteenth line insert "government" after "foreign"

on page 176 last line "forearm" should read "firearm"

on page 180 fourteenth last line "lor" should read "or"

on page 183 ninth line "legislation" should read "legislature"

on page 187 seventh last line "guarantied" should read "guaranteed"

on page 188 tenth last line delete "was"

on page 189 section 2 (3)   "on" should read "in"

on page 190 eight last line delete "of" "

on page 191 ninth last line "that" should read "than"

on page 200 second last line delete "for"

on page 204 tenth line   "Central" should read "Circuit"

on page 212 sixth line "as" should read "is"

on page 212 tenth last line add "it"

on page 216 tenth line should read "....acquitted of."

on page 217 nineteenth line insert "on" between "determine" and "his"

on page 217 twentieth line "imitative" should read "initiative"

on page 218 third last line "not" should read "no"

on page 222 sixth line delete first "a"

271